"Brings together a vast range of scholarship and anecdote to produce the first comprehensive history of the Jewish delicatessen. Both culinary and cultural history, this book will be of interest to scholars and common readers alike, the former for its incisive interpretations of modern Jewish foodways and the latter for its ability to recreate a time and place that was 'home' for so many twentieth-century Jews in America. Its evocation of deli menus alone will get your mouth watering."

&a DAVID KRAEMER, author of *Jewish Eating and Jewish Identity through the Ages*

"In *Pastrami on Rye*, Merwin finally addresses the pressing question overlooked in his first book on New York Jews (*In Their Own Image*): but where did they eat? This fun and informative examination of the New York Jewish deli is half history and half love story; *batampte und geshmacht*, with a heaping helping of *sakhel*—you'll *kvell* before you *plotz*!"

&a ERIC MICHAEL MAZUR, co-editor of *God in the Details: American Religion in Popular Culture*

"Merwin's long-awaited history of the deli delivers like the best deli fress: this is a book that nails the mustard-slicked soulful flavor of this cultural gem, with a heft of academic substance that leaves the mind thoroughly satisfied (and the body starved for chopped liver)."

&a DAVID SAX, author of *The Tastemakers: Why We're Crazy for Cupcakes but Fed Up with Fondue*

Pastrami on Rye

Pastrami {on} Rye

AN OVERSTUFFED HISTORY OF THE JEWISH DELI

Ted Merwin

NEW YORK UNIVERSITY PRESS

New York and London

New York University Press

New York and London
www.nyupress.org

References to Internet websites (URLs) were accurate at the time of writing. Neither the author nor New York University Press is responsible for URLs that may have expired or changed since the manuscript was prepared.

Library of Congress Cataloging-in-Publication Data
Merwin, Ted, 1968–
Pastrami on rye : an overstuffed history of the Jewish deli / Ted Merwin.
pages cm   Includes bibliographical references and index.
ISBN 978-0-8147-6031-4 (cloth : acid-free paper)
1. Delicatessens—United States--History. 2. Jews—United States—
Social life and customs. 3. Jewish cooking—History. I. Title.
TX945.4.M47   2015
641.5'676--dc23   2015010490

New York University Press books are printed on acid-free paper, and their binding materials are chosen for strength and durability. We strive to use environmentally responsible suppliers and materials to the greatest extent possible in publishing our books.

Manufactured in the United States of America

10 9 8 7 6 5 4 3 2 1

Also available as an ebook

For my wife, Andrea,
and our three daughters,
Hannah, Sarah, and Leah

When the American soldier abroad speaks with nostalgia of "God's own country," I suspect he is thinking of New England fish chowder, ham and eggs, and pumpkin pie, rather than the Constitution, the Metropolitan Museum of Art, or the Smithsonian Institute. The Frenchman, dreaming of *la belle France*, really has in mind frog's legs *à l'Aurore* or *suprêmes* of chicken Richelieu and not the Louvre or the Sorbonne. When an Englishman, stationed in one of the Empire's far flung mandates, dreams of this plot of earth which is England, he is not thinking of the mother of parliaments, Shakespeare or the British Museum, but of roast beef, boiled-to-death vegetables and suet pudding—although why I cannot imagine. And so it is with us Jews who frequently speak of the heritage of Israel when what we really have in mind is—yes—Jewish delicatessen.

🙞 CHARLES YALE HARRISON, "From the American Scene: One Touch of Delicatessen" (1946)

Contents

Preface

Growing up in the affluent Long Island, predominantly Jewish, suburb of Great Neck in the 1970s and '80s, I listened eagerly to my mother and her cousin Marcia reminiscing about working Sunday evenings waiting tables and busing dishes in Uncle Ben's deli in Williamsburg, Brooklyn. I heard about the hustle and bustle, the interactions between the working-class customers and the wise-cracking old Jewish waiters, the kibitzing at the deli counter with the jocular countermen in their white paper hats.

Partly as a connection to my grandparents, who did not keep kosher but who ate nothing but traditional eastern European Jewish food, I grew to love eating in delis, although the suburban ones that were close to my home had a more pretentious atmosphere with their Art Deco lighting, glass columns, and blond wood paneling. The fatty, scrumptious food was mouthwatering—the peppery pastrami, the chewy corned beef, the sour seeded rye bread, the fluffy matzoh balls in parsley-flecked chicken broth, the crunchy fresh pickles, the tangy coleslaw.

Part of what entranced me about delis was the set of elaborate, almost theatrical rituals that governed the making of the sandwiches. There was an intricate, elegant choreography to

xi

the movements of the counterman as he sliced up the meat. He took the soft, succulent beef from the steam table and sliced it by hand with a flourish, piling up the slices in the center of the bread—sour, chewy rye studded with black caraway seeds—as if building a monument on a town square. He slid the sandwich down the counter to you in a single, graceful motion, like a pitcher delivering a fastball to home plate.

You took the plate to your table, dipped a little wooden paddle into a small glass jar, and painted the bread with thick, impatient strokes of mustard. You opened wide and took a big, cavernous bite. The meat didn't melt in your mouth—it crumbled into it, imploding into it, your teeth plowing through the fat and muscle, your taste buds slapping again and again into the sheer rosiness of it, bursting into a long, drawn-out, happy song.

My parents had no formal connections to the Jewish community. They didn't belong to a synagogue, didn't celebrate the High Holy Days, and didn't send me to Hebrew school. But on Sunday nights, especially when my grandparents were visiting, my mother would dispatch me around the corner to Middle Neck Road to a kosher-style deli pompously called Squire's. I was delegated to pick up an unvarying order: a pound of roast beef, a pound of turkey, a dozen slices of rye bread studded with caraway seeds, a can of vegetarian baked beans, and a squat cylindrical take-out container of gravy. We made our own sandwiches around the round, wooden kitchen table. When we took the first bite of deli, our Jewishness came in like the tide. Before long, nothing but crumbs were left on that table, as if a biblical plague of locusts had devoured everything in sight.

I was always left wanting more.

When I first started to learn about Judaism as a student at Amherst College, it wasn't the food that attracted me—there wasn't much good nosh in western Massachusetts—but the simple, lilting Hebrew songs about peace and goodwill, the sense of fellowship with other Jewish students, the restrained, regal elegance of the Sabbath and holiday rituals, the scrappy emphasis on social justice, and the unwavering focus on moral self-improvement.

I never took a course in religion at Amherst, but I ended up writing my senior thesis as a play about intermarriage between Jews and Christians in early nineteenth-century Philadelphia, where the boundaries between the two groups seemed remarkably fluid and a large percentage of Jews married outside the faith. When I first started writing and teaching about Jewish food, I realized that the deli had served both as a place for the reinforcement of American Jewish identity and as a comfortable space for non-Jews to sample Jewish culture. But no one, to my surprise, had traced the history of the deli in New York or pinpointed its heyday. No one had peered through the greasy, garlicky, gassy, and gluttonous lens of the pastrami sandwich into the role of Jewish deli food in American culture.

Although my family did not belong to a synagogue, did not observe Jewish law, and celebrated few Jewish holidays, eating in delis offered me a sense of Jewish identity that I found in few other places. Whenever we celebrated a family occasion, my grandmother invariably ordered a tongue sandwich, which, in retrospect, seems entirely appropriate; it was as if the tongue that she ate was connected in a double sense to her own tongue—both her gift of gab and her parents' native language (Yiddish is known as the *mameloshen*, the mother's tongue), which, to her deep regret, was not being transmitted to her grandchildren.

I grew up at a time when the deli had long since ceased to function as a major gathering place for the Jewish community, when, even in Great Neck, it was J. P. King's, the Chinese restaurant on Grace Avenue, that was a more popular hangout spot than Squire's. But the deli sandwiches remain more salient in my memory than the moo shu pork or the beef lo mein at the Chinese eatery; they connected me to my people and to my past in a way that the Chinese dishes, however delicious, never could.

I knew that these foods from the Jewish deli were the same foods that my grandparents had eaten during their own upbringing, the foods with which they had celebrated births, weddings, and funerals—the foods that enabled them to build and sustain community with other second-generation Jews at a time when Jewishness was not simply an aspect of their identity or experience but the central, defining, and ineluctable feature of their existence.

Eating in delis was, for them, a laid-back, unfussy, grass-roots experience that required no education, no upper-class breeding, no intricate knowledge of manners and mores. Eating in delis, which were permeated with both the aura of abundance and the culture of celebrity, made Jews feel that, for them too, the American Dream was at long last eminently within their reach—so close, you might say, that they could taste it.

Acknowledgments

Authors often compare writing a book to birthing a child. Writing this one was more like raising an unruly child to adolescence. In the more than ten years that it took me to research and write it, my wife, Andrea, and I had three children: Hannah, who is mentioned in the manuscript as a kindergartner, when she tasted deli for the first time, just had her bat mitzvah. (And no, we didn't serve deli; my wife drew the line.) Our middle daughter, Sarah, never tires of reminding me that my wife wrote a whole manuscript in just two months while serving on the staff of Camp Ramah in the Poconos; she is dubious that someone could spend such a long time on a single project. And our youngest, Leah, seems to have most inherited my affinity for eastern European Jewish food, especially kasha varnishkes (buckwheat groats with bowtie noodles, for the uninitiated).

First and foremost, I owe a gigantic debt of gratitude to my editor at NYU Press, Jennifer Hammer, who initially suggested that I write a book on this topic and who kept an unbroken faith in it all along, as it went through multiple rounds of peer review. I feel a strong connection to NYU, partly because my father worked there for decades, editing the alumni magazine at the NYU Medical School, and partly because my grandmother volunteered on Fridays at the Student Activities office of the same school, selling discount theater tickets to the medical students. This is what enabled my family to attend Broadway and off-Broadway shows on a regular basis throughout my childhood, and I credit my love of theater (the field in which I earned my Ph.D.) to these early theatergoing experiences.

I'm also very much indebted to Professor Darra Goldstein at Williams College, the former editor of *Gastronomica*, for her help and encouragement. And I am exceedingly grateful to my former agent, Michele Rubin, and to my new one, Susan Ginsburg, at Writers House in New York. My freelance editor, Alice Peck, suggested the book's title.

I've had a tremendous amount of fun—and a lot of good pastrami sandwiches—working on this project, including interviewing dozens of deli owners and executives of kosher sausage companies, who were generous with their time and anecdotes. I'm also grateful to Marty Silver, former executive vice president of Hebrew National, for allowing me unfettered access to his company's archives in Jericho, Long Island. And I'd like to convey my appreciation to Ziggy Gruber, Brian Merlis, and Marlene Katz Padover for their help in locating and reproducing images for the book.

I'm indebted to many librarians and archivists, including Shulamith Berger at the Special Collections of Yeshiva University Library, Jeremy Megraw at the Billy Rose Theater Collection of the New York Public Library, and Dan Sharon at the Spertus Institute in Chicago (who, after one research trip to the library, mailed me articles for years whenever he ran across something that was germane to my topic). And I want to thank David Sax, author of *Save the Deli*, for always making time to chat about delis and to help me to track down an elusive interviewee.

I thank my terrific editor at the *Jewish Week*, Rob Goldblum, who has given me helpful feedback, endless encouragement, and weekly opportunities to stretch my wings as a writer by enabling me to pen a wide variety of articles, including the personal essays and reflection pieces that are my forte. I thank

Provost Neil Weissman at Dickinson College, as well as the college's Research and Development Committee, for the resources to travel and share my ideas with academic and popular audiences alike. And I thank my students, who, even as they are required to revise draft after draft of their own essays, have pushed me to become both a better writer and a better teacher of writing.

Helpful feedback and valuable suggestions came from Simon Bronner, Hasia Diner, Jenna Weissman Joselit, Melissa Klapper, Sharon O'Brien, Arthur Sabatini, and Paul Zakrzewski. In addition, many of the ideas in this book come from people who have heard me speak, and I want to thank both the organizers of these programs and the audience members—it is always invaluable for me to get feedback on my work and to share my abiding love of this subject with people for whom the deli was a central feature of their own childhoods, a setting for some of their most cherished memories of family and friends. Even as the deli itself continues to fade into obscurity, these memories will endure.

My greatest thanks, of course, go to my wife, Andrea, who shares all of my hopes and dreams—and, occasionally, my sandwiches. Her love and support make everything that I do not just possible but pleasurable and fulfilling. She wrote about the power of and symbolism of food in Judaism long before it ever occurred to me as a research topic of my own. I love her with all my heart—and quite a bit of my stomach.

Introduction

Is anything more emblematic of New York City than the overstuffed pastrami sandwich on rye? The pickled and smoked meats sold in storefront Jewish delicatessens starting in the late nineteenth century became part of the heritage of all New Yorkers. But they were, of course, especially important to Jews; the history of the delicatessen is the history of Jews eating themselves into Americans. The skyscraper sandwich became a hallmark of New York. But it also became a potent symbol of affluence, of success, and of the attainment of the American Dream. As the slogan for Reuben's, an iconic delicatessen in the theater district boasted, "From a sandwich to a national institution."

This book traces the rise and fall of the delicatessen in American Jewish culture. It traces the trajectory of an icon—a journey that originates in the ancient world and rockets through the Middle Ages to postrevolutionary France, lands briefly on the Lower East Side, gathers steam in the tenements of the outer boroughs, and is catapulted out to the cities and suburbs of America, with a one-time detour into outer space. Along the way, we learn what happens when food takes on an ethnic coloration and then gradually sheds that ethnic connection when it acculturates into America.

We learn how Jews retained the taste and scent of brine—that of the seas that they had crossed in order to get to America and of the oceans that so many settled along, first in New York and later in Miami Beach and L.A.—in the foods that they ate. Because of the utility of salt in seasoning and preserving food, it has played an enormous role in the history of Western civilization, as writer Mark Kurlansky has found.[1] It is little wonder, then, that it became essential to Jewish culture. Indeed, for a substantial part of the twentieth century, kosher sausage companies and delicatessens cured more than just meat and pickles—they sustained an essential part of Jewish culture, enabling it to survive and thrive in America.

Reinvented in the New World, including in ways that were in stark tension with Jewish religious Orthodoxy, the pastrami, corned beef, salami, bologna, and tongue that were sold in storefront New York delicatessens became, for a time, a mainstay of the American Jewish diet, taking on a primacy that they had never enjoyed in eastern European Jewish culture. Indeed, for the scholar Seth Wolitz, the deli was no less than the "epitome of the Jewish culinary experience in New York. It was the first (and most beloved) venue for Jewish food outside the home and a favorite neighborhood institution."[2]

These Jewish eateries were known for the staggering amount and variety of food on display; the delicatessen, in the words of the food historian John Mariani, "represented American bounty in its most voluptuous and self-indulgent form."[3] Smoked and pickled meats, from their roots in central and eastern Europe, held a special place even within Jewish "cuisine," which extended from *kreplach* (dumplings) and *knishes* (savory pastries) to *kishke* (stuffed beef intestines, also known as stuffed derma) and *p'tcha* (calf's-foot jelly, also called *studen* or *cholodetz*), of which the actor Zero Mostel quipped, "no matter what you call it, a pleasant gas stays with you all day."[4]

The delicatessen, whether in its kosher or nonkosher variant, was a second home for many American Jews, especially those who were the children of immigrants, who had begun to define their Jewish identity in a secular rather than religious fashion. Before the establishment of the State of Israel, before even the dispersion of Jews across the North American continent, the cramped, bustling delicatessen became a focal point of Jewish identity and remembrance—a capacious, well-trodden, metaphorical homeland for the Jewish soul. Given the identification of New York City with its large and prominent Jewish population, the delicatessen became an all-purpose symbol of Jewishness. As a delighted customer once exhaled upon entering the Second Avenue Deli, "Ah, I smell Judaism!"[5]

While the kosher delicatessen symbolized ethnic continuity, the nonkosher delicatessen symbolized the movement of Jews into the mainstream of American society. By the 1930s, the kosher delicatessen in particular became ubiquitous in the outer boroughs of New York, while the kosher-style delicatessen became synonymous with the showbiz culture of Manhattan. This book focuses on New York partly because it was where the majority of American Jews lived until the 1940s and partly because the Jewish delicatessen essentially began in New York and became emblematic of both New York and Jewish life. Gotham's Jewish delis were "the emperors of all food that is hand-held in New York," the screenwriter Richard Condon noted, the city that was "the capital of the greatest sandwich-consuming country of the world."[6] New York may be dubbed "The Big Apple" (a term used in connection first with horse racing and later with other kinds of urban entertainment), but throughout most of the twentieth century, a pastrami sandwich was more likely than a piece of fruit to trigger thoughts of New York. Both, however, are about sex: the apple represents temptation in Western culture, and the pastrami sandwich, as we will see, became the ultimate symbol of carnal desire.

In part because of the prevalence of Jewish food in the city, everyone who lives in New York "is Jewish," insisted the travel writer Daniel Stern in the 1960s, calling Jewishness a "pervading atmosphere, a zest, a style of life." Even visitors, he averred, become Jewish for the time that they are in New York. If you are already Jewish, he added, then "while you're here, you'll be *very* Jewish."[7] This sentiment jibes with the experience of Hilton Als (a theater critic for the *New Yorker*), who confessed that, as an African American boy growing up in the 1960s in Brooklyn, he felt like an "anxious Yeshiva student" in the company of his father, whom he describes as a "brown-skinned, well-dressed, mustachioed rebbe." Als fondly recalled his Sunday outings with his father; they would take a bus from their apartment to the Lower East Side, where they would shop for "briny sour pickles, pastrami, brisket, cheesecake, and celery soda: Jew food for the brain."[8]

It is difficult to overestimate the importance of the delicatessen—what the food writer Joan Nathan calls *"the* Jewish eating experience in America."[9] A delicatessen owner in Boston disclosed that elderly Jews come to her establishment for their last meal. "They're practically on respirators," she whispered, "but they want that last taste of deli before they die."[10] As the essayist Jonathan Rosen writes in *The Talmud and the Internet*, the great German poet Goethe begged, on his deathbed, for "more light"—Rosen's grandmother, by contrast, pleaded for pastrami.[11] Or, as the late comedian Soupy Sales (né Milton Supman) jested, if he had his life to live over, he would "live over a delicatessen."[12]

Judaism has almost always revolved around meat. Two thousand years ago, eating meat was a religious activity for Hebrews, since they ate it only as part of the Temple offering that was sacrificed by the priests. This was called the *shelamim* (full) offering, and it was intended to bring joy to all who consumed it, since it represented the expiation of sin for the community. However, the freshly roasted flesh had to be consumed within two days for it to supply what the rabbis deemed to be the proper quotient of happiness.

The question arose: Could freshly roasted meat also be eaten on the somber evening before the Ninth of Av, the fast day that commemorates the double destruction of the Temple, first by the Babylonians and then by the Romans? The rabbis decided, based on the two-day rule of the *shelamim*, that the meat would need to be cured for at least two days in order not to cause undue joy. They authorized the consumption of only pickled meat, along with new (unfermented) wine, thereby introducing corned beef into Jewish cuisine.[13] And is it merely coincidental that the priests were obliged to consume the tasty leftovers of the sacrificial offerings with mustard, foreshadowing the little mustard pot on the table of every Jewish delicatessen?[14] The ancient priests were, in a sense, forerunners of the New York delicatessen owners and countermen; by preparing meat, they presided over an activity that was central to the community's workings and self-definition.

Jews also have a long-standing connection with sandwiches; indeed, it was a rabbi who purportedly invented the first one, although he did not call it by that name. Hillel the Elder, who lived during the time of King Herod and the Roman emperor Augustus (and who gave his name to the national Jewish student organization), devised a creative way to fulfill the injunction in the Torah that the Israelites should eat matzoh and bitter herbs to commemorate their enslavement to the Egyptian pharaohs. He enclosed the herbs, along with a goodly portion of paschal lamb, inside the bread, making a lamb-herb wrap. Indeed, the unleavened bread that Hillel used to make that first sandwich was likely not the stiff, fragile, crumbly stuff that is matzoh but rather a thick, soft, chewy flatbread like Indian roti, Mediterranean pita, Mexican tortilla, or Middle Eastern lavash.

Hillel dubbed his innovation the *korech*, basing it on the ancient Hebrew word *lekarech*, which means "to encircle or envelop"; the term was also used to refer to a book binding or a funeral shroud. The modern word *sandwich* first appeared in an English cookbook in 1773 after John Montagu, the Fourth Earl of Sandwich, asked his servant to bring him pieces of meat between two slices of toast so that he could keep playing cards without taking a break. In 1840, the British historian Edward Gibbon witnessed in London what he called a "sight truly English," namely, "twenty or thirty perhaps, of the first men in the kingdom, in point of fashion and fortune" at a café and gambling club called the Cocoa Tree. Gibbon described them as "supping at little tables covered with a napkin, in the middle of a coffee-room, upon a bit of cold meat, or a sandwich, and drinking a glass of punch."[15]

A century later, in New York, the overstuffed delicatessen sandwich loomed large in Jewish Americans' understanding of who they were both as Jews and as Americans. The food historian Bee Wilson has noted that the sandwich lends its structure to everything from sponges to aircraft design;[16] it may not be too far-fetched to suggest that the delicatessen sandwich engineered a secular rather than religious way of being Jewish, one that helped to fuel the meteoric rise of Jews in our society.[17] Upwardly mobile Jews defined themselves in opposition to delicatessen fare, against its immigrant, low-class, plebeian connotations. By the concluding decades of the twentieth century, they had disavowed the delicatessen, disencumbering themselves from cured beef and pickled cucumbers in favor of a more gourmet, more international, and healthier cuisine.

The delicatessen was a victim of its own success. By flattering Jews' social and economic aspirations, it helped to propel them into the middle class. A satirical oil painting that hangs in the basement of Ben's Kosher Deli on West Thirty-Eighth Street depicts the restaurant as, incorrectly, located on the same street as some of the most iconic, four-star restaurants in Manhattan, including the 21 Club, Tavern on the Green, Sardi's, and the Four Seasons. The whimsical image gestures to the ambivalence that Jews have about forsaking the deli to eat in more gourmet restaurants, trading their traditional "peasant" food for upward mobility—if only they could have their pastrami and eat it too, the painting seems to say.

But when did the delicatessen become an important institution in Jewish life? Although delicatessen meats (or meats of any kind) were not a major part of the eastern European Jewish diet, historians have suggested that the centrality of the delicatessen to the American Jewish experience began with the immigrant generation on the Lower East Side of New York. The historian Hasia Diner argues, for example, that it was Jewish immigrants who "learned to think of delicatessen food as traditional."[18] But while Diner is correct about the retrospective elevation of delicatessen foods into a pivotal part of Jewish heritage, her timing is off. Smoked and pickled meats were too expensive for immigrants, and the immigrant Jewish mother was typically loath to bring in take-out food; it vitiated her role as the cook for the family. It was not the immigrants but their children who made the delicatessen their own. Even as second-generation Jews were still excluded from the upper echelons of American society, the deli made them feel like part of the "in crowd"—they had became more successful and developed a less religious Jewish identity.

Then again, as Diner emphasizes, eating out was itself an unfamiliar activity for Jews, who were not used to eating in restaurants, whether in eastern Europe or on the Lower East Side; they coined the word *oyesessen* at the turn of the twentieth century to designate this exciting new recreational activity.[19] The delicatessen enabled Jews to eat out in a Jewish way, by enjoying *in public* the foods that they associated with their heritage. Furthermore, unlike synagogues and fraternal organizations, many of which were organized on the basis of immigrants' towns of origin, delicatessens enabled the descendants of Jews from different social classes and different Ashkenazic (eastern European Jewish) nationalities to forge a common American Jewish identity. In the kosher delicatessen, the freethinker (atheist) and the *frum* (observant) Jew could literally break bread—typically rye with caraway seeds—together, as could the top-hatted capitalist and the leather-capped socialist. The delicatessen was, as the historian Jenna Weissman Joselit has observed, a "neutral Jewish place" that "signaled Jewishness in the public square, transcending traditional divisions between different types of Jews."[20]

Every minority group had its own dedicated social space in America. The sociologist Ray Oldenburg coined the influential phrase "third place" to refer to casual gathering places such as coffee shops and pool halls that occupy an intermediate realm between home and office. These are spaces, he observed, that level social distinctions among patrons, foster civic engagement, and provide a platform for mutual emotional support. As the theme song for the 1970s television show *Cheers*—set in a bar in Boston—goes, it's the place "where everyone knows your name."[21]

Third spaces function like the eighteenth-century town commons; the historian Sharon Daloz Parks has noted that the grassy square around which villages in New England were built was where people gathered "for play and protest, memorial and celebration, and worked out how they would live together." For Parks, the commons is indispensable to healthy communal life; she observes that "wherever there is consciousness of participation in a commons, there is an anchored sense of a shared life within a manageable frame."[22]

The Irish imported to America the pub, a venue that was, in the words of the historian Sybil Taylor, a combination "grocery store, funeral parlor, concert hall, restaurant, bar, political forum, congenial meeting place, courting corner, and, most of all, a place for talk."[23] The scholar Jennifer Nugent Duffy has underscored the role of the pub in promoting "vital economic, political, and social exchanges," especially for overwhelmed Irish immigrants who dwelled in overcrowded tenement apartments and needed a place to let off steam.[24]

Italian immigrants formed "social clubs" in Little Italy, such as the Saint Fortunata Society, established in 1900, where they smoked, played the bowling game of boccie, and cooked together. In 1896, the *New York Times* reported on the plethora of Italian societies and clubs, which boasted a combined membership of tens of thousands of immigrants. Whether by providing an urban hangout or by sponsoring dances and picnics, they provided a way for Italians to reminisce about the Old Country and forge new American identities in a supportive and nurturing environment.[25]

Most of these immigrant gathering places were established by, and catered to, men. The delicatessen, although it began as a take-out store and not a restaurant, was no exception; the first delicatessens likely to a large extent served single, immigrant, Jewish men who could not cook for themselves.[26] In general, Jews tended to come to America as whole families, since their homelands had become too inhospitable to Jews to permit them to stay; men from other immigrant groups often returned to their countries of origin with the money that they had earned.

But because delicatessens are oriented around the consumption of red meat, the iconic Jewish eatery did take on a manly vibe, one that was exploited, as we shall see, by vaudeville routines, films, and TV shows about Jewish men using the delicatessen to shore up their precarious sense of masculinity. The food writer Arthur Schwartz has pointed out that, in Yiddish, the word for "overstuffed" is *ongeshtupped*; the meat is crammed between the bread in a crude, sensual way that recalls the act of copulation.[27] The delicatessen, after all, is a space of carnality, of the pleasures of the "flesh"—the word for meat in Yiddish is *fleysh*.

Beyond the gender and sexual politics of the delicatessen, it was not, by any means, the only "third place" in American Jewish life. The synagogue was called in Hebrew *bayt knesset*, or "house of assembly." Settlement houses for the immigrant generation and Jewish Community Centers, YMHAs (Young Men's Hebrew Associations), B'nai B'rith (a kind of Jewish equivalent to the Masons, beginning in the mid-nineteenth century), and other institutions offered classes and lectures, put on cultural events, and provided gyms and other recreational opportunities—including sponsoring athletic teams. The Yiddish theater brought together immigrant Jews on a frequent, sometimes nightly, basis. But Jews bonded with especially great intensity around food; as the historians Annie Polland and Daniel Soyer have pointed out, delicatessens "became such an iconic New York institution that their presence marked a Jewish neighborhood more clearly than even that of a synagogue."[28]

Delicatessens were thus prime venues for both Jewish and non-Jewish candidates to campaign for political office. As J. J. Goldberg, the former editor in chief of the *Forward*, noted, "For most of the twentieth century, wooing the Jewish vote meant walking through Jewish neighborhoods, donning a skullcap, and being photographed while eating a kosher knish."[29] After Henry Morgenthau Jr., a Jewish candidate, lost his 1962 bid to unseat Governor Nelson Rockefeller, a Baptist who frequently campaigned for the Jewish vote in kosher delicatessens, Morgenthau ran into the African American civil rights activist Bayard Rustin on a corner. Rustin was eating a knish. Morgenthau asked him what he was eating. Rustin replied, "I'm eating the reason that you're not governor."[30] And George McGovern became the butt of ridicule when, during the 1972 presidential campaign, he ordered a glass of milk to accompany his chopped-chicken-liver sandwich at a kosher delicatessen in New York's garment district.[31]

The delicatessen enabled second-generation Jews to refuel themselves and reinvigorate their own tradition, at the same time as it facilitated their entrance into the mainstream of American society. The comedian Harpo Marx claimed that performing on Broadway was a special thrill because, while in New York, he had "two homes-away-from-home, Lindy's or Reuben's." In these delicatessens, he exulted, "I was back with my own people, who spoke my language, with my accent."[32] Even as the New York–style delicatessen spread out of New York and took root in other cities, it was known as a place of fellowship, friendship, and good cheer. "The deli is where you go to be Jewish," the food writer Jonathan Gold reflected. "You live a secular life, but you show up at Junior's [in Los Angeles] on a Sunday morning and suddenly all your Jewish stuff comes in."[33]

A successful delicatessen, whether in or out of New York, was defined by what one deli owner in L.A. called its "hubbub"—its casualness, conviviality, and sense of community.[34] "Owners traditionally were there to humor their customers," reflected Bill Ladany, president of the Vienna Sausage Company in Chicago. "It was as important to be friends as to make chicken noodle soup."[35] Non-Jews immersed themselves in an environment in which Jewishness rubbed off on them as well. As the food writer Patric Kuh observed, "You might hear Spanish, Mandarin, Korean or Tagalog in an L.A. deli, but everyone is essentially talking Yiddish."[36]

But by the mid-twentieth century, Jewish culture was itself in the process of changing, of becoming progressively more Americanized. The Jewish deli began to absorb more and more "American" foods, with many delis ultimately serving more turkey than either corned beef or pastrami. Indeed, by the 1960s, suburban Jewish delis offered entire take-out feasts for Thanksgiving, enabling Jews to carve out an American identity that relied on the consumption of take-out turkey sandwiches rather than a bird roasted at home. "Jewish New York," the genealogist Ira Wolfman has found, "reveled, and was revealed, in its food. Like much of American Jewish culture, Jewish food was a hybrid—a mishmash of old-world cooking and customs, Jewish dietary laws, and an ongoing accommodation with American life."[37]

Indeed, Jews ate "deli" at every stage of their American lives. Brises (circumcisions), bar mitzvahs, weddings, and shivas (gatherings after a funeral)—all were marked not just by carefully prescribed religious rites but by the consumption of corned beef, pastrami, rolled beef, tongue, and other deli meats catered by a local deli. Indeed, deli owners became expert at producing endless round platters of sandwiches—platters that were held together with frilly toothpicks and swathed by sheets of colorful, crinkly cellophane.

A typical Brooklyn wedding or bar mitzvah reception in the 1950s was a far cry from many of the lavish, ostentatious affairs of today. The party was held at home; kosher delicatessen platters were set out in the backyard, and the bathtub was filled with ice, soda, and beer.[38] "We would have family parties in the [photography] studio downstairs and all the relatives would come and Uncle Louie would cook," one Jewish New Yorker recalled, noting that her uncle's corned beef was the main dish at her wedding reception. "He would have a clothes boiler and put whole corn beefs [*sic*], pastrami, and spices in them and cook them all day. The relatives and me would gorge themselves on meat, pickles, and soda water. Nothing since could ever compare."[39]

Seven decades after the historian Arthur Schlesinger's seminal investigation into the previously unacknowledged but pivotal role of food in American history (from the Boston Tea Party and the Whiskey Rebellion to the Lend Lease program during the Second World War),[40] food studies has become its own branch of the academy. Scholars in this field, led by Warren Belasco, Carole Counihan, and Darra Goldstein, view food as a nexus of history, sociology, ethnicity, and culture.[41] "Food," as the anthropologist Claude Lévi-Strauss famously put it, "is good to think."[42] One might add that food is especially "good to think" about in terms of ethnic identity; for the anthropologist Arjun Appadurai, food is a "marvelously plastic kind of collective representation."[43] Indeed, the pastrami sandwich was a kind of palimpsest—a blank screen onto which succeeding generations of Jews projected different images of themselves and their group as they became progressively more acculturated into American society.

Scholars tend to focus not just on the food itself but on "foodways"—the *social context* in which food is prepared, served, and consumed—as well as the historical and sociological meaning with which food is endowed. Thus, at a time when Jews were stereotyped as uncouth and uncivilized, it is significant that they created an unusual type of eatery, one that in some ways fulfilled the very ideas that other Americans had of them. The deli was a place where they could eat with their hands, talk with their mouths full, fill their bellies, and enjoy the pleasure of each other's company in a raucous and convivial setting.[44] The historian Barry Kessler sums this up in the title of his article on the tumultuous delicatessens of Baltimore: "Bedlam with Corned Beef on the Side."[45]

The most significant recent academic works about Jewish food include the historian Hasia Diner's chapters on eastern European and immigrant Jewish food in her exemplary, cross-cultural study *Hungering for America* and David Kraemer's wide-ranging survey *Jewish Eating and Identity through the Ages*. But there has been no full-length study of the Jewish delicatessen. Historians have given the towering deli sandwich—and the place in which it was consumed—surprisingly short shrift. As the historian Michael Alexander declared, "It's about time historiography took serious notice of deli life."[46]

The deli has fared far better in popular writings. Nick Zukin and Michael Zusman's *The Artisan Jewish Deli at Home* (based on Kenny and Zuke's Deli in Portland, Oregon) and Noah and Rae Bernamoff's *Mile End Cookbook* (based on the Mile End Deli in Brooklyn and Manhattan) have joined earlier, anecdote-filled recipe books from the Second Avenue Deli and Junior's. Also worthy of note are Sheryll Bellman's lavishly illustrated coffee-table book on classic American delis, Arthur Schwartz's tantalizing guide to eastern European Jewish dishes, the journalist Maria Balinska's well-rounded history of the bagel, Laura Silver's foursquare history of the knish, Jane Ziegelman's enticing "edible history" of immigrant life in one New York tenement building on the Lower East Side, and the travel writer David Sax's edgy elegy *Save the Deli*.[47]

The publication of these volumes, along with popular food columns in Jewish newspapers such as the *Forward* and the *Jewish Week* and cover articles on Jewish food in *Moment* magazine, the *Baltimore Jewish Times*, and other Jewish publications, testify to the continuing interest in Jewish gastronomy and a growing sense that Jewish food connects Jews—and also appeals to non-Jews—in a way that few aspects of Judaism continue to do.[48]

Social scientists have adopted three main approaches to the study of food and foodways. The first is a functional approach, which looks, in part, at the role of food preparation and consumption in the formation and maintenance of group identity. The second is a structuralist approach, which treats food as a signifying system, as a "language" of its own and which, especially in the work of Roland Barthes, also theorizes a semiotics of media images of food and food advertising.[49] (The structuralist approach also emphasizes the fact that foods are arranged hierarchically within a culture, with particular foods eaten to mark special occasions.) The third is a developmental approach, which investigates how certain foods became part of the diet of specific peoples (and how other foods were shunned), examining the history of each group and the evolutionary and environmental processes that helped to determine its diet.

The approach in this book is eclectic; it borrows from each of these perspectives in analyzing the changing place of the delicatessen in American Jewish culture. In line with the functional approach, I view the deli as playing a crucial role in American Jewish life, one that helped to facilitate Jews' joining the American mainstream. Vis-à-vis the structuralist approach, I see the foods and foodways associated with Jewish delicacies as helping to organize the reality of Jewish life, both through the actual consumption of deli meats and also through the—often comedic and heavily eroticized—-images and representations of the deli in popular culture. Finally, with regard to the developmental approach, I view the passionate embrace of the deli as tempered over time as other social and economic factors led Jews away from the deli and toward other, more exotic-seeming, "gourmet" and healthier kinds of food. In each case, I see many layers of cultural and social meaning crammed into the overstuffed deli sandwich.

The research for this project took place over more than a decade, and it took many forms. I began by doing dozens of interviews with current and retired deli owners both in New York and along the Jewish retirement corridor in southeast Florida, between West Palm Beach in the north and Miami Beach in the south. While continuing to conduct interviews, both in person and on the telephone, I then did archival research in both corporate and public archives, ranging from the Hebrew National Company's files at its headquarters in Jericho, New York, to the

Dorot Division of the New York Public Library, the Center for Jewish History, the New York City Municipal Archives, the Jewish Theological Seminary, and the Yeshiva University Archives. I made extensive use of both Yiddish- and English-language newspapers, trade journals (especially the *Mogen Dovid Delicatessen Magazine*), and books. I found a plethora of photographs of delis in the collections of the Bronx Historical Society, the Brooklyn Historical Society, the Brooklyn Public Library, and the New York State Archives.

The final stage of the research involved finding cartoons, film clips, television episodes, and other examples of the reflection of the Jewish deli in pop culture. I found material at the Paley Center for Media (formerly the Museum of Broadcasting), the Jewish Museum in New York, the Billy Rose Collection of the New York Public Library for the Performing Arts, the George Eastman House (Rochester, New York), and the Academy for Motion Pictures Arts and Sciences (Los Angeles). I also found copious references to delicatessens in memoirs, novels, short stories, plays, and poetry—these helped immensely to round out the role of the delicatessen in American Jewish culture.

Throughout the research process, I collected hundreds of items of memorabilia relating to every aspect of deli culture throughout the United States—including neon signs and clocks, seltzer and soda bottles, menus, photos, placards, postcards, matchbooks, and even a scale and a slicing machine. Part of my collection was featured in "Chosen Food," an exhibition, funded by a grant from the National Endowment for the Humanities, on Jewish food that began at the Jewish Museum of Maryland and transferred to the Jewish Museum of Atlanta.

Will the deli survive for even one more generation? On a visit to my hometown, I took my five-year-old daughter to Kensington Kosher Deli on Middle Neck Road (Squire's, alas, is long gone), where I ordered a brisket sandwich for us to share. She barely nibbled at it. When I asked her if she didn't think it was the best food she had ever tasted, she patiently explained that her favorite food is Indian, followed by Chinese, followed by a dinner that her mother recently made that she "fell in love with and wanted to marry."

While I share her enthusiasm for her mother's cooking, I realized with a sharp pang of regret that she and her two sisters will almost inevitably grow up without having the same fondness for deli food that I did. Her metaphor of "marrying" food stuck with me, though. Will Jews ever again feel the same deep connection to deli food that they did throughout so much of the twentieth century, or have they found new gastronomic spouses and partners? Then again, as Rabbi Carol Harris-Shapiro has put it, "Jews keep fishing in the same ethnic waters. Perhaps some day they'll pull up gefilte fish again."[50]

={ 1 }=

According to the Customer's Desire

An illustrated advertising postcard from a Belgian butcher and food shop from the mid-nineteenth century is decorated with colorfully plumed birds, clusters of grapes, and an iron cooking pot on the bottom. A petite oval at the top, as if a window into an upper-class home, shows a nattily dressed gentleman sitting at a table with knife and fork in hand, preparing to dig into a feast of fancy foodstuffs. The caption, in French, lists all the meats, cheeses, pâtés, and other items that are available for purchase from the shop, which promises that everything will be prepared "according to the customer's desire."[1]

Perhaps it should not surprise that the pastrami sandwich became an object of such potent and piquant obsession in Jewish culture, given that the very word *delicatessen* derives originally from the Latin word *delicatus*, meaning "dainty, tender, charming, enticing, alluring, and voluptuous." Indeed, the Romans often used the word to refer to sexual attractiveness, as in the expression *puer delicatus*, the "delicious" boy, who was the recipient of an older man's erotic attentions. It entered medieval French as *delicat*, meaning "fine," and by the Renaissance morphed into *delicatesse*, signifying a fine food or delicacy. It was picked up as *delicatezza* in Italian and *Delikatesse* in Ger-

Advertising card for a Belgian gourmet store from the mid-nineteenth century (Collection of Ted Merwin)

man, both also denoting an unusual and highly prized food. It entered English only in the late 1880s, with the influx of Germans into the United States, and then only in the plural form, *delicatessen*.

The origin of the delicatessen as a food store derives from the democratization of gourmet eating in Europe. This occurred at some times through political upheavals such as the French Revolution, after which many chefs found themselves out of work, and at other times as a result of papal decrees. Pope Gregory XIII, who was invested in 1572, inveighed against the bishops and cardinals of his day for eating sybaritically despite their purported devotion to austerity and self-abnegation, and he mandated that they could employ no more than one chef apiece.[2] Unemployed chefs opened Italian specialty food shops called *salumerie* in which cured and smoked meats were sold to members of the haute bourgeoisie who, unable to afford their own chef, still desired to eat like a king—or a pope. Among the specialties of these stores were cured meats, which were especially popular in Italy. According to the *Harleian Miscellany* of 1590 (first collated and edited in the mid-eighteenth century by Samuel Johnson), "the first mess [course] or *antepast*, as they call it, that is brought to the table, is some fine meat to urge them to have an appetite."[3]

Delicatessens competed to provide the most unusual foodstuffs from around the globe. Their ostentatious, symmetrical window displays, which typically featured the head of a wild boar (the origin of the name for Boar's Head, an American company that was founded in 1905) were likened, by the Norwegian composer Edvard Grieg, to a symphony.[4] The most opulent German delicatessen of all, Dallmayr, which opened in Munich during the late seventeenth century (and is still in existence), made daily deliveries to Prince Luitpold of Bavaria. By the late nineteenth century, when the newly unified country flexed its imperialist muscles, delicatessens were also known as *Colonialwaren*, since most of their products were brought back from German colonies abroad. Dallmayr, for example, introduced the German public to bananas, which it imported from the Canary Islands.

France was not far behind in the realm of imported delicacies. After the French Revolution, the Israeli food and wine expert Daniel Rogov estimated, seventy royal chefs were guillotined, eight hundred opened restaurants, and no fewer than sixteen hundred opened gourmet food shops called *charcuteries*, which specialized in cured and smoked meats.[5] In addition, many of the workers in fine luxury goods transformed themselves into purveyors of fine food and drink. According to a French scholar, Charles Germain de Saint Aubin, writing in 1795, most of the haberdashers, embroiderers, jewelers, goldsmiths, and other high-end artisans in Paris opened food stores, bars, and restaurants; he notes that they had "crowded into the center of Paris to such an extent that it [was] not unusual to find a whole street occupied by nothing but their shops."[6]

By eating spiced and pickled meats, along with other gourmet foods, the Parisian bourgeoisie were able to show off their rising economic and social status, just as second-generation Jews were to do in New York a century and a half later by patronizing the delicatessens in the theater district, as we will see. Long before the birth of the overstuffed delicatessen sandwich, these meats had begun to symbolize the achievement of economic and social aspirations, of rising to an elevated status in society.

Pickled Meat in the European Jewish Diet

Cured meats and sausages entered the Jewish diet during the tenth and eleventh centuries, when Jews were living in the Alsace-Lorraine region of France. When they moved eastward in large numbers in the eighteenth and nineteenth centuries at the invitation of the Polish kings, they brought along what the Yiddish writer Abba Kanter called "this-worldly articles such as Dutch herring, smoked and canned fish, . . . and German sausage."[7] Pastrami, as mentioned earlier, was a Romanian specialty; it originated in Turkey and then came to Romania through Turkish conquests of southeastern Europe, in the area of Bessarabia and Moldavia. The name seems to derive from similar words in Romanian, Russian, Turkish, and Armenian— *pastram, pastromá, pastirma,* and *basturma,* words that mean "pressed."[8] Indeed, meat was preserved by squeezing out the juices, then air-drying it for up to a month. Turkish horsemen in Central Asia also preserved meat by inserting it in the sides of their saddles, where their legs would press against it as they rode; the meat was tenderized in the animal's sweat.

The eighteenth-century French gourmet Jean Anthelme Brillat-Savarin—who famously said, "Tell me what you eat and I will tell you who you are," frequently paraphrased as "You are what you eat"—quoted a Croat captain to the effect that when his people are "in the field and feel hungry, we shoot down the first animal that comes our way, cut off a good hunk of flesh, salt it a little (for we always carry a supply of salt in our sabretache) and put it under the saddle, next to the horse's back; then we gallop for a while, after which," he demonstrated, "moving his jaws like a man tearing meat apart with his teeth, '*gnian gnian*, we feed like princes.'"[9] The etymologist David L. Gold discovered a longer form of the word, *pastramagiu*, in both Turkish and Romanian, that referred to the person who both made and purveyed the salty, smoky, reddish meat. Interestingly, the ethics of the *pastramagiu* were suspect; it was a term also used to refer metaphorically, according to a Romanian dictionary, to a "bum, loafer, scalliwag, vagabond; rascal, rogue, or scamp."[10]

Given widespread and grinding poverty, meat consumption of all kinds among eastern European Jews was extremely low; historians have speculated that the average consumption of meat per household among the Jews of Poland was about a pound a week during most of the nineteenth century, with poor families eating almost none.[11] As Hasia Diner (the *Hungering for America* author) has noted, beef was especially expensive because of a hefty sales tax. This tax had been originally instituted by Jews themselves in order to provide funds for communal life but then taken over in many areas by the government. The despised tax, called the *korobka*, thrust most meat out of reach of the poor.[12]

In "Tevye Strikes It Rich," the Yiddish writer Sholem Aleichem describes what happens after Tevye the Dairyman (later the hero of the pathbreaking 1964 Broadway Jewish musical *Fiddler on the Roof*, by Jerry Bock, Sheldon Harnick, and Joseph Stein) gives two rich Russian Jewish ladies a lift home on his wagon. The family sets out an immense banquet to celebrate their safe return. Tevye is wide-eyed, realizing that he could feed his family for a week with the crumbs that fell off the table. He is finally invited to join the feast, which includes food that he "never dreamed existed," including "fish, and cold cuts, and roasts, and fowl, and more gizzards and chicken livers than you could count."[13]

Smoked and pickled meats remained rare delicacies for most eastern European Jews well into the twentieth century.

They were viewed as a special treat, as one notes in the exuberant klezmer tune "Rumenye, Rumenye" (Romania, Romania). Aaron Lebedeff, who wrote and performed the song, was the most celebrated Yiddish vaudeville star in New York in the 1920s. He punctuated his rendition with popping noises to imitate the sound of uncorking bottles for his favorite meal back in the Old Country, which comprised "*a mameligele, a pastromele, a karnatsele—un a gleyzele vayn*" (a little polenta, a little pastrami, a little sausage—and a small glass of wine). As the sound of the clarinet goes into ecstatic whoops, the singer recalls the pleasure of eating just a tiny bit of each of his favorite foods.[14] Similarly, the painter Mayer Kirshenblatt, who grew up in the Polish shtetl of Opatow in the 1920s, noshed on corned beef only when his uncle brought it back to his own shtetl, Drildz, from business trips to a larger town, Radom.[15]

For wealthier Jews, pickled beef was a part of their regular diet. Hans Ullman, who grew up in northern Germany in the early years of the twentieth century, recalled the double-walled wooden shed that stood on his family's farm and that was used to cure meats. Sawdust filled the space between the inner and outer walls of the building. In the winter, the shed was filled with ice from the mill pond, and the ice was covered with more sawdust. Beef was placed in earthenware pots, which were filled with brine and then submerged in the sawdust. After the beef was cured, it was immersed in a series of baths of fresh water to remove as much salt as possible. It was then minced by a servant girl who used a hand-cranked machine that turned the beef into meat loaf or patties.[16]

Geese and poultry were more available than beef, given the relative lack of grazing land in eastern Europe that was available to Jews, who were barred by the czar from owning land. In Yekheskl Kotik's memoirs of a privileged late nineteenth-century upbringing in the eastern European town of Kamenits, the author recalled his Aunt Yokheved slaughtering up to thirty geese at once. She cured the geese in a barrel for a month and then served pickled goose meat and cracklings to everyone in her extended family.[17]

In eastern Europe, Jews were much more likely to own drinking places than delicatessens; indeed, according to the historian Glenn Dynner, the vast majority of taverns in Poland were leased by Jews from the nobility.[18] As the memoirist Aharon Rosenbaum recalled of his hometown of Rzeszow, Poland, "There were a lot of taverns in Rzeszow. . . . Given the opportunity, men would sit down and discuss politics or municipal affairs. The best known tavern with the best mead belonged to Yekhiel Tenenbaum whose wife Khana would serve her tasty *kigels* [*kugels*, in Lithuanian Yiddish] and *cholent* [a hearty stew usually served on the Sabbath] to the guests."[19]

While few in number, delicatessens did exist in eastern Europe. Memorial Books (*Yizkor Buchs* in Yiddish)—collections of records and memoirs of eastern European Jews compiled by Holocaust survivors in the 1940s after their towns had been destroyed by the Nazis—often mention delicatessens, where prepared or imported (typically canned) foods were sold. But they make little distinction between them and ordinary grocery stores, such as in an 1891 business directory from Nowy Sacz, Poland, that lists no fewer than thirteen grocery/delicatessen dealers.[20] Similarly, a description of the shops next to the market square in the Ukrainian town of Gorodenka reads, "Some stores sold leather and boots, and only a few grocery stores like those of Yankel Haber and Shlomo Shtreyt met the ordinary needs of the citizens of the city. They sold a greater and colorful selection of supplies; some even sold delicatessen."[21] But what was meant by "delicatessen" is not clear.

A memoir of Jewish life in Mlawa, Poland, offers a tantalizing clue. It notes that a particular store "also served as a delicatessen. One could eat a piece of herring and polish it off with a slice of sponge cake, drink a glass of tea or a glass of soda with syrup which was measured out in small wine glasses made of white metal. . . . The Gentiles drank beer and brandy there and gorged themselves on derma and cabbage."[22] And in the

Interior of an early twentieth-century delicatessen / grocery store in Russia
(Collection of Ted Merwin)

town of Kelem, Lithuania, the businessman Yerachmiel Imber
owned two different stores, a grocery store and a delicatessen,
the latter called Vitmin. This was, in the words of the Mlawa
memoirist, "a new and different type of shop in such a small
town like Kelem. In it one could buy such things as candies in
all varieties, tropical fruits, and other imported and fine delicacies." In neither of these establishments, it seems, was meat on
the menu.[23]

The Delicatessen Migrates to the New World

When did delicatessens first come to the United States? Even
before the Revolutionary War, Thomas Jefferson, who was
known for his epicurean tastes, lauded the gourmet food
stores that he patronized in Philadelphia.[24] But the first real
influx of what were actually called "delicatessens" began with
the successive waves of central European immigration in the

mid-nineteenth century; indeed, Germans and other central Europeans became the largest ethnic group in New York. The first delicatessen owners in New York were from Germany and the neighboring Alsace-Lorraine region of France.

Among the most successful delicatessen owners was H. W. Borchardt, who had opened an iconic food store in Berlin in 1853. In the German capital, Borchardt purportedly served customers from as far away as Asia; he claimed that the sultan of Turkey employed him to cater meetings with foreign princes. Upon his arrival in New York, he opened a store on Grand Street on New York's Lower East Side. His shelves brimmed with cooked meats, hard cheeses, fancy canned foods, imported teas, olive oil, and other high-end groceries. According to the writer Edwin Brooks, "Everything capable of making a mouth water was there—and at prices prohibitive to the average person's pocketbook."[25]

The very first use of the word *delicatessen* in the *New York Times* occurred in 1875 in the context of an amusing lawsuit. A dyer, August Rath, had fallen in love with the daughter of a German delicatessen owner named Caesar Wall. "August dyed for a living in Jersey," the journalist quipped, "while Caesar ministered to the living in the form of sausages, sauerkraut and other delicatessen." On a shopping trip to the store, August met Caesar's virginal daughter, with whom he promptly fell in love, especially after being given her delicate lace jacket for cleaning. Before the nuptials were solemnized, August was invited to become a partner in the business. But when the daughter began to bestow her attentions on another man, August wrathfully withdrew both his funds and his affections.[26]

German delicatessen stores in New York did a brisk business, especially at Christmas time, by purveying dozens of kinds of sausages, smoked goose breast, apricot jam, honey cake, and plum duff. For an authentically German Christmas, the *New York Tribune* reported in 1900, a visit to a German delicatessen was essential since "it takes the German many years to become so thoroughly Americanized that he does not want the regulation German Christmas table luxuries, and these constitute the Christmas stock of the delicatessen dealer."[27]

Patronizing these small, mostly family-owned German delicatessens, the *New York Times* journalist L. H. Robins recalled, was an exotic pleasure; indeed, "to visit them and breathe their unfamiliar good odors had the tang of an adventure in foreign parts. New Yorkers used to do it just for the thrill." The recipes were "handed down in the old country from generation to generation of hausfrau."[28] The German section of the Lower East Side was called *Kleindeutchland* (Little Germany); if one went down there at daybreak, the *New York Herald* noted, "before it is fairly light, you will see the worthy burghers astir, opening the windows of the small delicatessen stores."[29]

According to the etymologist Edward Eggleston, writing in 1894, the term *delicatessen store* was still used exclusively in New York, demonstrating that the English tongue, as spoken in America, had borrowed relatively few words from German at that point.[30] But by the 1920s, the critic H. L. Mencken already observed the "profound effect" of the German migration on American culture, as shown by the nationwide adoption of many German words for food and drink.[31] Furthermore, the delicatessen trade, like many other occupations, had a colorful, exuberant lingo of its own. The etymologist H. T. Webster reflected in 1933 that "delicatessen men," like shoemakers and undertakers, had an occupational vocabulary that was "as little understood by outsiders as if it were Choctaw."[32]

Not all delicatessens were German ones, however. In 1885, the *Brooklyn Daily Eagle* complained that a neighborhood food store on Mott Street in Manhattan's Chinatown was making "no attempt to sell foods made or grown in this country, there being sold what the Germans would call a 'delicatessen.'"[33] A Chinese journalist, Wong Chin Foo, took exception to this idea that the Chinese delicatessen was in any sense inferior to a German one; he extolled the store's "perfumed ducks, pickled oysters and beautifully roasted and powdered pigs, with pink ears and red nostrils." Foo opined, moreover, that the Chinese delicatessen, of which there was but one for the city's ten thousand Chinese residents, was far superior to its numerous "Caucasian" counterparts, in that the latter "always sells stale meat and rotten cheese," while the former was known for its freshly killed pigs, chickens, and ducks. Foo insisted that while the European-style delicatessen required an initial outlay of hundreds of dollars and brought in little, the Chinese delicatessen cost a mere twenty dollars to purchase the meats and yielded "big profits." And, he observed, an "ordinary hallway" could accommodate a good-sized Chinese delicatessen store.[34]

Whatever the delicatessen's country of origin, its fare was widely perceived as exotic. A journalist for the *New York Tribune* who toured the food shops of the Lower East Side in 1897 found a "profusion of uncommon, foreign-looking eatables" sold in delicatessens, including smoked beef, smoked jowls, fresh ham, meat jelly, liver pudding, Russian caviar, and pumpernickel bread. These shops, the observer noted, had "gradually come to take the place of the English bakeshops," adding that they would "roast any desired article for their patrons, from a small bird to a boar's head elaborately decorated." The writer singled out the kosher delicatessen shops on the Lower East Side, in which he discovered smoked goose meat of various kinds, along with potato, beet, cabbage, parsnip, and herring salads in stone crocks. The kosher delicatessen is a "source of much comfort to those who live 'by the family,'" he explained, "and whose time is too valuable to devote to cooking."[35]

Food experts picked up on the parade of ethnic edibles that were making an entree into New York. As the historian Donna Gabaccia has noted, "cross-over" eating was common in New York and other cities in the late nineteenth century, as ethnic groups avidly enjoyed each other's cuisine.[36] This tradition, as Gabaccia has found, went back to the colonial era, when the English, Spanish, Dutch, and Native Americans occasionally sampled each other's foods.[37] But by the turn of the twentieth century, according to the journalist George Walsh, a proliferation of "queer foreign foods" had surfaced in American cities to sate the appetites of recent immigrants. Walsh reflected that "the early tastes which we cultivate are hard to eradicate, and the foreigner turns to the food of his fatherland with great relish, even though coarse and unsavory compared with the food of his adopted land."[38]

Walsh made no mention of Jewish delicatessens, but he limned the French, German, and Italian delicatessen shops that he discovered in New York, Philadelphia, and Chicago—stores that, he observed, had begun to attract "Americans" as well as immigrants.[39] In the growing number and variety of these stores, Walsh espied blood sausage from Italy, pigs' knuckles from France, air-dried beef from Spain, tree and sea mushrooms from Japan, dried chickens and ducks from China, cabbages from Scandinavia, tamales from Mexico, and cinnamon and clove cakes from Palestine. While he considered none of these items to be particularly appetizing, Walsh was impressed by the growing diversity of the urban food scene, in which, he conceded, "all of these odd dishes of the foreigners in our midst tend to broaden our own national bill of fare."[40]

Nor was Walsh alone in omitting Jewish delicatessens from a round-up of local food stores. Forrest Chrissey, the author of a book on American food published in 1917, also overlooked them in his chapter on "tempting table delicacies" purveyed in delicatessen stores of various nations. Chrissey catalogued Hanover tea sausage from England, candied cherries and goose liver sausage from France, guava jelly from the West Indies, pimento peppers from Spain, vermicelli from Italy, birds' nest soup from China, and even canned kangaroo tail from Australia—but no corned beef or pastrami.[41]

Indeed, there were relatively few kosher delicatessens in New York during the period of mass migration from eastern Europe—this despite the fact that Jewish immigrants owned a variety of mom-and-pop food businesses such as grocery stores and butcher shops. In 1899, an oft-cited survey of the Tenth Ward of the Lower East Side (which, with more than seventy-five thousand people crammed into a mere 109 acres was the most densely populated place on earth) found only ten delicatessens and ten *wurst* (sausage) stores—the latter likely overlapped with delicatessens to some extent in terms of their wares.[42] Indeed, delicatessen stores were themselves known as *wurst gesheftn*—sausage stores. By contrast, there were 131 kosher butcher—*schlacht*, in Yiddish—shops, suggesting that most Jewish families preferred to cook their meat at home. Indeed, in the entire immigrant ghetto, there were more than a thousand kosher butcher shops, selling an impressive total of six hundred thousand pounds of kosher beef a week.[43]

The Jewish delicatessen was an outgrowth of these kosher butcher shops. Some kosher butchers had started selling prepared foods, displaying pickled meats and frankfurters on hooks, along with shelves of beans, ketchup, crackers, and soup.[44] From the outset, the delicatessen stores tended to be long and narrow, with a counter running down one side. From this, kosher delicatessens developed, in which meats could be sliced hot, with hot dogs and potato knishes cooked on a grill in the window.

Katz's, which opened in 1888, was perhaps the first "true" Jewish delicatessen in New York. Originally opened under the name Iceland's Delicatessen in 1888 by two brothers of Reuven Iceland, an important Yiddish poet, the store quickly thrived. In 1903, after the Iceland Brothers were joined by Willy Katz, the store was renamed Iceland and Katz. In 1910, Willy Katz and his brother, Benny, bought out the Icelands. Redubbed Katz's, the deli then moved across to the west side of Ludlow Street. It was soon joined by other delicatessens, both on the Lower East Side and throughout the city.

Patricia Volk, the author of the lyrical memoir *Stuffed*, a chronicle of her family's life in the restaurant business, claims that her paternal grandfather, Sussman Volk, a miller from Vilna, introduced pastrami to America. Having failed to make it as a tinker, Volk left the cookware business in 1887 and opened a butcher shop on Delancey Street. A friend asked Volk to store a suitcase in his basement while he returned home to Romania

Employees of Katz's Delicatessen standing outside the store on Houston Street in the 1930s (Courtesy of Malene Katz Padover and Marvin Padover)

for a visit. In return, he gave Volk his pastrami recipe, which Volk used to such success that he had to open a delicatessen to meet the demand.[45] While Volk's story is apocryphal, the author Marcus Ravage has corroborated it to the extent that at the turn of the twentieth century, Romanian delicatessen stores appeared with their "goose-pastrama and kegs of ripe olives and tubs of salted vine-leaves."[46]

Some housewives pickled and smoked their own meat at home. But the process was so complex and time-consuming that few chose to do so. The first American Jewish cookbook, published in 1871 by Esther Levy and directed mostly to upper-class German Jewish women who had servants, contains directions for doing both. To cure a piece of kosher meat, Levy explains, first "make a pickle of salt, strong enough for an egg to swim on top of the water; add some salt-petre, a little bay salt, and coarse brown sugar."[47] After boiling all of these ingredients together and skimming off the fat, the meat is pressed down in a tub for a week or two. Smoking the meat presented particular challenges for the home cook; after the meat has been pickled for exactly sixteen days, Levy directs, either "send it out to be smoked" or, if the cook insists on doing it herself, "place it over a barrel, containing a pan of ignited sawdust, for some hours every day, until nicely browned."[48]

Poverty and Pickled Meat

For Jewish immigrants, the family budget dictated how much meat could be consumed. When kosher beef prices suddenly spiked from twelve to eighteen cents a pound in 1902, enraged Jewish women led a three-week boycott that began by picketing the downtown slaughterhouses. Protests erupted in Brooklyn, Harlem, Newark, Boston, and Philadelphia. Some of these were directed against delicatessens on Rivington and Orchard Streets, where rioters grabbed meat and poured kerosene on it. A few weeks later, after Orthodox rabbis also endorsed the boycott, the prices reverted to previous levels. But, as the historian Paula Hyman has written, the episode demonstrated the power that women had when they banded together; it became a model for later activism by both Jewish and non-Jewish women.[49]

On the whole, Jewish immigrants did eat better in America than they had done in eastern Europe. But many were still desperately poor and had few funds either for food or for the ice that was needed to keep it from spoiling.[50] For example, hunger was a constant companion for the future boxing promoter Sammy Aaronson, who lived on the Lower East Side until the age of ten, when his family moved to Brownsville. "Eating was always a struggle," Aaronson recalled in his memoir. "We lived on pumpernickel, herring, bologna ends and potatoes." His mother sent him to a Hester Street delicatessen, where he purchased a "steering wheel"–sized pumpernickel bread for a dime. The Aaronson family enjoyed hot food on Friday night, when they enjoyed a thin meat soup from the butcher's leftovers and bones. On Saturday nights, they scored the ends of salami, bologna, or garlic wurst or even some higher-quality meat if it were "late enough at night when the guy wanted to clean out his shelves."[51]

As the historian Moses Rischin noted, immigrants were obliged to "husband" their energy, time, and money in order to eat meat for their Sabbath dinner on Friday nights.[52] This often meant eating quite meager meals during the week. Those who spent their hard-earned funds on delicatessen food were castigated by social workers who tried to educate them about the importance of thrift.[53] Sara Smolinsky, the protagonist of Anzia Yezierska's autobiographical novel *Bread Givers*, was starving from working in a sweatshop, to the extent that, she says, "Whenever I passed a restaurant or a delicatessen store, I couldn't tear my eyes away from the food in the window. Something wild in me wanted to break through the glass, snatch some of that sausage and corned-beef, and gorge myself just once."[54]

Jewish parents' attitudes toward food were often conditioned by their own childhood memories of want in eastern Europe. When they could, Jewish mothers routinely overfed their children, especially their sons. Indeed, providing one's children with excessive amounts of food became ingrained in American Jewish culture. "In the swelling and thickening of a boy's body was the poor family's earliest success," noted the critic Alfred Kazin. "'Fix yourself!' a mother cried indignantly to the child on the stoop. 'Fix yourself!' The word for a fat boy was *solid*."[55] The boy's heft concretized the sturdiness of the Jewish family's position in society—it demonstrated the "solidity" of their grasp of an American identity.[56]

Eating Out in New York

Despite the poverty of immigrants, they did enjoy eating food away from home. While delicatessens were not yet a prominent part of the urban landscape, other kinds of eateries and places of leisure were woven into the fabric of life in the city. New Yorkers went out to a staggering variety of places, including, according to the historian David Nasaw, "restaurants, lecture halls, and lodges; beer halls, bawdy houses, brothels and dance halls; billiard rooms, picnic groves and pleasure gardens located just outside the city; and thousands of concert saloons and cheap variety theaters."[57] Rather than enabling immigrants to "escape" reality, the scholar Sabine Haenni has suggested, eating out and other leisure activities furnished a useful take on reality, one that enabled immigrants to "negotiate the massive upheavals, dislocations, and disruptions attending urban immigrant modernity."[58]

Buying and consuming delicatessen food was thus part and parcel of becoming American—and even, for some, of learning English. The writer Maurice Hindus, who arrived from Belarus in 1905, when he was a young teenager, learned English by taking sandwich orders from the girls who worked in a garment factory and fulfilling them at a local delicatessen. After struggling for a week, Hindus's facility with English rapidly improved, to the extent that the well-meaning boy would "only rarely get them so badly mixed that the girl who ordered a frankfurter without mustard received a corned-beef sandwich with mustard."[59]

Food also played an essential role in mitigating feelings of homesickness; as the historian Susan J. Matt has noted, "urban ethnic enclaves offered immigrants the cushion of the familiar, for the numerous grocery stores, bakeries and restaurants provided the opportunity to purchase a taste of home."[60] Matt quotes the Romanian-born author Marcus Ravage, who moved from New York to Missouri, where he "suffered unendurably from hunger" because "everything tasted flat." He lamented that he "missed the pickles and fragrant soups and the highly seasoned fried things and the rich pastries made with sweet cheese that [he] had been brought up on."[61]

There were a plethora of opportunities to eat out in New York, including inexpensive restaurants (such as the "penny" restaurants in Brooklyn, which actually sold meals for a nickel), pushcarts (which carried bagels, pickles, and other familiar eastern European Jewish items), and outdoor food stalls. Most popular of all was the candy store, with its all-important soda fountain. "Subsisting on a scatter of pennies," the historian Irving Howe recalled, "the candy store came to serve as an informal social center in the immigrant streets." The delicatessen, "while important," Howe concluded, "seldom served as the center for either adolescents or grownups as the candy store did."[62]

The candy store was the social center of the neighborhood. "To the boy home from work in the office or factory, and to the school boy, with nothing to do in the evening, the candy store serves as a club-house, where he can meet old friends and make new ones," the sociologist Benjamin Reich observed in 1899. Many of these stores had back rooms that were advertised as ice-cream parlors but that also served as venues for club meetings and performances by teenager amateur comedians testing out their vaudeville routines.[63]

The Tenth Ward boasted more than fifty confectionary shops at the turn of the twentieth century—fully five times the number of kosher delicatessens. The playwright Bella Spewack, who moved four times during a tumultuous childhood on the Lower East Side, did not mention eating in delicatessens in her memoir, *Streets*, but did recall with great fondness the candy store on the corner of Lewis and Stanton Streets, where her mother bought her hot chocolate on cold winter nights.[64] And while the delicatessen and candy store may have seemed quite different from each other, a bizarre combination of the two occurred at Luna Park, the Coney Island amusement park, where two German sisters named Bauer opened a "candy delicatessen" that sold marzipan versions of delicatessen products, including frankfurters, sausages, and sauerkraut.

Candy stores, the historian Jillian Gould has pointed out, were "not merely about a commodity. Rather, they were as much about the pivotal role they played within the community. . . . What happened around the store crystallized what was happening in the neighborhood at large."[65] Immigrant Jews flocked to candy stores for seltzer or soda water, known colloquially as "two cents plain." Gould dubbed the candy store the "local communications center," where tenement dwellers could use the telephone (at a time when few families had their own) or converse with the other denizens of the neighborhood.

Also important were coffeehouses; by 1905, according to Howe, there were "several score of these cafes, or, as they were sometimes called, coffee-and-cake parlors, on the East Side."[66] As in fin de siècle Vienna, where it was proverbial that *Der Jud gehört ins Kaffeehaus* (the Jew belongs in the coffee house), Jewish New Yorkers found the cafe to be a congenial haunt. For a dime, plus a nickel tip, one could order a glass of tea and a slice of cake, in an atmosphere filled with Yiddish and Hebrew writers, actors, scholars, and artists. In David Freedman's comic 1925 novel *Mendel Marantz*, a successful Jewish immigrant purchases a whole tenement building on the Lower East Side, where he establishes a combination delicatessen and coffeehouse. The crowd of nouveau riches manufacturers and businessmen relax at tables with samovars; they play cards or chess, while "munching tongue and bologna sandwiches and drinking bottles of celery-tonic."[67]

Fried-fish stalls, similar to those in London (which had been opened by Sephardic Jews—from the Iberian Peninsula—who appear to have invented "fish and chips"),[68] also made their appearance in New York in the "tenement house districts" such as the Lower East Side. Such stands sold cooked fish, eels, oysters, or crab for a few pennies. Most immigrant Jews, of course, would have eschewed the shellfish. "Like the delicatessen store," the *New York Times* observed, "these fried fish shops are a boon to the woman who doesn't want to cook, or who for some reason or other cannot do so at a particular time." There were only a few seats in the store, so it was assumed that the customer would take the food away. "A specially cooked order that may be taken hot to the tenement a few doors away costs a little more than cold cuts," the *Times* reported, pointing out that what a restaurant would sell for a quarter retailed for no more than ten or fifteen cents at a fish stand. On the other hand, the newspaper conceded, bread was not included.[69]

During the 1880s, some soda fountains, which were also commonly found in drug stores, had begun to serve sandwiches and evolve into what were called luncheonettes. Luncheonettes were found not just on the street but also in department stores, dime stores (such as Woolworth's), and railroad depots. In the first two decades of the twentieth century, luncheonettes—where customers generally sat at a counter—then evolved into lunchrooms, where table service was added. The historians John A. Jakle and Keith A. Sculle have suggested that lunchrooms were "the kind of business that many immigrant families could aspire to early in the twentieth century."[70] But they still remained tied to their origins as candy stores. For example, Schrafft's, which began in Boston in 1898, was a candy manufacturer that opened soda fountains as outlets for its products. In 1915, it had a dozen stores in the New York area; two decades later, it boasted three dozen stores, dispersed along the Atlantic seaboard.

In competing with all these other options for dining out, relatively pricey delicatessen food was at a disadvantage, even in the Jewish community. The immigrant Jewish woman's kitchen was her castle. Tenement apartments on the Lower East Side were structured with the kitchen literally at the center.[71] It was the accepted role of a wife and mother to cook for her family, not to purchase prepared food. To take out food was a tacit admission of inferior cooking skills. It was also difficult for many Jewish women to trust that prepared food was prepared under kosher auspices. This was a reasonable fear, given repeated scandals, as we shall see, related to the manufacture of kosher food.[72]

Nevertheless, immigrant Jews were under pressure to change what they cooked at home to more Americanized fare. Cooking instructors in the settlement houses, where the immigrants were taught the English language and instructed in American customs, emphasized the importance of relinquishing spicy, dark, odoriferous ethnic foods in favor of bland, white, odorless American ones. Garlic, which was often used in Jewish cooking, came in for particular censure; there were long-standing prejudices, dating back to the Middle Ages, against Jews as being stinky because of the garlic that they consumed.[73]

Gleaming white kitchens in the settlement houses, as well as the starched white aprons in which the eager pupils were clad, reinforced the whiteness and blandness of the foods that they prepared. As the historian Sara Evans has noted, home economists working in the settlement houses extolled the virtues of "white sauce," which she suggests, "found an analog in the concept of the American melting pot, which dissolved the pungent spiciness of diverse American cultures."[74]

These attitudes against the foods of immigrant cultures made delicatessen meats a hard sell. Because the kosher delicatessen was not yet an entrenched part of immigrant life on the Lower East Side, and because the family had little capital to invest, the parents of one young Jewish immigrant, Samuel Chotzinoff, struggled to establish their delicatessen in business. The Mandlebaum Sausage Factory on Houston Street installed them in business, and a soda manufacturer lent them a soda fountain. A relative hand-lettered the curving words "Kosher Delicatessen" on the plate-glass window in the front, while an impromptu window display was concocted of salamis hung by cords from the ceiling, pieces of uncooked corned beef and pastrami, and a basket of artificial flowers. A back room behind the store was equipped with a tin clothes boiler to cook the meats. When Chotzinoff lifted the boiler's lid, he remembered, "the fatty, bubbling water spilled over on the floor, and the delicious aggressive aroma of superheated pickled beef would mingle with and soon overpower the prevailing insistent, native, musty, dank smell of perspiring, decaying paint and plaster."[75]

Everyone in the family, including the children, worked in the store. When Samuel was authorized by his parents to wait on customers, he became adept at using the slicer so that he could give "paper-thin" slices of meat to the customers and much-thicker slices for himself. But after nine months of ups and downs, including a major setback in the form of a robbery and a subsequent shake-down for protection money, the family was forced to close the store.

The delicatessen business was so competitive and the profit margin so slim that many delicatessen owners shared the fate of the Chotzinoffs. A perusal of business directories from the period shows many delicatessens going in and out of business in less than a year, as in Moishe Nadir's short story "Ruined by Success," in which a Jewish immigrant who opens a delicatessen store receives no customers, despite a floral wreath that he places in the window to wish himself abundant patronage.[76] "For Sale—Cheap," ran a typical classified advertisement in 1888 in the *New York Herald*. "A fine delicatessen and kosher wurst store, with horse and wagon and outdoor trade."[77]

Rise of the Kosher Sausage Companies

Isaac Gellis had manufactured sausages in Berlin, where he won a contract with the Union army to supply beef to the troops. He arrived in New York in 1870, more than a decade before the massive exodus of Jews from eastern Europe, and opened a sausage factory on Essex Street. His secret was to use bull meat, not cow or steer as other kosher meat purveyors did. If smaller pieces of meat broke off from the large meats being smoked, he would sell these at retail. Gellis later boasted in his advertisements that he had helped Jewish immigrants to adjust to life in America by providing "good, real, kosher meat products."[78] Gellis was the only major manufacturer in New York—there were midwestern companies such as Vienna Beef, Sinai Kosher, and Oscherwitz that had started in the late nineteenth century—until Hebrew National began to capture an increasing share of the market for processed kosher meat.

Hebrew National was founded in 1905 by a Russian immigrant named Theodore Krainin, who had arrived in New York in the 1880s. Isadore Pinckowitz (later known as Isadore Pines), a meat peddler, bought the company in 1928 and began manu-

A corner kosher delicatessen in 1911 in East Harlem, on Lexington Avenue
and East 104th Street (Courtesy of Brian Merlis / Brooklynpix.com)

facturing hot dogs and sausages on the sixth floor of his tenement house at 155 East Broadway. The company soon opened
its own retail stores. When Motl, the hero of Sholem Aleichem's
picaresque Yiddish novel *Motl Peyse dem Khazns* (*Motl Peyse,
the Cantor's Son*), immigrates with his family to America, he
describes how his brother, Elye, gets a job selling "haht dawgz"
for the "Hibru Neshnel Delikatesn," which "has stores all over
town. If you're hungry, you step into one and order a haht dawg
with mustard or horseradish."[79]

Hebrew National's main competitor, Zion Kosher, emerged
in the years after the First World War when the entrepreneur
Max Anderson, who was peddling meat, pickles, and sauerkraut to delicatessen stores, decided to open up his own meat
factory. He and his partner, Leo Tarlow, launched a company
called Always Tasty (after the first initials of their last names)
that manufactured nonkosher meat. They eventually decided

to go into the kosher meat business, first by renting space in an old seltzer factory and then opening their own factory in the Hunts Point section of the East Bronx.

Hebrew National and Zion Kosher jostled for market share with a growing number of smaller kosher provisions companies. Indeed, by the 1930s there were more than a dozen different, independently operated kosher sausage companies located on the Lower East Side, near the slaughterhouses where they purchased their meat, including Schmulka Bernstein's, Jacob Branfman, Barnet Brodie, Hod Carmel, European Kosher, Gittlin's Kosher Provisions, Isaac Gellis, Hygrade, National Kosher, Remach Kosher Meat Products, Mt. Sinai Kosher Provision Supply, Ukor, and 999 Real Kosher Sausage. The delicatessen industry grew fast in order to meet ever-increasing demand for its products. Each company advertised itself as offering the highest quality and most sanitary meats under the strictest rabbinical supervision. As a Yiddish-language ad for Barnet Brodie put it, the company's products were "made from the best meats," were "under the supervision of the rabbis of Greater New York," and were, last but not least, "famous for their taste and quality."[80]

A Store Becomes a Restaurant

At the turn of the twentieth century, some delicatessen stores installed tables, either inside or out on the sidewalk. For example, the delicatessen store owned by Chotzinoff's family had only three tables. At the grand opening, the relatives who were occupying the tables started to get up to let some of the bona fide customers sit down; Chotzinoff's father waved them back down again, under the logic that the more crowded the store seemed, the better it would be for business. Meanwhile, the delicatessen counter did a booming business.

Was a delicatessen with tables a store or a restaurant? This was a question that even the courts had a difficult time answering. In a case before the New York Supreme Court in 1910, a delicatessen owner on the Lower East Side sued a fellow business owner who opened a restaurant next door to her store; the new neighbor argued that because his establishment had tables, it was a bona fide restaurant, not a delicatessen. The judge decided that a delicatessen could indeed have tables; he pointed out that delicatessens could come in all types, comparing them, "in their infinite variety," to Cleopatra![81]

This issue bedeviled even the kosher delicatessens that spread outside the city; the owners of one in Scranton, Pennsylvania, in 1914 were sued by their landlord for conducting a restaurant, in violation of the terms of their lease, because they occasionally permitted customers to sit at the family table at the rear of the store. The judge decided that their establishment could not be considered a restaurant; he found that the "agreement between the parties with respect to conducting a kosher restaurant is not violated by the selling of dried fish, frankfurters, or other articles usually kept in a delicatessen store, even though such articles are eaten upon the premises by the purchasers." He compared the situation to one in which customers purchase cold snacks in a country store and consume them in the building, cracker-barrel style.[82]

With or without tables, delicatessens became targets of a nationwide campaign to enforce Sunday closing laws. According to the historian Batya Miller, the last two decades of the nineteenth century witnessed the rise of evangelical and social-reform-minded Protestants, who deemed it their religious obligation to force others to observe the Sabbath.[83] This was supported by the U.S. Supreme Court, which in 1885 ruled that a Chinese laundryman in San Francisco could be compelled to close his shop on Sundays, under the rationale that the government has a right "to protect all persons from the physical and moral debasement which comes from uninterrupted labor."[84]

These laws, which date back to the early seventeenth century in Virginia, required that businesses be closed on Sundays in observance of the Christian Sabbath. (They were called "blue laws" since they were written on blue paper in New Haven during the colonial era.) They posed a significant problem for many Jewish business owners throughout the country; if they were closed on Saturday in observance of their own Sabbath, then closing on Sunday deprived them of essential weekend business. Even if they were not formally prosecuted, Jewish storekeepers were often the victims of police extortion if they refused to obey the Sunday closing law.[85]

More than 150 owners banded together in 1895 into a formal association of delicatessen dealers to prevail upon the city to allow them to remain open on Sundays. Police Commissioner Theodore Roosevelt informed them that they could sell their products until ten o'clock in the morning—when church services typically began—and could fill deliveries throughout the day if they had been received before that hour. This pleased most of the butchers and grocers, who were happy to have the day off; they argued that anyone who needed provisions for the day could purchase them before ten o'clock. But the delicatessen dealers, especially those who owned smaller neighborhood stores, explained that they needed to stay open all day on Sunday in order to serve their less affluent customers who did not own refrigerators.[86]

Few delicatessen owners were pacified by Roosevelt's making an exception for delicatessens that had tables in their establishments. But they got a sympathetic hearing from Excise Commissioner Julius Harburger, who fulminated against the Sunday law, informing the delicatessen owners at a public meeting in July 1895 that their stores "are a necessity to the people; they are part of the people; they are the existence of the people."[87] His rhetoric became even more overheated in a speech a month later to his constituents, declaring that "under monarchical forms of government, under despotic powers, the people are not hampered, molested, or coerced, as we are under the restrictive policy of the Sunday law," which, he said, led to "the discomfort of three-quarters of our city's population, and the loss of millions of dollars."[88]

Sunday closing laws nevertheless continued in effect, with protests continuing for years. In 1899, the editor of the *New*

York Times sympathized with the delicatessen owners, and he penned a series of ringing editorials in their defense. The first noted that Sunday was the biggest day of the week for the delicatessen trade. "Everyone who lives in New York knows that it is the custom of some nine-tenths of the householders of New York, not alone of German birth, to give their servants Sunday evening off, and on that day to skirmish, as it were, for their evening meal."[89]

After lambasting the statute that prevented the consumption of delicatessen food on Sundays in the metropolis. the editor spoke up for the "scores, if not hundreds of thousands," of New Yorkers who purchase food from delicatessens on Sundays. Nor, he pointed out, can city dwellers necessarily buy the food ahead of time, since "Sunday is their visiting day. If unexpected visitors arrive and there is 'nothing in the house,' the dispatch of a messenger to the dealer in cooked food is the natural and ready recourse of the host and hostess."[90] An advice columnist declared that a housewife would be appropriately frugal if she would "fit up her reserve shelf against the coming of the unexpected guest, and so forestall the hurried trip to the delicatessen store, which is such a drain on both time and pocketbook."[91]

The government also recognized that exceptions needed to be made. A bizarre compromise was worked out February 1899 in which the delicatessens could remain open on Sundays if, like caterers, they sold only complete meals, rather than uncooked food or individual items. Thus, delicatessens would refuse to sell a package of meat by itself, but if a loaf of bread were added to the order, then the sale could take place.[92] Furthermore, if customers desired to carry out the food, then they were obliged to pretend that the delicatessen was delivering it to them, agreeing to act as the agent of the store in bringing it home! After considerable wrangling over the next several months, the courts finally relented, permitting delicatessens to purvey cooked food on Sundays. Two hundred euphoric delicatessen owners celebrated their victory in a park in Upper Manhattan.[93]

Interior of Youngerman's Delicatessen on Marcy Avenue in Williamsburg, Brooklyn, in 1918 (Courtesy of Brian Merlis / Brooklynpix.com)

Nonetheless, the delicatessen raids resumed in 1913 under the direction of Rhinelander Waldo, Tammany's corrupt police commissioner. These were more successful, since the delicatessen dealers were induced to participate by being made "delicatessen deputies," which enabled them to spy on their competitors and have them served with summonses. Again, only "prepared" food could be sold; it was left up to the policeman on the scene—who was often obliged to rely more on his taste buds than on the statute books—to decide what constituted this type of edible. But rather than having to close all day on Sunday, delicatessens were permitted to remain open before 10 a.m. and from 4 p.m. to 7:30 p.m., in order to capture the lucrative Sunday-evening dinner trade.

The tide was turning in terms of American eating patterns. The home-cooked Sunday dinner, a staple of American life, es-

pecially for rural, churchgoing families, had largely been transformed, in the urban setting, into a take-out delicatessen meal.
In 1920, an anonymous social critic in *Life* magazine satirically
compared a typical 1890s Sunday-school picnic to one of his
own day; he contrasted the earnest "packing of the [homemade]
chicken sandwiches and the frosted cake" in the earlier period
to his own generation's lackadaisical, last-minute visit to the
delicatessen.[94]

Cleanliness, Sin, and the Kosher Delicatessen

Some Jews, however, resisted the incursion of delicatessen
food into their diet. While elderly immigrants, by contrast,
"frowned on delicatessen and clung to their accustomed boiled
and sweet-and-sour meats," according to Samuel Chotzinoff,
the younger generation "took to delicatessen for its spiciness,
preferring it to the bland, boiled meats their mothers served at
home."[95] Eating delicatessen food could be, for these younger
Jews, a rebellious act. The critic Alfred Kazin noted that the
pungency of delicatessen sausages carried, for him, an erotic
charge. "Wurst carried associations with the forbidden, the
adulterated, the excessive, with spices that teased and mad-
dened the senses to demand more, still more." Only on Saturday
nights, when the holy Sabbath gave way to the profane weekday,
could this food "be eaten with a good conscience." Indeed, this
was food that was "bought on the sly" and was "supposed to be
bad for us"—associated with the fact that it was "made in dark
cellars," far from the light of day.[96]

While the spiciness of delicatessen meats may have been
a boon to some customers, spices had been, since the mid-
nineteenth century, the object of opprobrium in American
culture. Progressive reformers had found that spices were frequently used to disguise the fact that food was spoiled or tainted.
Furthermore, there were long-standing associations between
the eating of spicy foods and excessive drinking. John Harvey
Kellogg, founder of Kellogg's cereal company, and his wife, the

temperance advocate Ella Eaton Kellogg, insisted that the ingestion of spices and condiments led inexorably to a craving for alcohol. The association stemmed, perhaps, from the practice of placing bowls of spices on the counters of saloons; patrons chewed them to mask the smell of alcohol on their breath.

As Ella Kellogg opined in her popular cookbook *Science in the Kitchen*, "True condiments such as pepper, pepper sauce, ginger, spice, mustard, cinnamon, cloves, etc. are all strong irritants" that are "unquestionably a strong auxiliary to the formation of the habit of using intoxicating drinks."[97] Following the theories of an influential Presbyterian minister, Sylvester Graham (the inventor of Graham Crackers), the Kelloggs also feared that eating both meat and spicy food with any regularity would lead to sexual fantasies and masturbation; John Kellogg developed Corn Flakes in order, he declared, to promote sexual abstinence.[98]

Delicatessen owners throughout the country were thus obliged, from time to time, to confront the widespread perception that their fare was both unhealthy and unclean. The social worker Lillian Wald, who founded the Henry Street Settlement House, instructed immigrant Jewish mothers to refrain from serving smoked and salted meat to their children and to feed them fresh fruits and vegetables instead. A dietician who visited a kosher delicatessen in an unnamed western city in 1928 was shocked by the gluttony that she observed, noting that one obese female customer would "make a good addition to the growing army of Jewish diabetics," and she fantasized about pulling the woman's son out of the delicatessen and into a healthier, more rural place—where he could be furnished with less salty, sugary, and fatty victuals.[99]

While the cleanliness of the deli was also highly suspect, these concerns could be allayed, delicatessen owners were told, if they dressed in the proper clothes. In the pages of the *Mogen Dovid Delicatessen Magazine*, the main trade journal for the delicatessen owners in New York, store owners were reminded that anyone handling or serving food was compelled, by municipal legislation, to wear white. An organization called the Sanitation League informed the dealers, quoting a former city health commissioner who had been elected to the U.S. Senate, Royal S. Copeland, that "the man who is *slovenly* and who makes a poor appearance because of improper uniform or clothing, is sluggish and inefficient mentally and physically." According to Copeland, "if you compel workers to wear clean 'spic and span' uniforms or outer garments, you improve their morale as well as their disappearance [*sic*]. . . . It is thus of real importance to all distributors of food or drink to 'trade up' in the matter of the appearance of their men."[100]

Kosher meat companies and delicatessens competed to offer the products that were seen as the cleanest and healthiest. In a Yiddish advertisement in the *Mogen Dovid Delicatessen Magazine* in August 1931, Barnet Brodie trumpeted its "modern, sanitary factory" that produced corned beef, tongue, pastrami, salami, bologna, and frankfurters that were not just "famous for their taste and quality" but that were supervised by the rabbinical authorities in the city.[101] Krainin, the founder of Hebrew National, lamented in an article in a popular magazine, the *Jewish Forum*, that no rabbi had seen fit to explain to the general public that the kosher laws prohibited the consumption of meat from unhealthy or diseased animals; Krainin defined this as the essence of the kosher system.[102] Indeed, the Chelsea Delicatessen, located on Ninth Avenue between Twenty-Second and Twenty-Third Streets, advertised itself as providing "Cleanliness, Quality and Service Above All" in the furnishing of "sandwiches and salads of all cuts and preparations"—cleanliness came first, and everything else followed in its train.[103]

Balancing out the reputedly unhealthy qualities of delicatessen food, along with its fattiness and saltiness, was the drink of choice that accompanied it. Dr. Brown's Cel-Ray Tonic was first distributed (according to company lore) in 1869 by a doctor who gave out spoonfuls to children on the Lower East Side to help alleviate their digestive problems. The bright-green soda was sold only in delicatessens until the 1980s, when it became available in supermarkets. (The name was changed to "soda" in the 1920s when the government, which was cracking down on the sale of patent medicines, objected to the use of the word "tonic.") In addition to the use of celery in treating physical ailments, it was also widely employed to reduce anxiety. A Victorian "guide to life," published in 1888, recommends that all people who are "engaged in labor weakening to the nerves should use celery daily in the season, and onions in its stead when not in season."[104] The food writer Leah Koenig has pointed out that carbonated beverages, in general, reminded customers of the hot-spring health spas that used mineral water to relieve both physical and psychological distress.[105]

Popular culture also depicted delicatessen food as unhealthy. A mean-spirited 1920s vaudeville monologue, "In the Delicatessen Shop," features a delicatessen owner with a very heavy, mock-Yiddish accent who tries to cater to her customers' needs while attempting to control a brood of children who are playing games with the food, as well as putting both the cat and the baby inside the counter. "Mine gracious! Izzy! Such a poy!" she finally bursts out. "Coome vrum dot counter behind. Vhen papa come he should spunish you vit a stick. How you oxpect your mamma to zell to de gustomers vhen dey seen you rolling dem epple pies on de floor around?"[106]

This was a routine almost certainly written for non-Jewish entertainers known as "Hebrew" comics who traded on anti-Semitic attitudes.[107] The food sold in the delicatessen is portrayed as not fit for human consumption, just as Jews were typically portrayed as unsuitable for participation—unkosher, one might say—in American society. The Jewish deli owner is a laughing stock, her products—and her very personhood—irrevocably tainted. As the historian Matthew Frye Jacobson has noted, Jews were disparaged as racial outsiders who had the potential to pollute the racial stock of America.[108]

These stereotypes made Jews themselves unpalatable to "native" Americans; one commentator at Harvard University in the early 1920s justified strict quotas on Jewish admissions by calling Jews an "unassimilable race, as dangerous to a college as indigestible food to man."[109]

Fraud in the Kosher Delicatessen Industry

Beyond the kosher delicatessen industry's doubtful reputation for the healthfulness and purity of its products, it was also tainted by large-scale scandals that erupted around the selling of nonkosher meat as kosher. Since kosher meat was more difficult to obtain and always commanded a higher price than nonkosher (*treyf*, in Yiddish) meat, meat companies and delis often misled their customers by switching the two. At a time when kosher meat was in tremendous demand—in 1917, the national consumption of kosher meat reached 156 million pounds—there was big money in this kind of scam. Individual rabbis gave their *hecksher* or stamp of approval to the process under their supervision. Yet in 1925, a study by the state found that fully 40 percent of meat sold as kosher in New York City was actually *treyf*.[110]

It is little wonder, though, because until 1916, when the Union of Orthodox Rabbis forbade the practice, it was not uncommon for both kosher and nonkosher meat to be manufactured in different parts of the same factory. But when companies decided to produce only kosher meat, they often cut corners regarding the supervision of the process. Such was the case with Sunshine Provision Company, which switched in 1922 from the production of nonkosher meat to kosher meat but was found using hog casings for its "kosher" sausages; fully 95 percent of the meat that the company was selling as kosher was actually *treyf*.[111]

The most egregious case of fraud occurred in 1933, when the owners of one of the most prominent kosher meat companies, Jacob Branfman and Son, were indicted for selling nonkosher meat, which was delivered to the factory late at night, after the kosher supervisor (the *mashgiach*) had gone home. An undercover investigator testified that he had observed through binoculars as a worker draped oilcloth over the Branfman name on one of the company's trucks while barrels of nonkosher brisket were being loaded into it. A police raid found two and a half tons of nonkosher meat sitting in the factory.[112] When the case came to court, the judge ruled that "to expose for sale" means "to have in stock," even if the product is not displayed.[113] The conviction meant that not only did delicatessens have to discard all the meat they had purchased from Branfman, but rabbis instructed thousands of customers to throw out all the cooking vessels, dishes, and silverware that had come in contact with the offending products.

Delicatessen owners also often tried to trick their customers by passing off nonkosher meat as kosher; they thus saved the hefty price difference between the two types of meat. Some played on the similarity in Hebrew between the words for "kosher" and "meat"—the two words vary only by their initial letter (and even those initial letters look very similar). Rather than offering "kosher meat," then, some delicatessen owners fooled customers by putting "meat meat" in their windows; they knew that few customers would notice the subtle difference, and they could deny that they had offered kosher meat for sale in the first place. The editor of the *Mogen Dovid Delicatessen Magazine* defended the practice, arguing that if stores use Hebrew lettering or put a Star of David in their window or print advertising, it is simply because they "mean to advise that Yiddish may be spoken in their places, that a Jewish atmosphere prevails, etc." To require that Hebrew lettering must not be used in a deceptive manner, he argued disingenuously, suggests that Jews are unfamiliar with their own language.[114]

A revised law then required meat dealers to label their products "kosher" or "on-kosher" with four-inch signs and to display additional signs in their windows making clear which type of meat was offered for sale. These laws complemented the existing consumer-protection statutes, first passed in 1915 and upheld by the U.S. Supreme Court ten years later, that stated that it was illegal for a food dealer to represent goods as kosher when they were not.[115] As an English-language editorial in the *Yiddishes Tageblatt* demanded in 1922, as yet another bill was proposed to regulate the advertising and selling of kosher meat, "butchers, provision and delicatessen dealers who display the word 'kosher' must live up to that sign."[116]

Some delicatessen owners kept up the battle; they argued that the word *kosher* was difficult to define and can admit of a range of meanings, beyond only the strict Orthodox interpretation. For example, many delicatessens remained open on the Jewish Sabbath, in violation of Jewish law. Even if the meat itself were strictly kosher, selling it on the Sabbath rendered it impure in the minds of traditional Jews. When the state decided to continue to rely on the guidance of Orthodox rabbis and laymen to define "kosher," more than four hundred kosher delicatessen owners joined in a protest meeting in Brownsville. The owners complained that the new regulations were reminiscent of the despised Russian *korobka*, and they accused the legislature of kowtowing to a small segment of the Jewish community at the expense of the majority of Jews in the city.

Samuel Caesar, the president of the kosher delicatessen owners' association, reminded the union men at the rally that most of them were members of the Workmen's Circle, a fervently socialist Jewish organization. How, Caesar thundered, could the owners permit a "small group of rabbis the right to force Orthodox Judaism" on them? In defining the kosher delicatessen owners as secular Jews battling against the forces of religious Orthodoxy, Caesar insisted on the delicatessen as a place where different understandings of Jewishness could coexist.[117]

This redefinition of the delicatessen in secular terms foreshadowed the development of the delicatessen into a kind of "secular synagogue" for second-generation Jews—one in which the delicatessen transcended its immigrant Jewish origins. As we have seen, the delicatessen, which had been largely unknown in eastern Europe, was also not particularly entrenched in Lower East Side immigrant Jewish life. At the same time, Jews were themselves marginalized by other Americans. In the next chapter, we will see how Jews began to conquer their pervasive sense of inferiority by turning Jewish delicatessen food from a low-class, suspect item into a high-class one of glitz and glamor.

As the delicatessen continued to gain traction in the culture of New York, different orientations toward Jewish religion and culture would produce not just different kinds of kosher delicatessens but a "kosher-style" type of delicatessen as well that reflected the desire of many Jews to create a new balance between their Jewish and American identities, one in which the nature of Jewish food itself would be redefined to serve the purpose of acculturation into American society.

={2}=

From a Sandwich to a National Institution

DELICATESSENS IN THE JAZZ AGE AND THE INTERWAR ERA

In the Marx Brothers' first Broadway show, *I'll Say She Is!*, which catapulted the vaudeville performers to stage (and later film) stardom, the delicatessen played a starring role. The 1924 revue was about a bored rich girl who promises her hand in marriage to the suitor who gives her the greatest excitement. The climax featured Groucho as a famous French hero. Playing Napoleon to Lotta Miles's Josephine, Napoleon was surprisingly, anachronistically, and quite bizarrely fixated on Jewish delicatessen foods:

> NAPOLEON: Get me a bologna sandwich. Never mind the bologna. Never mind the bread. Just bring the check. Get me a wine brick.
> JOSEPHINE: Oh! It's you. I thought you were at the Front.
> NAPOLEON: I was, but nobody answered the bell, so I came around here.
> JOSEPHINE: Well, what are you looking for?
> NAPOLEON: My sword—I lost my sword.
> JOSEPHINE: There it is, dear, just where you left it.
> NAPOLEON: How stupid of you. Why didn't you tell me? Look at that point. I wish you wouldn't open sardines with my sword. I am beginning to smell like a delicatessen. My infantry is beginning to smell like the Cavalry.[1]

What makes this skit deliciously ironic is its presentation of a "Jewish" Napoleon. After all, it was the great French leader who helped to emancipate the Jews, offering them French citizenship in return for their promise to keep their religion to themselves. This enabled the rapid assimilation of most of the Jews of France and also served as a model for other European governments in their approach to the "Jewish Question"—the problem of how to integrate Jews into European civil society. In return, Napoleon became a staple of Jewish folklore.[2]

By contrast to this victorious bigwig, the demasculinized Groucho Marx version of Napoleon can't keep track of his sword, and he doesn't seem to know where he is going. Even when he finds his sword, he discovers that his presumably unfaithful lover has been using it, quite promiscuously, as a can opener. He's "hot" for Josephine, but his body smells like a delicatessen. He is sinking inexorably back to his "Jewish" roots, which put him at odds with his role as a French hero and lover. The call of the delicatessen is ultimately too strong; after this repartee, he gestures to the band leader to strike up the famous French song "The Mayonnaise"—a joke, of course, on the French national anthem, "La Marseillaise."

The call of the delicatessen likewise reverberated stentoriously for the children of Jewish immigrants who acculturated into American society during the Jazz Age and for whom the Jewish eatery and its fare became symbols of success. Rising prosperity after the First World War led to the pell-mell exodus of Jews from the Lower East Side. Newer Jewish neighborhoods sprang up in Harlem, the Bronx, and Brooklyn—neighborhoods in which the delicatessen became a crucial gathering space for a generation of lower-middle-class Jews who were eager to participate in American society while still maintaining loyalty to their ethnic roots.

Even as the membership of the Ku Klux Klan peaked, Henry Ford fulminated against Jewish "control" of American banking and entertainment, and stringent new immigration restrictions were passed that essentially ended the influx of eastern

European Jews, second-generation Jews found a congenial gathering place in the delicatessen, a place where they could feel, in Deborah Dash Moore's influential phrase, "at home in America,"[3] and where they could congratulate themselves on having transcended their immigrant origins. The ability to consume meat was, as we saw for the bourgeoisie in late eighteenth-century Paris, a visible index of upward mobility. The sandwich-making business, in particular, appeared to be a quick route to riches. "There are sandwich impresarios in every city in the country," the drama critic George Jean Nathan asserted, "who—up to a few years ago poor little delicatessen dealers—now wear dinner jackets every evening and own Packard Sixes."[4]

The serving of "overstuffed" sandwiches in theater-district delicatessens presaged the contemporary hot-dog-eating contests sponsored annually by Nathan's on the Fourth of July, which, like the Thanksgiving feast, are a celebration of American bounty and excess.[5] The anthropologist Robert Abrahams has suggested that American holidays are typically marked by taking ordinary things and "stylizing them, blowing them up, distending, or miniaturizing them"—he lists the "lowly firecracker, the balloon, the wrapped present, the cornucopia, the piñata, the stuffed turkey, and Santa's stuffed bag." The overstuffed delicatessen sandwich could certainly be added to that catalogue of cartoonish items that burst their boundaries, release repressed energies, and create a carnival atmosphere of raucous celebration.[6]

The exaltation felt by second-generation Jews that they had finally "arrived" in America was spurred by the very atmosphere of the nonkosher, theater-district delicatessens, which were imbued with the glitz and glamor of celebrity—as shown in everything from the showbiz pictures on the walls to the sandwiches that were named after the theater and film stars of the day. Allan Sherman and Bud Burtson's unproduced 1947 musical *The Golden Touch* satirizes the stardust atmosphere of these delis; it revolves around a nonkosher delicatessen in the theater district called Cheesecake Sam's that caters to "up-scale" customers such as "the most important shipping clerks and celebrated soda jerks! A boulevardier from Avenue A! The distingue of Rockaway! A furrier from Astoria."[7]

The Stage Delicatessen, which opened in 1935, was thus aptly named; it was the Jewish *customers* who used it as a platform to display, through conspicuous consumption of large quantities of pickled meat, their own growing visibility in American society; the Stage Delicatessen's unofficial slogan was "Where Celebrities Go to Look at People."[8] Its clientele imbibed the show-business atmosphere like slabs of brisket soaking up barrels of brine on their way to becoming corned beef and pastrami. As the vaudevillian Joe Smith joked in one of his routines, "Max's Stage Delicatessen," the food was "so high-class that if you get an ulcer from eating here, it'll have on a tuxedo."[9]

At these vibrant, humming eateries, ordinary New Yorkers hobnobbed with the rich and famous. Harpo Marx described the lively crowd at Lindy's and Reuben's as a mix of the down on their luck with the very successful—"cardplayers, horseplayers, bookies, song-pluggers, agents, actors out of work and actors playing the Palace, Al Jolson with his mob of fans, and Arnold Rothstein with his mob of runners and flunkies. The cheesecake was ambrosia. The talk was old, familiar music."[10] Second-generation Jews dined amid that lively "music" in order to have some of the stardust rub off on themselves.

It may seem odd that the humble sandwich epitomized life in New York during the opulent, ostentatious Jazz Age. But sandwiches were all the rage. The drama critic George Jean Nathan reported in 1926 on the "sandwich wave" that had "latterly engulfed the Republic." He found 5,215 stores in New York City alone that specialized in sandwiches, which he discovered had become "one of the leading industries of the country, taking precedence over soda-water, candy, chewing gum, and the *Saturday Evening Post*." Furthermore, the sandwich appealed, in one form or another, to everybody, in every social class and occupation in society, including, Nathan noted, to "the shopgirl

Cover of Reuben's menu with caricatures of stage and film stars—note
the slogan in the lower lefthand corner. (Collection of Ted Merwin)

and the lady of fashion, the day-laborer and the Brillat-Savarin." As a result, Nathan found no less than 946 different kinds of sandwiches, made from ingredients ranging from snails to spaghetti.[11]

The menus in the theater-district delicatessens were typically very long, with hundreds of items available every night. As Jim Heiman pointed out in his history of twentieth-century American menu design, "being handed an oversized bill of fare became an event in itself, subtly suggesting a restaurant's importance by the seemingly endless choices offered to a customer."[12] It made the customer feel important too, to know that his or her options were so vast; the composer Oscar Levant once jokingly asked a waiter at Lindy's if he could take a delicatessen menu home, in order to give him something to read.[13]

During the 1920s, which the novelist and historian Jerome Charyn calls the "delicatessen decade,"[14] Jewish eateries participated in this culture of conspicuous consumption. "If you take a glance into the plate-glass window," noted the humorist Montague Glass of a delicatessen in downtown Manhattan, "you will see such a display of food, tastefully decorated with strips of varicolored paper,[15] as Rabelais might have catalogued for one of Gargantua's heartier meals." The turkeys, he added, are "interspersed with spiced beef, smoked tongue, plump kippered white fish, and festoons of frankfurters." Glass compared the decor to that of an old-fashioned Pullman railroad car, which employed such expensive materials as inlaid mother of pearl, stained glass, satinwood, and mahogany.[16]

Some delicatessen exteriors were even more attention grabbing and ostentatious. Arnold Manoff, a worker for the Federal Writers' Project who interviewed Arnold Reuben in 1938, compared the interior of Reuben's with the opulent lounge of the Radio City Musical Hall, noting that as the pedestrian strolls up Fifty-Eighth Street toward Fifth Avenue,

> suddenly the wall of brick to your left is ended and the periphery of your eye catches a huge pane of glass curtained in cream folds and

shrubberied formally at the bottom. A red blazing neon sprawls over the window REUBENS. Typical. This is REUBENS! Who is Reuben that his name should stand alone without a word of explanation, without even a first name, without a Company or Inc after it? What the hell! You don't mind GENERAL MOTORS; Money! Power! Industry. Well, all right, REUBEN. Twenty Five feet long, five feet high on 58th Street, Right next to the Savoy Plaza, the Sherry Natherland [*sic*]. Nearby Central Park, the old Plaza, Fifth Ave. Nearby Park Ave. A ritzy restaurant, if you judge by what you can't see from the outside.[17]

The immense neon sign connoted brashness and brazenness, opulence and ostentation; it joined in the nightly visual symphony of the lights of the skyscrapers of Manhattan. The delicatessen's location among the iconic hotels that surround Central Park also places it in the most august company imaginable— old-money, Protestant New York society. To the writer, there was evidently something incongruous about such an obviously Jewish name being so prominently emblazoned on the midtown Manhattan scene, at a time when Jews were still viewed by many as grasping, ill-mannered interlopers in American society. Yet the sign still suggested that a Jew and his restaurant had, however improbably, reached the pinnacle of American society.

During the Jazz Age, Broadway was itself at its zenith. The number of new shows more than doubled from 126 in 1927 to 264 in 1928—the all-time peak.[18] Theater tickets were relatively inexpensive; many New Yorkers attended theater on a weekly basis, and they also patronized the palatial movie theaters that were also located near Times Square.

No ethnic group was more involved and invested in popular culture than were the Jews, who provided the lion's share of the creative talent, financial backing, and real estate for the entertainment business.[19] And no New York eateries were more emblematic of show-business culture than were the theater-district delicatessens, which transformed the ordinary sandwich into a fancy meal. According to Rian James, who penned a popular dining guide to New York in 1930, Reuben "raised the in-elegant dime sandwich to a wholly elegant dollar status!" James noted that in Reuben's, you can "see all Broadway parade before you."[20]

After his performances at the Winter Garden Theater, the famous Jewish singer Al Jolson, the most popular Jewish entertainer of his day (best known for his 1927 film *The Jazz Singer*), would invite the entire audience to accompany him to Lindy's for a pastrami sandwich. The bootlegger Arnold Rothstein, infamous for fixing the 1919 World Series, did all his business at delicatessen tables at Lindy's, where he was such a fixture that when he was gunned down outside the restaurant in 1928, many people thought that he had been an owner of the restaurant. By controlling the city's underworld from his table at Lindy's, the historian Michael Alexander has noted, Rothstein demonstrated that a Jew could be influential and admired, despite being a criminal, while remaining squarely within his own ethnic milieu.[21]

The owners of these delicatessens were colorful and obsessed with public attention. By promoting the image of their restaurants as filled with stars of every description and a general air of comic mayhem, they seemed to have themselves missed their calling to be on the stage. Arnold Reuben, for example, was described as having an "aggressive, brusque appearance" with a twitching face, from which "words roll out of his mouth in a spitting, swishing thick torrent. . . . Intonations mixed Yiddish, Broadway wise guy, clipped executive style, and big-man, really boy-at-heart, petulant, lisping, ain't-I-charming manner."[22]

Max Asnas, who opened the Stage Delicatessen in 1937 after a stint as a counterman at the Gaiety, was a short, rotund man with a waddling gait and deep voice overlaid with a thick Yiddish accent. The "sage of the Stage" was known for his quick comebacks. When the comic Jack E. Leonard accused one of the waiters of spilling mustard on his expensive coat, Asnas retorted, "You think this is cheap mustard?" An elderly female patron who asked if the establishment was kosher was told that it was so nonkosher that even when Asnas bought kosher meats, he sold them as nonkosher. "And where did you get the accent?" she pursued. "This I got from the customers," he rejoined.[23]

Asnas, who spent much of his time at the racetrack, was, despite his diminutive height, larger than life. The former Hollywood press agent Leon Gutterman called Asnas a "philosopher, philanthropist, comedian, gag expert, show business critic, psychologist, psychoanalyst, and 'pastrami pundit' all in one man."[24] Everybody who was anybody, it seemed, knew him. In "When Mighty Maxie Makes with the Delicatessen," a song written by the Broadway composer Martin Kalmanoff, Asnas is proclaimed the "toast of the town," and the Stage, it is noted, is where "you'll find debutantes with poodles eatin' hot goulash and noodles" and where the "corned beef and pastrami can keep them all fressin' [gobbling] till it's time to close down."[25]

The length of a delicatessen menu was matched by the extravagance of the dishes. A sample menu from Reuben's Delicatessen from the 1920s begins with a selection of oysters, clams, and other shellfish, then proceeds to a section on hors d'oeuvres that features beluga caviar and pâté de foie gras. After a "Steaks and Chops" section that lists pork chops along with lamb chops and chateaubriand, the menu offers various kinds of ham and rarebit. Even a humble Jewish favorite such as *matzoh brei* (a matzoh and scrambled egg combination, traditionally eaten during the week of Passover, when the consumption of leavened bread is forbidden) was gussied up as Matzoth Pancakes with Jelly a la Reuben, while chopped liver was reinvented as Chopped Chicken Livers with Truffles and Mushrooms. In addition, more than two dozen "named" sandwiches are also listed on the menu, each costing about a dollar. Beginning with the Al Jolson Tartar Sandwich, which paid tribute to the greatest Jewish star of the era, the menu includes sandwiches named after the playwright Sammy Shipman, the silent film star Lina Basquette, and the orchestra leader Paul Whiteman.

Reuben claimed that when he created a sandwich, he tried "to make it fit the character and temperament of the celebrity" after whom the sandwich was named. The custom began, he said, when a showgirl named Annette Seelos, who had just been hired for a small part in a Charlie Chaplin film being filmed in New York, came into his "shtoonky delicatessen store" on Broadway and Seventy-Third Street and asked him for a free sandwich; he obliged by putting Virginia ham, roast turkey, Swiss cheese, and coleslaw on rye bread. But although she wanted to have the sandwich named after her, he decided to name it after himself.[26]

It was Reuben's exuberant, enticing ambience that made it into a key place for Jews to show off their rising economic and social position in America. An ad for Reuben's in a program of the Ziegfeld Follies from the early 1930s urges theater patrons to dine at the restaurant after the show, since "no evening's entertainment is complete without a visit to Reuben's—where delectable food is served in charming atmosphere—where persons who have 'arrived' foregather to meet their friends." The ad suggests that the restaurant is extremely high class and caters to an affluent customer base; it contains silhouettes of upper-class men in top hats and wealthy women in fashionable mink coats.[27]

This was the mirror that the delicatessen reflected to its largely lower-middle-class Jewish customers; it showed them not as they were but as they desperately, urgently desired to be. The window of the nonkosher delicatessen store provided a glimpse into an intensely Jewish space, but one that held the promise of magical, almost mystical, transformation. It reassured Jews that they had begun to "make it" in America.

Using the slogan "where a sandwich grew into an institution" (later replaced, by the early 1930s, by the even more exalted "from a sandwich to a *national* institution"), Reuben's thus walked a thin line between proclaiming the overt Jewishness of its milieu and projecting an enticing image of acculturation. By claiming that it had become "institutionalized" in American life, the delicatessen implicitly suggested that Jews themselves were beginning to join the framework of American society, to become part of the very structure of American life by downplaying their religion in favor of a more secular way of being Jewish.

Perhaps the most showbiz-style delicatessen of them all was Lindy's, which was opened on August 20, 1921, by the German immigrant Leo Lindemann and his wife, Clara, who had met when he worked as a busboy in her father's restaurant, the Palace Cafe at Broadway and Forty-Seventh Street. Lindemann and his wife attended the opening night of Broadway shows, and the stars reciprocated by patronizing his restaurant. By the end of the decade, the enterprising deli owner opened a second location across the street and two blocks uptown. (By the late 1930s, he expanded the second restaurant to serve 344 people, with tables turning over ten times a day.) The delicatessen also captured a lot of business during the dinner break between the two parts of Eugene O'Neill's *Strange Interlude* at the nearby John Golden Theatre. Lindy's was famous for making sandwiches with entire loaves of rye bread sliced lengthwise and for serving huge slices of strawberry-topped cheesecake.

Lindy's was immortalized in a series of interwar short stories by the journalist Damon Runyon, later adapted into the 1950 Broadway musical *Guys and Dolls,* in which a delicatessen called Mindy's was the gathering spot for a collection of colorful gangsters. Runyon's genius was to realize that the theater-district delicatessens were places where lower-middle-class Jewish men went to feel more successful, masculine, and American. (Runyon rarely strayed from this milieu in his work, once noting, "As I see it, there are two kinds of people in this world; people who love delis, and people you shouldn't associate with.")[28] Take, for example, the opening of "Butch Minds the Baby," about a gangster's comical struggles in looking after an infant: "One evening along about seven o'clock, I am sitting in Mindy's restaurant putting on the gefilte fish."[29]

Putting on the gefilte fish? Where, in heaven's name, was he putting it? Actually, the expression "putting on the gefilte fish" is a play on the expression "puttin' on the ritz," meaning to assume upper-class airs. Irving Berlin's famous song "Puttin' on the Ritz" asks, "Have you seen the well-to-do / Up and down Park Avenue / On that famous thoroughfare / With their noses in the air."[30] But it is also a play on an earlier expression, "puttin' on the dog," which refers to the practice of cradling a poodle or other small dog on one's lap as an emblem of a luxurious life-style free from physical exertion; many prosperous Victorian women, including Queen Victoria herself, had their portraits done with dogs on their laps. The expression was current in America during the Victorian period; Lyman Bagg, who gradu-ated from Yale in 1869, used the expression in describing how students showed off at his alma mater: "To put on the dog, is to make a flashy display, to cut a swell."[31] The elevation of gefilte fish helped Jews to enter the American mainstream, to swim with the changing tides of American social and economic life.

In line with the desire of Jews to become more American, delicatessens often promoted an image of upscale dining that was quite incongruous with their actual fare. The cover of a blue-and-white 1945 menu from the Rialto Restaurant and Deli-catessen displays a pen-and-ink drawing of an elegantly dressed couple being served by a tuxedo-clad waiter holding a covered chafing dish; the man and woman sit under an immense fern as they drink their cocktails and gaze at each other in the light of a small, shade-covered lamp on their table. However, the Rialto's offerings were considerably less lofty than such an image of fine dining might suggest; the menu items ranged from tongue and cheese sandwiches to pastrami omelets. It seems unlikely that any of this food was served from chafing dishes! The exterior of the menu represented how Jews wanted to be seen on the out-side; the interior revealed how they actually felt and operated on the inside, still tied tightly to their ethnic origins.

This contradictory self-image may have led, in some ways, to the growth of Jewish popular culture. The burgeoning Jewish audience, as well as the many Jewish members of the entertain-ment industry, led to an increasing number of plays and films that centered on New York Jewish life and that showed the travails—both external and internal—that Jews faced in becom-

Cover of Rialto Delicatessen menu from 1945 (Collection of Ted Merwin)

ing American.³² Because it was almost de rigueur for comedy sketches and scenes that centered on Jewish life to take place in delicatessens, the Jewish eating establishment often became the place for the working out of these conflicts.

For example, *Kosher Kitty Kelly*, a 1925 Broadway musical that was turned into a silent film in 1926, showed the Jewish eatery as a place for different ethnic groups to come together. The Yiddish-accented deli owner Moses Ginsburg is friendly but disreputable; he secretly peddles alcohol in milk bottles. Ginsburg's "stricktly" kosher delicatessen store has a diverse customer base that includes African Americans, Greeks, a Swede (who turns out, unluckily for Ginsburg, to be a Prohibition agent), and a Chinese laundryman. Ginsburg also tries to serve the Jewish community by playing matchmaker; he attempts to get a Jewish girl named Rosie Feinbaum to give up her Irish beau, Pat O'Reilly, for a Jewish doctor named Morris Rosen. Unfortunately, Morris already has a girlfriend, Kitty Kelly, the Irish girl of the title.

Despite the characters' camaraderie, almost all of them are so intensely xenophobic that they believe that foreigners should be either kept out of the country or killed. Rosie fantasizes about marrying Pat in order to "get into a different atmosphere, away from [her] own people," where she could bleach her hair blond and stop being identifiably Jewish. Morris's mother, Sarah, goes to a meeting to find out how New York can be purged of "foreigners"—when she gets there, she is shocked to learn that they want to get rid of all immigrants, including the Jews! Meanwhile, the Chinese laundryman, Lee, whom the other characters call "the Chink," attends a gathering of the tongs, the Chinese gangs that aim to "kill all foreign devils" and take over the drug trade in the city. Everyone seems to get along fine only as long as they're all buying food—and drink—in the delicatessen, the all-purpose symbol of racial and ethnic harmony.³³

Jews and Irish also encounter one another in the 1926 silent film comedy *Private Izzy Murphy*, which marked the debut of the director Lloyd Bacon. George Jessel plays an enterprising

Advertising card from 1926 silent film version of *Kosher Kitty Kelly*
(Collection of Ted Merwin)

Jewish delicatessen owner who opens two stores, one in a Jewish neighborhood and one in an Irish section. In order to impress his Irish girlfriend, Eileen, with his bravado, Goldberg enlists in the army disguised as an Irishman. When his all-Irish regiment wins a big battle, the Jewish doughboy shares in the victory. The word "private" in the title is a pun; Izzy hides his true identity until he can demolish the stereotype that attaches to it, the stereotype of the Jew who is accomplished in business but not on the battlefield.[34] Both films, like the long-running film series *The Cohens and the Kellys* and the film *Clancy's Kosher Wedding*, capitalized on the popularity of Anne Nichols's *Abie's Irish Rose*, a record-breaking Broadway play that combined the ethnic humor of stereotypical Jewish and Irish characters.[35]

But Jewish delicatessen food did not automatically help to build bridges to non-Jews. In an early short talkie, *The Delicatessen Kid*, produced in 1929, the comic Benny Rubin plays the starstruck son of a delicatessen owner (Otto Lederer) who imitates the different singing and dancing styles of the various (non-Jewish) entertainers who patronize the store, who are modeled on such luminaries as Eddie Leonard, Bill "Bojangles" Robinson, and Pat Rooney. Much of the humor comes from the fact that these non-Jewish customers do not seem as appreciative of Jewish food as the father would like; one refuses to buy pickles along with his sandwiches, while another—the Bojangles character—asks in vain for pork chops.[36]

The Jewish Delicatessen Waiter

Even as delicatessens became both setting and theme for popular culture, they took on a highly theatrical vibe of their own. Beyond the celebrity atmosphere, one of the most entertaining aspects of the Jewish delicatessen was provided by the stereotypically snooty Jewish waiters, many of whom were former actors from the Yiddish or vaudeville stage. Jewish delicatessen waiters were frequently bossy and obnoxious to the customers; they told them where to sit, what to order, and how to behave. They acted, in other words, more like the famously snooty waiters in high-class Parisian restaurants than the servers that one would expect in a New York sandwich shop.

The short-tempered, sarcastic delicatessen waiter was always ready with a cynical remark that cut the customer down to size like an expert tailor taking a swipe at a garment. He expressed the resentment, always bubbling above the surface like the froth on a glass of seltzer, that the Jewish laborer felt for those who were starting to put on airs. The waiter was also left behind in a backbreaking occupation, serving his social betters with food that symbolized upward mobility.[37] As Diane Kassner, the bewigged and heavily-made-up waitress who worked for decades at the Second Avenue Deli, intoned with a mixture of stoicism and regret as she dumped matzoh ball soup from a tin cup into a customer's bowl, "You'll be the richer; I'll be the poorer."[38]

Many waiters labored for decades in the same restaurant; it was not uncommon for the waiters at Ratner's (which was a well-known dairy restaurant) to work into their eighties or nineties. It is no wonder that the waiters at Lindy's joked about writing a book about their experience, under the title "I've Waited Long Enough."[39] The Jewish waiter was, in Alan Richman's words, "as much as an American original as the workingmen who drove herds of cattle, laid railroad tracks, built skyscrapers." The only difference, he conceded, was that the waiter "just moved a lot slower."[40]

Why did customers want to be insulted or treated jocularly when they ate in Jewish delicatessens? Most Jews were probably able to discriminate between what was truly nasty or inattentive treatment and what was essentially an appeal to a common "language" or way of interacting, in which raised voices and sarcasm were a shared inheritance from Yiddish immigrant culture. Who else could talk to you so obnoxiously other than a close friend or family member? "A waiter in Lindy's," it was said, "is not only your servant. He's also your relative."[41] The waiter was a kind of surrogate uncle or grandfather for the duration of the meal; he paradoxically made you feel at home by treating you with undisguised contempt.

Furthermore, the hostile-seeming server was nothing new in American culture. An anonymous New York waitress, quoted in 1916, was asked about the effect of the work on her physical and emotional state. "Sore feet and a devilish mean disposition," she responded.[42] In the early years of the twentieth century, when women were first being hired in significant numbers as waitresses (until then, the idea of having women serve male customers carried awkward sexual connotations), the stereotype of the ill-mannered "hasher" developed. "Almost everyone agreed that the 'hasher' (girl who waited table) of a generation ago was an untidy, uneven-tempered, unpredictable creature," noted one observer during the Depression. "She didn't have charm." But by the 1930s, an important change had occurred, in that "pulchritude and personality are just as necessary to the food-dispenser as pork chops and *pastrami*."[43]

Many non-Jews also enjoyed being ribbed by the waiters, despite the disparity between the way in which they were

Tuxedoed waiter at the Rialto Restaurant and Delicatessen, along with chef and two countermen (Courtesy of Ziggy Gruber)

treated in non-Jewish restaurants and the delicatessen waiters' brusqueness. The sociologist Harry G. Levine recalled that his Irish and Scotch-Irish mother, who hailed from Hibbing, Minnesota, after she saw a Broadway show made a beeline for the Stage or Lindy's, where she could look forward to an equally diverting performance from a different breed of entertainers, the "bossy, know-it-all waiters," whom Levine said were no less salient in his memory than "the Formica tables, the walls lined with pictures of celebrities [he'd] never heard of, the glass cases filled with enormous cheesecakes, and the multimeat sandwiches named after comedians."[44]

The Jazzy "Delicatessen Wife"

Outside the theater district, the appeal of the delicatessen spread rapidly, as take-out food suddenly jumped in popularity. While the immigrant Jewish wife was expected to cook for her family, the second-generation Jewish wife began to pay others to cook for her and her family. A Yiddish song recorded in the late 1920s by Pesach Burstein, "Git Mir Di Meidlach Fun Amol" (Give Me the Girls from Yesteryear), lamented that modern Jewish women danced to jazz music, smoked cigarettes, and fed their men with gassy food from the corner delicatessen. If only, the singer fantasized, he could find one of the virtuous old-time girls—non-Jewish girls, it seems—with blond hair, beautiful braids, and the inclination to prepare home-cooked meals for her beau.[45]

Even after marriage, it seemed, Jewish women continued to take food out from the local delicatessen. As the homemaker Ethel Somers complained in 1927, "In this age of delicatessen lure, simple home dinners are becoming all too uncommon. . . . They are commonly shunned."[46] Sometimes it fell to the husbands to do the delicatessen shopping, perhaps because their wives were out of the house. "Already some of the young men who married last June are dropping in at the delicatessen about dinner time to get a few sandwiches," a humor column in *Life* magazine noted sarcastically in 1929.[47]

At a time of expanding freedoms for women, many conservative commentators viewed delis as enabling women to evade their household responsibilities. What would women do if they no longer had to spend the afternoon shopping and cooking for dinner? Either they could keep working after marriage, or they could use their afternoons for leisure pursuits such as playing cards, going to film and theater matinees, clothes shopping, reading novels, and attending meetings and classes. As a Brooklyn Jewish mother in Daniel Fuchs's proletarian novel *Homage to Blenholt* noted sarcastically, "all the young ladies, they don't cook like the older generation. Lunch they eat in the delicatessen stores with the baby carriages outside, and in the night when the husbands come home from work, they throw together pastrami, cole slaw, potato salad, and finished, supper."[48]

These New York housewives were, to some extent, following in the footsteps of the feminist and social reformer Jane

Addams, who founded Hull House in Chicago, a settlement house with a heavily Jewish clientele. As early as 1904, Addams had advocated the ordering of all food from take-out stores in order to release women from "domestic servitude." As *Everybody's Magazine* reported, "She would have your meals delivered at the house-door, just as the returned washing is. Your beefsteak would be 'done' as your linen is. Cooking is drudgery and should be 'done' on the outside. . . . [She] [f]ound great bake, soup, meat, delicatessen shops."[49]

Women could join the workforce and still, through taking out food, have dinner on the table when their husbands walked in the door. This, according to the journalist L. H. Robins, helped to create the "beehive" nature of the New York economy, which generated greater wealth than any other city on earth. But it was not just that the wives were earning money that made the husbands tolerant of all the take-out dinners they ate from the delicatessen. Robins insisted that most husbands would rather keep their wives from toil, thus preserving their beauty, than sit down to a home-cooked repast at the end of each day.[50]

The effect of delicatessen food on customers' marriages was a matter of heated debate. One deli owner reported in 1925 that his interaction with his customers gave him intimate knowledge of what was going on in their homes; he boasted that he was a greater expert in marital relationships than were Brigham Young, King Solomon, and the local family court judge put together! The secret of a good marriage, he disclosed, was to live near a delicatessen, speculating that if the range were stolen from some of his customers' kitchens, it would take a month before they would notice the theft.[51]

Others, by contrast, viewed the delicatessen as destroying marriages and disrupting family life. At an annual convention in Baltimore of the General Federation of Women's Clubs, its president, Mrs. John D. Sherman, claimed that the "delicatessen wife," a term that she evidently coined, gave her husband grounds for divorce. She linked the buying of prepared food to participation in other "jazzy" activities, coupled with an alarm-

Cover of the *New Yorker* from March 28, 1936 (Courtesy of Condé Nast /
The New Yorker)

ing tendency to shirk the housework.[52] As Agnes V. Mahoney of the Industrial Survey and Research Bureau put it, it was precisely the reliance of many wives on the corner delicatessen and its "ready-cooked tin-can food" that had increased the incidence of broken homes.[53]

Florence Guy Seabury's satirical essay "The Delicatessen Husband" took up the situation of a man who "lives from can to mouth."[54] Since his wife works long hours as a chemist, he is delegated to do the household shopping. But he feels emasculated by the shopping experience, viewing delicatessens in particular as home wreckers and "emblems of a declining civilization." In short, he concludes, they are "generations removed from his ideals."[55] Nevertheless, by the turn of the twenty-first century, Seabury predicted, everything from clothing to newborn babies would arrive wrapped up in neat delicatessen-type packages. Seabury suggested that the proliferation of delicatessens represented a degree of progress since while a delicatessen husband might be "cursed with the task of bringing into his walled apartment his share of the canned tongue and chicken wings," he at least did not have to slaughter the animal himself or split the wood to make the fire for his own dinner and coffee.[56]

Delicatessen stores were also viewed as the unfortunate by-products of powerful new technologies that were rapidly reshaping American culture. One prominent critic, Silas Bent, assailed the toll on the mind and body that the "mechanized" way of living was beginning to take. Bent viewed the speed with which food could be produced and circulated as symbolic of the drastic changes in modern life. In a chapter titled "From Barbecue to Delicatessen Dinner," Bent traced these developments from primitive man's way of eating to the modern methods by which foodstuffs were circulated around the globe. The almost instant availability of an astonishing variety of food, Bent believed, caused a host of both physical and emotional problems. "The machine," Bent lamented, "is sending more and more of us out of the home into restaurants, cafeterias, clubs and hotels; it is making us soft and dyspeptic, hurried and worried."[57]

Those men who brought delicatessen food home without first requesting permission of the lady of the house risked becoming the target of considerable wrath. In Arthur Kober's short story "You Can't Beat Friedkin's Meats," published in 1938 in the *New Yorker*, Mrs. Gross is enraged when her husband brings home a large paper bag of cold cuts from the local kosher delicatessen for their Saturday lunch. "Mine cooking is no good, ha?" she explodes, before rushing out to throw the food in the face of the hapless delicatessen owner.[58] Similarly, in Jo Sinclair's major work of postwar fiction, *Wasteland*, a Jewish mother is horribly insulted when her grownup son purchases corned-beef sandwiches for his Friday-night repast rather than eat her cooking.[59]

Yet, by the interwar era, the delicatessen had become the quintessential urban store, preserving denizens from having to cook for themselves whenever they found it impractical or inconvenient to do so. By 1921, according to an advertising-industry trade publication, there were already 319 delicatessens in the Bronx, even though Jewish migration to the neighborhood had not yet reached its peak.[60] The humorist Montague Glass jokingly suggested that a "booster" sign be erected at the entrance to the city reading, "New York: Gateway to Westchester County," with the "information" that "New York City Contains 9,622,849 Delicatessen Stores (Estimated) and Over 38,658,031 Miles of Electric Railroad."[61]

Nor was the popularity of delicatessens limited to New York. As one journalist in Baltimore put it, a "studio apartment, with a cocktail shaker and a dinner furnished by the nearest delicatessen store, usually represents the sum total of standardized living among thousands of city dwellers in these modern times."[62] Tracing the history of the delicatessen store from its modest beginnings as a purveyor of "Swiss cheese and pickled lambs' tongues" to its gussied-up modern incarnation with its menu of "broiled guinea hen and mushrooms under glass to alligator pear salad and petit fours," she found that the delicatessen had come a long way in the sophistication of its fare and the elegance of its window displays. Indeed, she noted, delicatessen stores in America were judged superior to their European counterparts, given the greater variety of foods available in this country—"tomatoes, peaches, alligator pears and pineapples are rare and expensive luxuries abroad, while they are plentiful and comparatively cheap here."[63]

Just as before the First World War, Sunday night remained the delicatessen's busiest time of the week. Calling the delicatessen the "urbanite's pantry-keeper," Robins dubbed those delicatessens that were open on Sundays "oases in a desert of locked-up plenty." The delicatessen was, he noted, nothing short of a "life saver" for those who were entertaining unexpected guests, for families whose cook had walked out, for travelers who came back from vacation to an empty larder, for people who decided on the spur of the moment to have a picnic, for those who had planned to go the beach but whose plans were foiled by rain— actually "for almost any kind of New Yorker there is."[64]

Heyday of the Kosher Delicatessen

Meat was a mainstay of the Jewish diet throughout the Depression. According to Louisa Gertner, writing in the *Yiddish Daily Forward* in 1937, even in the summertime New Yorkers ate "more meat than [the population of] entire nations."[65] Much of this meat was sold in delicatessens. In S. J. Wilson's 1964 novel *Hurray for Me*, set in the early 1930s, a Jewish mother confesses to her family that she has not had time to make dinner. One of her sons suggests delicatessen "for a change." The mother scoffs at the suggestion, noting sarcastically that he eats deli every day for lunch. The son asks how she knows. Her tart reply: "Because I ate deli five times a week when I went to high school . . . and your father did, and so did everyone else. What else is there to eat when you go to school?"[66]

The number of kosher delicatessens alone was staggering. According to a list compiled in 1931 by Thomas Dwyer, commissioner of public markets, there were 1,550 kosher delicatessens in New York City, in addition to 6,500 kosher butchers,

1,000 kosher slaughterhouses for poultry, 575 kosher meat restaurants, and 150 dairy restaurants. All in all, he stated, there
were more than 10,000 kosher food dealers in the city.[67] Two
years later, Koenigsberg used the list as the basis for a plan submitted to Mayor Fiorello LaGuardia for the hiring of seventy
inspectors to enforce the kosher laws.

Furthermore, according to a study conducted by Samuel
Popkin for the *Mogen Dovid Delicatessen Magazine*, there were
more than twenty-three hundred delicatessens—both Jewish
and non-Jewish—in New York in the 1930s, representing almost a quarter of all those in the United States at the time.[68]
Popkin found that the total volume of sales in the delicatessen
industry had reached $40 million. But he asserted that only the
last eight months of each year were profitable for the delicatessen business, at least in the Northeast, since in these seasons
there is a tendency for people to eat outdoors; "many people
go to nearby parks and beaches and in all cases the most con-
venient and relatively appetizing lunch is delicatessen." Indeed,
the best season for delicatessen food is summer, when "jaded
appetites demand some spicy food," pointing them straightaway
to the local delicatessen.[69]

In upscale neighborhoods, such as the Upper West Side
(where, by the mid-1920s, more than half of the Jewish heads of
household were garment manufacturers), ethnic Jewish businesses of all types helped prosperous Jews to resist lingering
feelings of vulnerability in American society and to maintain
a powerful sense of ethnic solidarity. As David Ward and Oliver Zunz have noted of second-generation Jews, "The physical
attributes of the upper-class neighborhood they fashioned catered to their sense of urbanity and style, while its ethnicity, visible in the solid synagogues, kosher butcher shops, bookstores,
delicatessens and bakeries, nourished a sense of cohesion despite their minority status."[70] The Jewish labor leader David Dubinsky had only to be glimpsed on one of his frequent jaunts to
a kosher delicatessen in order to seem genuinely like one of the
union rank-and-file.[71]

Interior of Morris Wepner's Delicatessen in Upper Manhattan in 1920
(Courtesy of Paul Lewis)

Jewish delicatessens, Daniel Rogov has noted, tended to be located in older buildings and to have worn furnishings, tarnished silver, chipped plates, an antique cash register (and an even more antique person sitting behind it), and an overall down-at-the-heels atmosphere. As he put it, "Some maintain the mood, if not the actuality, of sawdust on the floors and nearly all feature large plate glass windows with no trace of draperies."[72] In Brooklyn, many of the delicatessens were constructed by Murray Hager, who was a well-known builder. The salamis hung in an arc in the window, the neon signs flashed the name of the deli and the company that supplied the meat (e.g., Hebrew National, Zion Kosher, 999), and there were towers of canned beans. They had light oak chairs with pink vinyl seats, wood-grain Formica on the tables, and a decoration over the entrance to the kitchen that typically featured plastic flowers overflowing from a plastic flower pot. As the restaurant designer Pat Kuleto recalled in 1990, "Until recently, there was no such thing as deli design. They were always started on a budget, so you'd simply buy the cheapest restaurant equipment. Then you'd put a few sandwich signs up on the wall, a few pictures of the owner, a couple of notices from the government and a few posters supplied maybe by the RC Cola Company or something. You'd turn the lights up real bright, hang a bunch of sausages around. . . . And that was it—they called it a deli."[73]

The main feature was, of course, the delicatessen counter, with the row of meats on display and hand-lettered signs on the walls advertising the prices. As the historian Ruth Glazer pointed out in the 1940s, delicatessens would "hide demurely behind window displays of dummy beer cans. But for those who have eyes to see there are steaming frankfurters and knishes on the grill and untold delights behind the clouded glass and shredded colored cellophane."[74] Some delicatessens were larger and more elaborately decorated than others. The larger, more famous kosher delicatessens—Grabstein's, George and Sid's, and the Hy Tulip—were in Brooklyn, with smaller, storefront-type delicatessens more typical of the Bronx.

Paradoxically, the number of kosher delicatessens grew even as fewer Jews kept kosher. An especially large decline of kosher observance, that of close to 30 percent, occurred between 1914 and 1924, as the second generation came to the fore. Ironically, this was at a time when almost half of the entire city's meat supply was slaughtered according to the kosher regulations, as government reports from 1920 show.[75] A survey done in 1937, after the publication of *The Royal Table*, the first popular guide in English to the Jewish dietary laws, found that the proportion of Jews keeping kosher had decreased even further than in preceding decades. It concluded that no more than 15 percent of the Jews in the United States kept strictly kosher, while 20 percent observed the kosher laws inconsistently and the other 65 percent—most of whom belonged to the Conservative

or Reform branches of Judaism—scarcely bothered to keep kosher at all.[76] As a review of the guide put it, the American Jew
has "seen the tempo and flow of America's modern industrial
life break down the rigid barriers between Jews and Gentiles
[and] kick his cumbersome dietary rituals into a cocked hat.
To keep up the pace, it is easier to go Reformed with its wor-
ship of Judaism adapted to eight-cylinder cars, subways and
cafeterias."[77]

Nevertheless, the kosher delicatessen remained essential for
those Jews who did continue to keep kosher, who still identified "kosher" with authentically Jewish, or who had more observant relatives with whom they dined on a regular basis. An
investigator for a study of New York foodways by the Works
Progress Administration concluded that the success of Rosen-
blum's Delicatessen on Manhattan's Upper West Side was
based largely on its reputation as a place where religious laws
were followed to the letter. He reported that the elder Rosen-
blum, who wore a skullcap and beard, ran the cash register but
seemed present "more for decorative than business purposes,
giving the place an air of religious orthodoxy." This was important, given that his two sons did not appear to be religiously
observant.[78]

However, while some delicatessens stopped selling kosher
meat, others became kosher for the first time in the 1930s.
Herb Rosenberg, whose father owned a deli in Brooklyn, recalled that as more Jews moved to Coney Island, the demand
for kosher delicatessen products increased significantly. Not
all the clientele kept kosher, and many were not Jewish. For
example, the black actor Lou Gosset was a regular at the
deli; his grandmother cleaned houses in the neighborhood
to support her extended family. But in order to compete with
the six other Jewish delicatessens on the twenty-three-block
stretch of Mermaid Avenue where Herb's father's store was
located, his father decided to make his store kosher. Pressure
from religious authorities was also a factor; Herb remembers

the local rabbi, who was preparing the boy for his bar mitzvah, trying to convince his father both to close on Saturdays
(which they did not end up doing) and to sell only kosher
meats.[79]

Some Jews strove mightily to convince their coreligionists
to maintain the dietary laws. "Borrowing heavily from an-
thropology to zoology," the historian Jenna Weissman Joselit
has noted, "its defenders alternately sanitized, domesticated,
aestheticized, commodified, and otherwise reinterpreted the
practice of keeping kosher."[80] But they had little effect on the
majority of their fellow Jews, for whom living in America
largely meant eating what other Americans ate. Many Jews
developed a workable compromise; they kept kosher at home
but relaxed their standards when they ate out, thus making
a distinction between their private and public lives. Indeed,
Mordechai Kaplan, a Conservative rabbi who founded the Re-
constructionist Movement, sanctioned the practice of keeping
kosher at home but eating out in nonkosher restaurants as a
way of balancing Jewish particularity with the need to live in
the larger society.[81]

The kosher delicatessen thus symbolized ethnic community
and continuity. According to Deborah Dash Moore, second-
generation Jews "continued to endow the urban environment
with ethnic attributes" such as food stores and restaurants.[82]
While she does not write about delicatessens in particular,
Moore notes that "even middle-class neighborhoods would
transmit a Jewish tinge to secular activities pursued within
their boundaries."[83] It is little wonder that, according to the historian Elliot Willensky, garlic was the "common gastronomic
denominator" for most of the ethnic cuisines of Brooklyn and
was the basic ingredient in the food used in the kosher delicatessens, which advertised their presence all the way down
the street. Even the sidewalks, he said, had a "translucence
that could be attributed only to regular—if unintentional—
saturation with well-rendered chicken fat."[84]

Pulling Together through the Depression

Many who worked in the delicatessen industry characterize it as a *mishpoche*, using the Yiddish word for "family." As one storekeeper, Isidore P. Salupsky, told his fellow delicatessen owners in 1932 in the pages of the *Mogen Dovid Delicatessen Magazine*, "With the present unemployment and bad times in general, some of our stores are hardly able to exist, many of the stores can hardly pay their bills; some of them are hardly making a living." The owners needed to band together, Salupsky implored, rather than undercutting each other with their prices.[85]

Among the hard-and-fast rules given to delicatessen owners in the pages of the *Mogen Dovid* were to avoid "knocking" a competitor's products, to maintain a neat appearance, to beware of becoming "too familiar" with the customer, to avoid displaying any "excitement," to refrain from shouting at the clerk or sweeping the floor when customers were present, to open the store on time in the morning, and to make periodic changes in the window displays.[86] It was essential, deli owners realized, to distinguish their products from ordinary groceries. Only if delicatessen meats could continue to be viewed as delicacies would the industry have a future, given the higher prices of prepared meats. An industry expert, writing in the pages of another trade publication, called *Voice of the Delicatessen Industry*, noted that these products were a "necessary luxury" for consumers and insisted that delicatessen "must not follow in the footsteps of groceries with their emphasis on volume and lower prices." The loyal customer, he explained, "looks upon delicatessen as choice food, as special relishes, and does not mind if he has to pay a bit more."[87]

Nevertheless, the work was backbreaking. Eighteen-hour days were routine, with unceasing physical labor. Herbert Krupp, who supplied kosher delicatessens in New Jersey, recalled having to reach into barrels of meat so cold that his hands almost froze, grabbing the fifteen- to twenty-pound slippery pieces of corned beef by a nub or flap of fat, called the deckle, and *schlepping* them into the store, where he flung them onto the scale to be weighed. (Owners were always suspicious that the meat had been "pumped," or filled with water to increase the weight.) Delicatessen owners who cured their own meat had to rotate the huge pieces of meat through basement barrels filled with brine and spices. Only after several days of curing could the meat finally be cut into manageable sections, cooked, and prepared for slicing.

In the wake of Prohibition, one almost guaranteed money maker was alcohol, so many delicatessens started selling beer. The future delicatessen owner Phil Levenson recalls standing on a Coca-Cola box as a young teenager selling hot dogs and beers for a nickel apiece in his father's deli in the Bronx. The hothouse (flower) workers in the Bronx Park neighborhood were so thirsty after work, he said, that he once sold two half barrels of beer from a four-foot bar in just a couple of hours.[88]

Delicatessen owners often enlisted their children to help in the store. The parents of Murray Lefkowitz, a powerful union organizer who represented deli employees, met because the older Lefkowitz mistook his future wife for her sister, whom he had recommended for a job in a meat-processing plant scrubbing dirt off beef tongues. Another job that was often given to children was to produce what was variously called a "poke," "toot," or "toodle," a small piece of wax paper twisted into a cone, filled with mustard, and crimped on the bottom. As Ruth Glazer noted, "As soon as the youngsters of the family are old enough to hold two 'toots' of mustard in one hand and a ladle of mustard in the other, they are pressed into service."[89]

Irving Goldfried's father had sold shoes in Poland before coming to the United States before the First World War. A friend recommended the deli business because the food sold fast: "You order your merchandise before the weekend, and already on Monday you have your money." So in 1932, he bought a sixty-seat delicatessen (including an apartment in the back of the store) on Saratoga and Livonia Avenues in Brooklyn for

Exterior of Gottlieb's Delicatessen on Myrtle Avenue on the Brooklyn-
Queens border in 1950s (Collection of Ted Merwin)

$5,000. The waiters were college students from the neighbor-
hood who needed money for tuition; the family worked behind
the counter while Irving's wife did the cooking. A hot dog, an
order of french fries, and a soda each cost a nickel, and customers drifted in on their way to the bus stop or public school
nearby. The elder Goldfried did not drive, so he walked a mile
to the factory to pick up ten or twelve briskets in a baby car-
riage. Irving learned to work long hours as well, peeling potatoes in the backyard while listening to swing-band music on the
Victrola.[90]

Grandparents, aunts, uncles, and cousins also got into the
act. Marty Grabstein, whose parents owned the popular Grabstein's Delicatessen in Brooklyn, told me that it was really
his grandmother who ran the place. He recalled her as a tiny
woman wielding a carving knife. She would bang on the table
and shout, "Morris, it's getting busy!" when she felt that her son
wasn't moving fast enough to seat the long lines of customers.[91]
It made sense to hire—or simply rely on—family members,

since finding good employees was often a struggle. Levenson quipped that his chef was "whoever walked in the door and stayed sober for two weeks." Family members were always assured of a free meal, known as putting the bill "on the cuff."[92]

Fred Molod's father sold his delicatessen on the Lower East Side and moved to the Bay Parkway section of Brooklyn, where he bought another delicatessen in partnership with his father-in-law, who had been a presser in a garment factory. Molod recalls that since they lived across the street from the store, his father did not even own a suit. "The only time that we closed early was at eight p.m. on Friday night," noted Molod. "We broke the fast of Yom Kippur by going back to the store and reopening for business."[93]

The Delicatessen as a "Secular Synagogue"

The critic Alfred Kazin, who grew up in the Brownsville section of Brooklyn, famously described going to a kosher deli as a quintessential secular Jewish ritual. As he memorably recalled,

> But our greatest delight in all seasons was "delicatessen"—hot spiced corned beef, pastrami, rolled beef, hard salami, soft salami, chicken salami, bologna, frankfurter "specials," and the thinner, wrinkled hot dogs always taken with mustard and relish and sauerkraut. . . . At Saturday twilight, as soon as the delicatessen store reopened after the Sabbath rest, we raced into it panting for the hot dogs sizzling on the gas plate just inside the window. The look of that blackened empty gas plate had driven us wild all through the wearisome Sabbath day. And now, as the electric sign blazed up again, lighting up the words JEWISH NATIONAL DELICATESSEN, it was as if we had entered into our rightful heritage.[94]

Before he had even taken a bite, the illumination of the sign closed a powerful emotional and spiritual circuit for Kazin, connecting him with his tradition. Where (and, we could add, with whom) Kazin ate affected him profoundly. There was also something almost sacred about the neon delicatessen sign itself. The mystical glowing letters, connected by the tubes carrying the phantasmically colored gas, held a kind of kabbalistic fascination for Kazin and his peers. Just as medieval rabbis called the letters of the Torah "black fire written on white fire,"[95] the shining letters of the sign hung in the air with the dazzling radiance of supernal energy.

The delicatessen became the seat of many of Kazin's deepest and most important memories. As the scholar Naomi Seidman has insightfully pointed out, Kazin's innovative form of storytelling is "not a map of the neighborhood, although the streets and landmarks and borders are duly and precisely recorded, but rather a map of a consciousness. . . . We are, Kazin seems to say, not so much what we eat but *where* we first ate, and slept, and walked; geography, in other words, is destiny."[96]

Nostalgia for the delicatessen became, in the decades after the Second World War, an essential feature of secular Jewish life for the second generation of American Jews, who grew up at a time when a third of the population of Brooklyn was Jewish and almost one-half of the overall Jewish population of New York lived in that borough. The delicatessen was where this secular Jewish identity, in large measure, took root; it was where the Jewish community came together and nurtured its relationship to Jewish heritage.

Like the lighted delicatessen sign, the illuminated movie screen also held great fascination for secular Jews in the outer boroughs. Going to a Saturday movie matinee, at a time when talking movies ("talkies") were still a relative novelty, was a cherished ritual for many Jewish children; there was seldom any contest between spending the Sabbath in the synagogue and spending it in the cinema. As Kazin noted, comparing the two, "Right hand and left hand: two doorways to the East. But the first led to music I heard in the dark, to inwardness; the other to ambiguity. That poor worn synagogue could never in my affections compete with that movie house, whose very lounge looked and smelled to me like an Oriental temple. It had Persian rugs, and was marvelously half-lit at all hours of the day."[97] And just as one could scarcely attend a Broadway show without also eating in a deli, a trip to the cinema typically involved a delicatessen lunch.

Delicatessens were often located near the movie theaters; for example, the RKO Movie Theatre in Ridgewood, Queens (on the border of Bushwick, Brooklyn), was across the street from Gottlieb's, a kosher delicatessen that stayed open late to serve the crowd streaming out of the cinema. Similarly, the Ambassador Theatre in Brooklyn was next door to Goldfried's; when the movie operators were hungry, they lowered a bucket from four floors up, and sandwiches were sent up on a rope and pulley.

Another movie theater, called People's Cinema (formerly, The Bluebird), was located diagonally across the street; a former patron of the People's recalled that kids would come in on Saturday afternoons with salami sandwiches, bottles of Pepsi, and cake and watch cartoons, westerns, and the installments in the "Little Tough Guys" or "East Side Kids" series about lower-class children and their adventures in the New York slums.[98] Barbara Solomon's father, who owned a deli in Sheepshead Bay, got four free movie passes a week because her father advertised the local movie houses by putting posters in the window. (Her father also provided the sandwiches for her dates.)[99]

Louis Menashe, a Sephardic Jew who learned to love Ashkenazic cooking, spent Saturday afternoons with friends at a movie theater on Broadway in Williamsburg, and then the group repaired to Pastrami King on Roebling Avenue and South Second Street, a block from his home. The hand-sliced pastrami was smoked with cedar (not the usual hickory) and flavored with fresh garlic (rather than the typical garlic salt). As Menashe recalled, "Press, the harried waiter, would ignore us kids—our tips weren't so good—but the long hungry wait was worth it."[100] Some customers sneaked deli sandwiches into the movie theater itself. While waiting on a long line to get into *Gone with the Wind* in 1939, a group of young people "got hungry": "so we bought hot pastrami sandwiches and pickles to take inside. The entire movie house stank of deli. An usher came up and said you can't do that, but what could we do? We ate it anyway."[101]

On summer weekends, beachgoers would stop at a deli to buy sandwiches for their picnic baskets. Paul Goldberg worked in his father's delicatessen in the Flatbush section of Brooklyn. He remembers that customers would come in carrying beach chairs and hampers. "We hoped that the food wouldn't turn green before they ate it," he admitted. When the beachgoing traffic dropped off, Goldberg's father hired a teenager to take sandwich orders from women waiting for their hair to dry in the local beauty parlor.[102]

Sunday night, in particular, was "delicatessen night" for many secular Jewish families, when extended families gathered for dinner in a kosher deli—or took food home. On the white dining-room tablecloth in the Bronx apartment in which the author Kate Simon grew up, she recalled, "appeared the traditional Sunday night company meal: slices of salami and corned beef, a mound of rye bread, pickles sliced lengthwise, and the mild mustard the delicatessen dripped into slender paper cones from a huge bottle. . . . The drinks were celery tonic or cream soda, nectars we were allowed only on state occasions, in small glasses."[103]

Nevertheless, the relationship that the kosher delicatessen had with Jewish religion was a complicated one, and one that bespoke the myriad ways in which American Jews attempted to balance their Jewish and American identities. Many of these establishments were open on the Sabbath and Jewish holidays, despite the prohibition in Jewish law against handling money or doing business on such occasions. This reflected a schizophrenic attitude toward religious observance, in which it became comfortable for Jews to observe the Sabbath selectively, picking and choosing the rules that they wished to follow.[104] Delicatessens did the same; Poliakoff's, an upscale kosher eatery that included deli sandwiches on its menu, and Lou G. Siegel's, a landmark kosher deli in Manhattan's theater district, transgressed Jewish law by opening for business on Friday nights but requested, by putting notices on their menus, that patrons refrain from smoking (also forbidden by religious law on the Sabbath).

The historian Jeffrey Gurock recalls that when he was growing up in the East Bronx, his parents, who belonged to an Orthodox synagogue, would take their sons to kosher delis whenever the family chose to eat out. "However," Gurock notes, "unlike their more scrupulous synagogue friends, my folks gave no thought as to whether the delis that we more generally frequented were open on Saturday. Nor did they ever peek into the back room to see if there was a *mashgiach* [kosher supervisor] on the premises." As long as the Hebrew phrase *basar kasher* (kosher meat) was displayed in the window along with the logo for Hebrew National, his family felt comfortable eating in the restaurant.[105]

For some Jews, eating in a delicatessen became almost a religion unto itself. The sociologist Harry Levine noted that his father, Sid, a self-described "gastronomic Jew" who grew up in a family of poor socialist Jews in Harlem, "worshiped only at delicatessens," where his "most sacred objects" included stuffed cabbage, chopped liver, salami, frankfurter, tongue, corned beef, and hot pastrami. Levine heard his father call himself a "gastronomical" Jew so frequently that the boy thought that it was a denomination of Judaism.[106] Susan Stamberg, a host of National Public Radio's *All Things Considered*, remembered, "Growing up in Manhattan in the 1950s, I thought the whole world was Jewish," particularly when her father took her and her siblings to the Lower East Side every weekend for knishes at Schmulka Bernstein's or Yonah Schimmel's. "We were ethnic Jews more than observant ones," she concluded.[107]

For some Jews, perhaps even nonkosher delis were too religious for comfort. In Jay Cantor's 2003 novel *Great Neck*, a Jewish survivor of the Holocaust, Richard Hartman, patronizes an empty German delicatessen named Kuck's (in Great Neck), where he takes out a roast beef sandwich with mayonnaise every night. "*I'm not a Jew of faith*, he thought, on the way back to his room, as he imagined the suburban householders who crowded Squire's Jewish delicatessen were, *or rather my faith is culture*, like (he liked to think) Freud's faith, or Kafka's or Proust's or Walter Benjamin's, all the old Talmudic fervor now focused on secular texts."[108]

During the interwar era, then, the delicatessen consolidated its hold on Jewish life—and on the overall culture of New York, at a time when gender roles were in flux and take-out food was starting to become popular. The nonkosher delicatessens in the theater district, which had been spawned as a way for Jews to eat mostly traditional food but to free themselves from the stringency of the kosher dietary laws, used their showbiz atmosphere to flatter Jews' sense of their growing importance in American society and to provide a secular avenue to Judaism. In the following decade, at a time when many small businesses were closing because of the ravages of the Great Depression, the outer-borough kosher delicatessens also continued to thrive and even to multiply. But even as the delicatessen became the Jewish hangout par excellence, it quickly lost its hold on Jewish life with the coming of another world war, which led to meat rationing and exposed Jews to other types of food, both at home and abroad. The delicatessen—and Jewish Life—would never be the same.

={ 3 }=

Send a Salami

DELICATESSENS DURING THE
SECOND WORLD WAR AND THE
POSTWAR EXODUS FROM NEW YORK

The entrance of the United States into the Second World
War in December 1941 ultimately transformed the relationship of many Jews to their religion. Obliged to eat army rations,
Jewish soldiers found it almost impossible to keep kosher on a
regular basis. In *G.I. Jews*, Deborah Dash Moore's book about
Jews in the army, Moore discusses the ways in which many
Jewish soldiers, especially those raised in kosher homes, were
compelled to modify their eating patterns in order to survive on
army rations. "Eating ham for Uncle Sam" became, Moore has
found, a patriotic act of self-sacrifice. But not all servicemen
were obliged to subsist on nonkosher food; the practice soon
developed of sending hard salamis, which keep for a long time
without refrigeration, to sons who were serving abroad. For the
most part, however, Jews learned that they could do without
familiar foods and still maintain their Jewish identity.

Louis Schwartz, a waiter in the Sixth Avenue Delicatessen
who was famous for selling more than $4 million worth of war
bonds, claimed to have invented the famous slogan "Send a
Salami to Your Boy in the Army," which became a permanent
catchphrase at Katz's Delicatessen and other delicatessens in
the city. The slogan seems to have originated with Hal David,
a lyricist whose Austrian Jewish parents owned a kosher deli-

catessen in Brooklyn; David is best known for a string of 1960s hit songs with the Jewish composer Burt Bacharach.[1] David penned it while serving in the army in the Central Pacific Entertainment Section, based at the University of Hawaii in Honolulu; the unit developed songs, sketches, and musicals to be performed for the troops throughout the Central and South Pacific. (The lyric continued, "Don't just send him things to wear / Send him something he can chew.")[2] The slogan carried a potent unconscious thrust; given the phallic associations that salamis have, sending one to one's son was perhaps unconsciously attempting to give him a boost of virility in order to enable him to win the war and return safely to the bosom of his family.

At a time when all things identified with Germany were suspect, the German origin of delicatessen food was potentially problematic. As the *New York Times* pointed out, the word *delicatessen* was "of Axis origin," along with frankfurters, hamburgers, and bologna. However, the *Times* added reassuringly, the situation was not one to fret about. After all, even King George and Queen Elizabeth had recently feasted on Nathan's hot dogs at a picnic in Hyde Park given by Franklin Delano Roosevelt. When the filler in the sandwich was a luncheon meat of foreign origin, it became happily domesticated—no longer a foreign intruder but a "perfect symbol of the American melting pot."[3]

Jews at home learned, however, that they could maintain their ethnic identity without corned beef and pastrami. The need to send large quantities of food overseas to feed the soldiers led to severe shortages on the home front. The government's Office of Price Administration (OPA) initially limited the supply of rubber and gasoline before moving on to food items, beginning with sugar and coffee. In 1942, the government instituted a "Share the Meat" campaign in which American were asked to limit their consumption of meat. But rationing still became inevitable, given the fact that up to 60 percent of the nation's meat supply was reserved for consumption by the military—the average consumption of meat by each soldier was a pound per day[4]—and by the Lend Lease Program that shipped enormous quantities of food (in the first half of 1943, forty-five million pounds of beef alone)[5] to the civilian populations of Europe. One soldier's wife admitted that she fantasized about eating steak more than she did about having sex.[6]

Jews were heavily represented in the meat-processing industry in New York, both kosher and nonkosher; indeed, of the five thousand employees in this business, one expert estimated, more than a quarter were Jewish.[7] But with the advent of meat rationing on March 29, 1943, both butcher shops and delicatessens no longer had access to much of their product. The major associations of kosher delicatessens calculated that the selling of meat products accounted for about 90 percent of their overall business, with about 75 percent of their sales in the form of sandwiches and 15 percent in the form of cooked dishes.

Beef rationing was instituted with an initial limit of twenty-eight ounces a week per person; it was estimated that the wealthiest third of the population consumed an average of five pounds of meat a week and the poorest third an average of only about one pound a week. Red stamps, issued by the government, were required to buy meat, fish, and dairy products; blue stamps were needed for canned fruits and vegetables. Each citizen, including children, received two ration books a month, containing forty-eight blue points and sixty-four red points.

Delicatessen items carried a premium above the point value of raw meat—two additional points per pound if unsliced and three additional points per pound if sliced.[8] If a patron bought cured meats from a delicatessen to make his or her own sandwiches, the red stamps were required. A meal consumed in a restaurant or prepared for take-out did not require stamps, so many delicatessen customers bought complete sandwiches.[9] Many citizens hoarded these stamps so that they could make a single large purchase. However, the numbers of points needed to buy particular foods fluctuated on a daily basis. As the memoirist Ruth Corbett recalled, it was cause for celebration when

A Brooklyn Jewish boy's rationing card from World War II
(Collection of Ted Merwin)

the number of stamps was reduced for a particular item, such as when thirteen kinds of kosher meats were taken down by one point.[10] Frankfurters were in such short supply that meat packers were enjoined to stretch their filling by using beans, potatoes, or cracker meal; they suggested substituting bread and gravy for meat.[11]

Nevertheless, the government recognized that the consumption of red meat by the citizenry was essential in order to maintain wartime morale. The historian Amy Bentley has argued that beef, long a symbol of status and wealth, increased in symbolic value during the war partially because of both governmental and private-industry propaganda.[12] The government instituted price ceilings on meat in order to prevent inflation, but this led to a decrease in supply and triggered an extensive black market. That black market was particularly pronounced in delicatessen meats, especially corned beef and tongue; the following year, four of the major kosher sausage companies in

New York—Zion Kosher, Real Kosher, Brownsville Kosher, and Benjamin Rachleff—were convicted. (Leo Tarlow of Zion Kosher was sentenced to a forty-day jail term, although the jail time was suspended.)[13] In May 1945, the delicatessen manufacturers, distributors, and retailers all threatened to strike in order to try to compel the OPA to make more meat available.[14]

In order to comply with federal guidelines limiting meat consumption, Mayor Fiorello LaGuardia requested that no meat be sold on Tuesdays in New York City, with the only exemption being for hot dog and hamburger stands, which were asked to encourage substitute foods like fish.[15] While many delicatessens had been open seven days of the week, they almost unanimously decided to close their doors on these "meatless Tuesdays," with a few remaining open only to sell beer. Irving Krasner, a jobber in the delicatessen business, married his wife, Selma, on a Tuesday and went back to work the next day, while Barbara Solomon's dad used his precious Tuesdays to take her and her brother for leisurely boat rides up the Hudson or on excursions to the Bronx Zoo.

Periodic shortages continued, even after the end of the war; about a tenth of the thousand kosher delicatessens in the city shut down in September 1946 for lack of meat. The delicatessen industry associations called a meeting to discuss closing down all of the stores for at least a month, given that the shops had only 10 to 20 percent of their usual merchandise. Kosher delicatessens were especially hard hit, with that reduction in their normal supply and with some meats, such as corned beef and tongue, virtually unobtainable at any price. Louis Schweller, the president of the Bronx Delicatessen Dealers Association, predicted that most of the thousand or so remaining kosher delicatessens would have to close. But also affected were the seven thousand or so delicatessens that were mostly indistinguishable from grocery stores. In all, according to Jack Kranis, attorney for the Joint Council of Delicatessen Store Dealers, as many as ten thousand employees—waiters, countermen, and kitchen help—could be left jobless.[16]

Customers shop for meat in Gellis Delicatessen in Manhattan during postwar shortages on October 9, 1946 (Copyright Bettmann/CORBIS)

Food writers in the press suggested using nonmeat substitutes, canned meat products, or such innovations as "corned beef spread." Restaurants and hotels were asked to "stretch" their meat by preparing hash and nonrationed meat such as kidney, liver, and tripe. A horse-meat dealer in Newark announced plans to open an outlet in Manhattan, incurring the wrath of former mayor LaGuardia, who called the consumption of horse meat "degrading and humiliating" and pointed out that eating horses had been rejected even by the "peasants of Europe and the coolies of China."[17] Fortunately, the shortages eased before horse meat became a staple of the New York diet.

That delicatessen food was seen as a special treat was shown by the ongoing efforts of the 52 Association, a group that started in 1945 after a restaurant owner picked up the tab for a group of blind sailors who had dined in his restaurant. The owner and his friends then created an organization in which fifty-two men would each be asked to contribute fifty-two dollars a year to pay for a weekly party for wounded veterans, serving food from delicatessens and gourmet food stores. By the early 1950s, the organization boasted more than two thousand members in New York alone and had expanded its efforts to include not just sponsoring the social events but helping the veterans to find jobs. According to one journalist, the organization's philosophy was that there is "not much wrong with a man's spirit that cannot be bettered by large portions of pastrami and cheesecake rendered under warm, friendly conditions."[18]

Murray Handwerker, the son of the founder of Nathan's, took an indirect path to bringing delicatessen into his store, which initially served only hot dogs, hamburgers, french fries, and chow mein. While serving overseas, he became introduced to foreign cuisines, as did many of his fellow soldiers. Upon his return, he decided to experiment with serving different foods. Murray took advantage of his father's vacation in Florida to start serving shrimp and clams. Only after he started making a profit from seafood did he bring in (nonkosher) delicatessen foods. "The postwar years were a turning point," he recalled. "Tastes were changing. And I, coming home from the war and going into the business, was part of that scene."[19]

While the war exposed Jews to other types of food, it also provided opportunities for non-Jews to learn about Jewish food. Lieutenant Colonel Harold Dorfman realized how much he missed delicatessen food when he served as navigator in a B-24 bomber on September 12, 1944. As the plane approached its target, the submarine pens of northern Germany, the pilot was ordered to inquire and record what was in each crew member's mind. Each responded, in turn, that he was thinking about his family back home—each, that is, except for Dorfman, who said that he was consumed with a desire for a hot pastrami sandwich. The response from the pilot: "How do you spell pastrami?" The crew endured an eight-hour attack by enemy gunfire by laughing and joking about the episode. But to actually taste the unfamiliar delicacy, most had to wait until they arrived in New York eight months later on their way back to Fort Dix.[20]

The "New York" Jewish Delicatessen, outside New York

After the Second World War, many Jews migrated out of New York, often in search of the warmer climes that they had discovered during their military service. Bringing their love of Jewish food with them, these newcomers established "New York–style" delicatessens all over the continent. While these delicatessens traded on the idea of "authentic" New York Jewish food, they each developed local variations on the theme. Many imported food from New York or hired delicatessen managers or workers away from New York, but they put the stamp of the local culture on the delicatessen and its menu.

Many Jewish New Yorkers relocated to Miami and L.A., where they found palm trees and wide-open spaces. By migrating to far-away cities that were known for their "leisure lifestyle," Deborah Dash Moore has argued, Jews remade themselves "from natives standing on the threshold of security and status into strangers seeking to establish networks to sustain themselves."[21] In the absence of well-developed social, professional, and religious networks, food still connected them to the life that they had left behind.

In some parts of the country, of course, Jewish delis were few and far between. When the actress Molly Picon returned to the United States from a series of performances in South America in the 1930s, she undertook a tour across the South and Southwest. "We continued driving straight through the Blue Ridge Mountains of Virginia, the Smokies, and south until we got to San Antonio. For four days, we'd be driving, and not one delicatessen on the whole trip!" she complained.[22] But almost every city that had a significant Jewish population had delicatessens, and these eateries were, as in New York, important gathering spots for an acculturating generation of American Jews.

In Baltimore, "Corned Beef Row" flourished on Lombard Street in Baltimore, with delis such as Weiss's, Sussman and Lev's, Awrach and Perl's, and Nates and Leon's. Baltimore had boasted delis since the turn of the century, with five delicatessens listed in the Baltimore city directory as of 1905 and seventeen as of 1910. One of the first, H. L. Kaplan & Company, began in 1897; by 1917, it advertised in a New York Yiddish newspaper, the *Yiddishes Tageblatt*, promoting its "high grade kosher sausage, smoked and corned beef, tongues, and pure chicken fat."[23]

Most of these delicatessens were located in East Baltimore, where the majority of the Jews lived. As in New York, most were strictly take-out stores until the interwar era, when they began to operate full-service restaurants as well. Sussman's Delicatessen had a separate counter on each side of the store, one for smoked fish and herring, the other for sausages and other meats. In 1926, its owner, Jacob Sussman, went into partnership with Carl Lev, a delicatessen dealer from New York. By the mid-1930s, they had installed seating booths, an Art Deco–style bar, and a ceramic-tile floor. A Viennese baker from New York prepared the bread, pies, and pastries.

Baltimore delicatessens, many of which, like the kosher delicatessen in Providence, doubled as soda fountains, were known for their variations on traditional sandwiches. The "Broadway Special" at Sussman and Lev's comprised tongue, spiced beef, corned beef, salami, sweet gherkins, and lettuce, all of which could be washed down with an Almond Smash soda. Over at Ballow's, Nathan Ballow served the ten-cent Easterwood Special, a half loaf of rye bread filled with bologna and mustard, as well as a bologna and hot dog combination. Nates and Leon's, founded by Nates Herr and Leon Shavitz, was known for its combination sandwiches, of which it ultimately developed 120, including an especially popular one of corned beef, coleslaw,

Interior of Sussman and Lev's Delicatessen in Baltimore from the 1930s
(Courtesy of the Jewish Museum of Maryland)

lettuce, and Russian dressing. Harry and Seymour Attman, who promoted their deli as the "home of fifty sandwiches," took ideas for combinations from the Carnegie Delicatessen in New York.[24]

In Boston, the G&G, owned by Irving Green and Charlie Goldstein, was an iconic deli on Blue Hill Avenue, in the heart of the Jewish working-class neighborhood, that, in the 1940s, served a decidedly nonkosher mix of ice-cream sodas, beer, potato pancakes, liverwurst and Swiss-cheese sandwiches, and chopped chicken liver accompanied by bread and butter. The historians Hillel Levine and Lawrence Harmon describe it as the central gathering place for the Jewish community, the Jewish version of the downtown Algonquin Club, where the Brahmins of Boston carried on their business. Candidates for local and national office knew that they needed to shake hands at the G&G in order to carry the Jewish vote; at the G&G, on every election night, a wooden bandstand was installed just outside the door, where the candidates and their supporters would make their last-minute pitches. Even John F. Kennedy, for example, according to Levine and Harmon, "made eye contact and munched french fries smothered in kishke grease with the best of them."[25]

Other nearby delicatessens were the downtown Essex Food Shop, which boasted the "biggest and best sandwiches in Boston"; the Modern Delicatessen & Lunch in the suburb of Roxbury, which carried three kinds of "solame" and two kinds of "frankforts"; and a chain called Barney Sheff's, located in Boston, Roxbury, and Revere. Other than Rubin's, which opened in Brookline in 1928, kosher delicatessens were never very popular in Boston, perhaps because of the centrality of pork and shellfish in the cuisine of New England. Indeed, one specialty of the Boston delis was the Swiss delicacy called *cervelat*—a mixture of beef, bacon, and pork rind packed into cow intestines and then smoked and boiled.

Chicago, a city famed for its stockyards and for providing dressed meat to the rest of the country, was also known for its delicatessens—even if they were rarely called by that name.[26] Manny's Coffee Shop and Deli opened in 1942 in the Maxwell Street area in Chicago, where the Jewish ghetto was still emptying out. When the New York Yankees came to town, the players got corned beef sandwiches and pickles from Friedman's Deli on Western Avenue, an establishment owned by the diehard Yankee fan Oscar Friedman. Friedman had befriended Yankees second baseman Bobby Richardson when Friedman was stationed in Sumter, South Carolina, during the Korean War, which happened to be Richardson's hometown. Friedman's son, Mark, recalled that each visit by the Yankees occasioned an exciting family outing to the stadium; before the game, they would deliver a paper sack of sandwiches and pickles to the Yankees' dressing room and get to meet Richardson, Tony Kubek, Elston Howard, Whitey Ford, and new manager Yogi Berra. Another celebrity customer of Friedman's was Nat "King" Cole, who performed with his trio at a nearby nightclub called the Rag Doll. Cole once insisted, despite the owner's objections, on ordering—and eating—a corned beef and sardine sandwich.[27]

The writer Joseph Epstein, who grew up in Chicago, recalled that Friedman's, which sported only ten or eleven tables, was a "meeting place after dates or a card game," a place where he found "older men, bedizened with pinky rings, talking about deals they had cut or bets they had won." Epstein frequently ended up there at one o'clock in the morning, when he and his friends "might tuck into a bowl of chicken kreplach soup, a corned-beef sandwich, and a Pepsi, maybe a couple of cups of coffee, a slice of cheesecake, possibly pick up a bit of halvah on the way out, a full fourth meal of the day, eating and arguing, before turning in for a perfect night's sleep."[28]

Delicatessens were particularly important as Jewish gathering places in Los Angeles given that Jews in the sprawling region tended to live much less closely together than they had in New York. Moore quotes a Los Angeles rabbi to the effect that the "sprawling atmosphere militates against the creation of a Jewish climate . . . in a given street or group or streets where people could come together informally and still be with like-minded persons."[29] The delicatessen also became the hangout of choice for the many Jews who worked in the film industry. "There could be no picture making," the film director Orson Welles flatly declared, "without pastrami."[30]

Canter's Delicatessen, which had first opened in Jersey City, New Jersey, in 1924, relocated to the Jewish suburb of Boyle Heights in 1931 and then moved to Fairfax Avenue—the heart of the Los Angeles Jewish community in the postwar years—in 1953. During the Depression, Canter's sold so many sandwiches for a dime apiece that a local bank borrowed money from it; by 1946, the deli was raking in a million dollars a year. Cohen's (also on Fairfax), Woloshin's (which was one of the few kosher delicatessens on the West Coast), Linny's, Lax's, Eat 'n Shop, Joseph's, and Nate 'n Al's were also hangouts for Jews in the entertainment industry. Both Lax's and Joseph's advertised themselves as offering what they called "choice Eastern delicacies," which neatly captured the identification of delicatessen food with both New York and eastern Europe.

In *Tough Jews*, a history of Jewish gangsters in America, Rich Cohen describes his father's ritual breakfasts with his friends from childhood (including the television news anchor Larry King) at Nate 'n Al's, where they act like big shots, call each other by mobster-sounding nicknames in their indelible Brooklyn accents, and act fearless and macho and mean. The deli roots them in a shared ethnic Jewish past, while it feeds their fantasies of machismo. As Cohen writes, "They fled Brooklyn thirty-five, forty years ago and have shed as many outward signs of their heritage as would be shed, yet still retain something of the old world, a final, fleeting glimpse of what their fathers must have been."[31]

Other Jews from New York opened delicatessens in Southern California. The grandmother of Murray "Boy" Maltin operated a restaurant during the Depression on the first floor of their apartment building on Mermaid Avenue in Coney Island. The family moved to Los Angeles when Maltin's father bought a hamburger stand on Lick Pier in Ocean Park and soon moved up to owning a delicatessen near the beach. During the Second World War, Maltin recalled, it was quite a scene on weekend nights, when the coins started pouring into the jukebox. A popular song of the day was a Johnny Mercer romantic ballad, "And Angels Sing," adapted from a klezmer tune by the trumpeter Ziggy Elman (né Harry Finkelman), sung by Martha Tilton, and performed by Elman with a band drawn from Benny Goodman's orchestra.

As Maltin remembered it, "The Yehuden [Jews] were slapping the mustard on the pastrami-and-slaw-sands, the corned-beef-with-sauerkraut-sands, the chopped-liver-and-pastrami-sands, the club-sands. On and on went the music; and a hundred conductors behind the deli counter, waving their arms in the air and slapping the rye with mustard spoons."[32] Maltin's father later bought a kosher butcher shop on Pico Boulevard (in the

Jewish section known as Pico-Robertson) and transformed it into a deli called Bonds (since it was bought with war bonds) that was the largest kosher deli west of the Mississippi; it had a seating capacity of 350 people, with its own bakery and a banquet that seated 200 guests.

As Jews moved to other parts of Los Angeles in succeeding decades, other delicatessens sprang up, including Zucky's in Santa Monica, the Stage Stop in Arcadia, and Art's in the Valley. A delicatessen in South Gate called Kosher Murphy's (trading on the long association between the Jews and Irish in popular culture) served kosher frankfurters and salami along with grilled ham-and-cheese sandwiches. Levitoff's, the "house of delicacies," offered "hot corned beef, hot tongue, and hot pastromi" at its two locations, one in Beverly Hills and the other on Sunset Boulevard in Hollywood.

Jewish delicatessens were also scattered throughout the Deep South. Mazo's in Charleston, South Carolina, was run by three brothers; the historian Marcie Cohen Ferris has found that there was "one uptown, a more 'genteel' operation downtown, and another location on Folly Beach."[33] Rosen's Delirama opened in Memphis, Tennessee, in 1905; by the early 1960s, it was advertising itself, on its Jewish-star-shaped menus, as "the largest, most modern, and most complete strictly Kosher Food Mart in the country."[34] Other delicatessens in Memphis included Abraham's (where the specialties included a pastrami Reuben and Hungarian meatballs on an onion roll served with hot slaw), Halpern's, and Segal's, which was a restaurant, caterer, and kosher butcher shop.[35]

As early as 1881, a grocery store in New Orleans had advertised "kosher smoked and pickled beef, sausages and tongues," as well as goose grease, New York salt pickles, and Passover cakes. But only after the Second World War did the city boast a number of full-service kosher delis, including Pressner's, which offered a "kosher smorgasbord" that included pastrami, tongue, salami, liverwurst, bologna, and an assortment of appetizing items such as smoked, fish, herring, and lox.[36]

In some southern cities, the delicatessen became a place of pilgrimage for both Jews and non-Jews. Harry Golden, who moved from New York to become the editor of the *North Carolina Israelite*, recalled the 1953 opening of the Brass Rail, a delicatessen in Charlotte. Church Street, the main business thoroughfare, "began to look like the Red Sea with wave after wave of Israelites crossing over each day for stuffed cabbage with raisin sauce, pumpernickel bread, chicken-in-the-pot, and boiled beef flanken." As the church bells pealed at noon, "We're Marching to Zion, Beautiful, Beautiful Zion," Jews and non-Jews alike began "pouring across Church Street to Izzy and Jack who are already slicing the hot pastrami."[37]

One southern delicatessen, however, became a flashpoint for racial animosity during the civil rights era. Charlie Lebedin opened a New York–style delicatessen in Atlanta called Leb's that refused to serve African Americans; the owner even turned away the singer Harry Belafonte, who came to town to do a benefit concert. In 1964, a series of sit-ins and protests at the delicatessen, along with other eateries owned by Lebedin, induced the Ku Klux Klan to support the owner. But when Lebedin joined the KKK in a protest of a local dinner to celebrate Martin Luther King Jr.'s receipt of the Nobel Peace Prize, the delicatessen lost the few remaining Jewish customers that it had.[38]

In 1941, when Judith Nelson Drucker's father retired from the garment business and moved his family to Miami, delicatessen foods were still not readily available there. "So whenever my father would go up to New York, he'd come back with a big box of salamis." The salami became, like them, a fish out of water. "We identified with the salami," she ruefully recalled. Nevertheless, Washington Avenue on the southern part of Miami Beach, according to a contemporaneous press account, sported "numerous vegetarian and kosher restaurants, delicatessens, and cafeterias where a bagel with a spot of cream cheese is 30 cents (the charge is 45 cents with lox) and herring and chopped liver are daily items on the menu."[39]

Sissi Perlman Feltman recalled that when her parents opened Joe's Broadway Delicatessen in the 1930s, it was "one of the few places to go besides Joe's Stone Crab," which was a famous seafood restaurant that was also owned by Jews. As in New York, Sunday was delicatessen night for many Jewish patrons. "It wasn't kosher, but it was an authentic deli," Feltman noted. "We had our own bakery in the back where we made our rye bread, and we cured our own pickles in big wooden barrels. We cooked big pots of brisket, and my brother was always stationed in the front window, carving a big roast beef."[40]

By the postwar era, the "Shtetl by the Sea," as Miami Beach was nicknamed, increased its population significantly, with many elderly Jewish "snowbirds" who wintered in Florida and returned to New York in time for the spring holiday of Passover. Other famous Miami Beach delis included Pumpernik's and Raphil's. One writer waggishly called Miami Beach "an extension of Lindy's, the Copa, Toots Shor's and the Gaiety Delicatessen, with sand."[41] The idea that others besides Jews might want to inhabit Miami during the winter months angered one Jewish hotel operator, who barked, "I'm sick of hearing that. We made Miami Beach a corned beef and dill-pickle stand and that's the way it's going to be!"[42]

Wolfie's, opened in Miami Beach in 1947 by Wolfie Cohen, sported a laid-back atmosphere with a singing waiter. The genial host, like his counterparts in New York, was known to approach a couple sitting at a table in stony silence; he would joke with them until they laughed and began conversing with each other. Jerry Cohen, the contractor who built Wolfie's, issued a challenge: "Find me a Jewish person in Miami Beach who didn't go to Wolfie's. . . . The Jewish culture of Miami Beach was all about eating. Even if you went out to dinner, you stopped off at Wolfie's before you went home. The way that New York had Lindy's, Miami Beach had Wolfie's."[43]

The delicatessens in Miami Beach were, like their counterparts in New York and L.A., known for their celebrity clientele. Barbara Raichlen (the wife of the barbecue guru Steve Raichlen)

Exterior of Wolfie's Delicatessen in Miami Beach in the late 1950s
(Courtesy of Brian Merlis / Brooklynpix.com)

told me that her father's deli, Raphil's, was the "place to see and be seen," with luminaries such as the gangster Meyer Lansky and the movie star Marlon Brando eating in the restaurant and its walls plastered with pictures of famous people. Al Jolson was known to frequent Joe's Broadway Deli. And it was in Pumpernik's, which was eventually bought by Wolfie Cohen and renamed Rascal House, that the future CNN host Larry King (né Zeiger) first started doing live radio interviews with celebrities.

The Delicatessen Summers in the Catskills

Playing a Viennese authority on mountain climbing on the pioneering 1950s television variety show *Your Show of Shows*, the New York Jewish comedian Sid Caesar proudly recalled climbing Mount Everest in 1935 with five other climbers and an ample supply of corned beef and pastrami sandwiches. Actually, he admitted, his group didn't reach the summit—or even the mountain. "How far did you get?" his interlocutor inquired.

"About as far as Twenty-Third and Broadway," Caesar replied, before they got caught in such terrible traffic that they could proceed no further.

Those Jews who stayed in New York did often succeed in bringing delicatessen sandwiches on trips with them, especially when they summered in the Catskills Mountains. Jews who could not afford to stay in Borscht Belt hotels—known for their gargantuan meals of traditional Jewish foods, including many deli-type delicacies—made do with rented bungalows called *kochaleins* (Yiddish for "cook for yourself"). Husbands would typically work during the week and come up to the mountains for the weekends. Each family, the satirist Harry Gersh recalled, arrived with a paper bag containing a dozen rolls, a loaf of pumpernickel bread, and a pound each of pastrami and corned beef. These were accompanied, according to Gersh, by pickles, mustard, sauerkraut, sour tomatoes, bagel, lox, cheese, and a whole white fish. While the women of the family took over the cooking from then on, everyone looked forward to the weekend, when the men would come bearing more delicatessen food. The fathers, Gersh disclosed, packed their clothes in loose packages and filled their suitcases with food from the delicatessen and appetizing stores. This was to keep the landlord, who profited from selling food to the tenants, in the dark.[44] The *New York Times* restaurant critic Mimi Sheraton, whose family summered in the Catskills when she was a girl, recalled that when weekend visitors arrived, "the customary gift was delicatessen," along with "towering boxes of cake."[45]

There were also Jewish delicatessens that opened up in the Catskills, including Kaplan's in Monticello, Singer's in Liberty, Cousin's in Ellenville, and Frank and Bob's in South Fallsburg.[46] The best known was Kaplan's on Broadway, famed for its immense sign with ten thousand flashing lightbulbs; performers were introduced in the hotels as "Broadway entertainment" only because they had eaten at Kaplan's just before the show.[47] Opened by Moe and Annie Kaplan in the years following the Second World War, the kosher-style deli got meat from Hebrew

Postcard image of Kaplan's Delicatessen in Monticello, New York
(Collection of Ted Merwin)

National and bread from local bakeries. (It also served cheese blintzes and cheesecake, but only with separate silverware and on separate dishes.) Among the waitresses were Ricki and Sari Kaplan, the nieces of the owners; their only other option for work, given limited opportunities for women, was the job of telephone operator. Celebrities such as Perry Como and Neil Sedaka ate at Kaplan's after performing in the local hotels. The comic Mac Robbins recalled that the entertainers from the hotels would take guests to a nearby delicatessen in exchange for a free lunch.[48]

In the summer, the bulk of the clientele at Kaplan's were those who lived in the bungalow colonies, along with parents visiting their children in the many summer camps in the area. But some customers would drive up from the Bronx on a lark to have a sandwich. The tables were large; strangers were often seated next to one another. The place got so busy that Sari Kaplan recalled that her sister would slip her a "potato chip" sandwich so that she could have a bite to eat in between serving tables. The one rule of family life, she said, was that "no one gets married, gives birth, or dies during the summer"—there was simply no time to do anything but take care of the business. In the winter, college students stopped at Kaplan's on their way to and from upstate universities such as Cornell and the state university campuses at Cortland and Binghamton. The entire front room of the store was decorated with college pennants; you got a free salami if you brought in a pennant that was not already up on the wall. The "college banner special" was chopped liver and roast beef on a seeded roll.[49]

Corned Beef in Space

While Jews went "up the mountains" and all over the country, often bringing delicatessen sandwiches along for the ride, it was a corned beef sandwich from Wolfie's Delicatessen in Cocoa Beach, Florida, that traveled the farthest distance of any delicatessen sandwich in history. In 1965, at the height of the space race with the Soviet Union, there was a fierce competition to be the first country to land a man on the moon. Gemini 3 was manned by John Young and Virgil Grissom; a fellow astronaut named Wally Schirra, who was known to be a prankster, had given Young the sandwich to smuggle aboard. This violated numerous rules of space travel because NASA was testing out various kinds of food to see if they could be safely consumed in space without either flying into the astronauts' windpipes or into the mechanical controls of the spacecraft.

The Russians, by contrast, believed that it was important for astronauts to experience some pleasure and relaxation through having good food on board and had already experimented with giving their astronauts toothpaste tubes of pâté, cheese, chocolate, and coffee, along with tiny pieces of bread, candied fruit jelly, and bits of salami. Indeed, the Russian cosmonaut Yuri Gagarin, on his first voyage in space, gobbled a bite-sized salami sandwich.[50] (It was important for astronauts to be supplied with high-quality food because, as the historian Jane Levi has noted, the shift of fluid to the head tends to hamper the senses of both taste and smell, and American astronauts, as opposed to Russian cosmonauts, had been noticeably skinnier and weaker, with less of their food eaten, when they returned to Earth.)[51]

In the middle of the Gemini flight, Young suddenly inquired if his partner was interested in a corned beef sandwich. After the astonished Grissom took a bite, he noticed nervously that crumbs of rye bread were starting to float around the cabin and that the smell of the beef was beginning to permeate the ship. "It became instantly obvious," he later recalled, "that our life-support system wasn't prepared to cope with the high powered aroma of genuine kosher corned beef." He reluctantly stowed the sandwich away.[52]

After the spacecraft landed, the astronauts were called on the carpet for their breach of the gastronomic rules of space. Representative George Shipley of Illinois complained that the sandwich incident was "disgusting." Comparing the spacecraft to a surgeon's operating room, he was appalled that the sandwich was permitted to pollute the sterilized space. George Mueller, the director of the Gemini Program, responded with a straight face that NASA frowned on "unauthorized objects such as sandwiches going aboard the spacecraft" and assured the congressmen that the agency had "taken steps, obviously, to prevent recurrence of corned beef sandwiches in future flights."[53]

In the end, the sandwich incident was not so much overstuffed as overblown. But it showed how iconic the delicatessen sandwich had become. What if the Gemini 3 had ended up on another planet, and aliens had picked up the corned beef sandwich and concluded that it was the staple food of earthlings?

The Second World War changed the relationship that Jews had to their own traditional fare, exposing them to other types of food and opening up new vistas for Jewish life in other parts of the country. Even as the delicatessens that Jews imported to other parts of the country enabled them to continue to gather and to connect to their heritage, wartime rationing taught Jews that they could do without delicatessen food. In the next chapter, we will see how upward mobility—of the social and economic kind, rather than the mountain-climbing or space-travel varieties—changed the relationship of Jews to delicatessen food even more, ultimately leaving the delicatessen in the dust.

=[4]=

Miss Hebrew National Salami

THE MOVEMENT TO THE SUBURBS
AND THE DECLINE OF THE DELI

In a classic *Mad* magazine cartoon from the 1960s, a family goes out to eat for the first time at an unbearably crowded, extremely chaotic Chinese restaurant. The meal is a nightmare: they can't get a table, their uncle can't decide what to order, the waiter ignores them, they stay so long that the table is removed, and then they tip the wrong amount. They are in a surrealistic environment, in which everything and everybody seems to conspire against them. Yet the very next Sunday night they find themselves once again standing in line at a chop suey joint. While the family is not explicitly marked as Jewish, the cartoon is filled with in-jokes for a Jewish readership; in the background, signs read, "Egg Foo Yong with Gefilte Fish" and "Chow Main Best! Liver Worst."[1] Jews were indeed developing a particularly intense relationship to Chinese food. The local Chinese restaurant became *the* neighborhood hangout on Sunday night, and going out for Chinese became a Jewish ritual in its own right.

Before long, it was the non-Jewish, ethnic restaurant rather than the delicatessen that served as a more popular gathering place for Jewish New Yorkers. But Jews still repaired to the delicatessen when they wanted to reconnect to their heritage. In the mid-1950s, the shortened form *deli* first came into widespread use. Joseph A. Weingarten noted in his 1954 dictionary of American slang that although he had never seen the word *deli* in print, it was common for people to say, "I'm having deli tonight" or "Mom, let's have deli." (He speculated that perhaps the word should be spelled "dely" or "delly" instead.)[2]

Beyond the attraction of Jewish New Yorkers to other ethnic cuisines, especially Chinese food, there were a host of other factors that led to the decline of the deli. While half of America's Jews still lived in New York City, rising crime rates along with the rapid construction of new highways and middle-income housing developments impelled many to move to the suburbs of western Long Island, southern Westchester, southeastern Connecticut, and northern New Jersey.[3] The Jewish movement to the suburbs, in which Jews were often in the minority, obviated the deli's role as a neighborhood gathering place. As Jews desired to be viewed on an equal footing with other Americans, they downplayed their ethnicity and culture in favor of Jewish religion. Indeed, Jews began to define their identity in opposition to the foods that had sustained their parents in Brooklyn and the Bronx and to develop a more sophisticated, more multicultural, and more gourmet palate.

When the Brooklyn Dodgers, a team especially beloved by ethnic minorities because of its perennial "underdog" status to the New York Yankees, abruptly decamped to Los Angeles, Jews were among those who felt the most betrayed. As the sportscaster Howard Cosell put it, on a trip back to his old neighborhood in Brooklyn, it was a particular shock to see that Radin's Delicatessen, located for decades near Ebbets Field (where the Dodgers had played) had closed. Radin's was, he recalled ruefully, "the 'Stage Delicatessen' of Brooklyn, the eatery for ballplayers. Hot dogs (crisp, all-beef ones) were always ready on the grill. The hot pastrami was unfailingly lean. You never had to ask, the tongue would be cut from the center. . . . Franklin Avenue without Radin's had to be like a man without a country."[4]

In 1960, there were still more than five dozen kosher delis in Brooklyn, with names like Schneier's or Schnipper's[5]—the kinds of names that the deli owners' sons had already changed when they graduated law or business school. But rising crime rates often made running a deli untenable.[6] In a particularly disturbing incident, a partly crippled deli owner on the Lower East Side killed two would-be teenage robbers with a carving knife when they invaded his cash register.[7] Paul Goldberg's father showed more restraint; when he caught someone trying to reach over the counter to grab a salami, he simply whacked him on the hand with the flat side of a knife. A Jewish lawyer recalled that it was the robbery of a deli in his neighborhood in East New York that was the last straw; his family no longer felt safe in the city.[8]

Some delis followed Jews to the suburbs; for example, when the Glen Oaks shopping center in eastern Queens was completed in 1950, Grodsky's Delicatessen could be found sandwiched among May's Department Store, F. W. Woolworth's, Dan's Supreme Super Market, and a slew of smaller stores.[9] Nevertheless, the historian Edward Shapiro has noted that in a typical postwar suburb, the local stores did not sell Jewish newspapers, there were no kosher butchers, synagogues were few and far between, and, last but not least, "corned beef sandwiches were not readily available."[10] The few delis that sprang up in suburban shopping malls still served as gathering places for segments of the Jewish population, but the community itself was weakened by dispersion and by the diminution of close ethnic ties. While Jews still sought to maintain a distinct ethnic identity, they did so in the context of a society that valued sameness and unity.

Other delis closed because the owners did not want their children to have to work the long hours that running a restaurant entailed. As the historian Karen Brodkin Sacks has noted, Jews "became white" by taking advantage of the G.I. Bill and federal home-loan guarantees—these programs enabled returning servicemen to go to college and to buy a house. This helped Jews to move squarely into the middle class and become professionals. Given their greater economic opportunities in American

Interior of Zarkower's Kosher Delicatessen in White Plains, New York,
in 1962 (Collection of Ted Merwin)

society, many children of deli owners viewed the prospect of
taking over the family deli with distaste, if not outright disgust.
In the Yiddish-English song "Sixteen Tons," based on Tennessee
Ernie Ford's coal miner's lament of the same title, the comedian
Mickey Katz changed the shoveling of coal to the piling up of
deli meats: "You load sixteen tons of hot salami / Corned beef,
rolled beef, and hot pastrami." He contracts a hernia from the
physical strain of shlepping these meats, along with cake, beef
intestines, and bagels.[11]

The choreographer Jerome Robbins, whose father owned a
kosher delicatessen on the same block as their apartment on
East Ninety-Seventh Street, had no interest in going into the
family business. As his biographer, Greg Lawrence, put it, "by
the time Jerome was born, the inherited dream of success had
magnified beyond anything that his lower middle-class father
might have imagined." Along with so many fellow Jews, he

"would embrace the idea of putting as much social distance as possible between himself and his origins."[12]

Susan Thaler, whose father owned Schlachter's Kosher Delicatessen on 176th Street and Walton Avenue in the Bronx, was mortified by her father's line of work. "Why couldn't he take weekends off instead of a school day so we could do things together like a family?" she asked plaintively in an essay in the *New York Times*. "Why couldn't he learn to speak English without an accent? Why couldn't he sell the store and get a real job in an office where he could wear a suit and tie and carry a briefcase? Why couldn't he be witty and tall and dapper like Mr. Anderson on 'Father Knows Best'?" Only later in life, when she had a child of her own, did she belatedly conclude that her father was "blessed" rather than cursed by his humble occupation.[13]

Other daughters of deli owners bedecked themselves in expensive clothes and jewelry in an attempt to conceal their humble origins, of which they had a lifelong sense of shame. As the humorist Harry Gersh conceded, they were simply absorbing the sensibility of their time; it was demeaning to admit that your father worked behind the counter of a store. "A delicatessen store man is different from a candy store man or a merchant, but not much," Gersh pointed out. "A little of the spice of the pastrami, a little of the fat he didn't trim off the corned beef enters his soul."[14] Deli owners were stereotyped as low class; on the jacket of Jackie Mason's 1962 debut album, *I'm the Greatest Comedian in the World, Only Nobody Knows it Yet!*, the comedian's heavy Yiddish accent is described as "midway between that of a Bronx taxi driver and a Lower East Side delicatessen proprietor."[15]

The Supermarket Delicatessen Counter

With the rise of atomic power and the coming of other scientific breakthroughs during the postwar era, frozen food was widely viewed as more modern and exciting than fresh food. Technology seemed to promise a future in which every food was appetizing, nutritious, and safe to eat. According to the historian Rachel Bowlby, every product was seen to be merely "awaiting its ideal package, to beautify it and to guarantee its cleanliness."[16] Many Jews "enjoyed kosher frankfurters, bagels, or a good piece of herring," the historian Alan Kraut notes, "but they preferred their consumables spotless and packaged for easy storage."[17] Using technology such as vacuum-packing and freeze-drying—originally developed in order to send food to the troops overseas—frozen food was placed in a water-proof plastic or foil pouch, known as a "hotback," that could be dropped in boiling water to reheat. "With our quarter-pound hotbacks of corned beef or pastrami that go into boiling water, you can have a hot pastrami on rye in a remote areas of Kansas," Jack Chase, a sales manager for Hebrew National, boasted to the *New York Times*.[18] When the sales staff of Zion Kosher went to call on supermarkets, they were armed with a laminated green card that showed photographs of their packaged products—everything from kosher frankfurters to liverwurst, kishka (stuffed derma), salami, and bologna.[19]

Ironically, these modern technologies were modern analogues of the smoking, salting, drying, and spicing that ancient peoples had used to preserve meat, fish, vegetables, and other foods.[20] By freezing pastrami (which is already twice preserved, given that it is made from brisket that is cured and then smoked), Hebrew National was preserving it yet again, but for modern mass consumption. By 1947, the company was selling cans of stuffed cabbage, meatballs in gravy, spaghetti sauce and meatballs, rice with braised beef, corned beef hash, and potato pancakes. These products, all of which cost less than a dollar a pound, could be found at more than three hundred stores in the New York area.[21]

The packaging of Jewish food was, however, nothing new. Since the turn of the twentieth century, matzoh, gefilte fish, and other staples of Jewish holiday fare had been available in boxes, jars, and other containers. As the historian Jenna Weissman Joselit has found, Yiddish newspapers had advertised such products as Uneeda Biscuits, Quaker Oats, and Proctor and

Sales card with images of packaged Zion Kosher Delicatessen products
(Collection of Ted Merwin)

Gamble's cooking fat Crisco (the availability of which, its makers proclaimed, represented the culmination of four thousand years of Jews waiting for a non-meat-based cooking fat that could be used for the frying of dairy products). In the 1920s, Joselit notes, "white bread, mayonnaise, and satiny-smooth Spry gradually assumed pride of place within the kosher kitchen, transforming it from an island of culinary superstition to a common meeting ground for tuna fish sandwiches and oatmeal cookies."[22] National consumer products were marketed to a Jewish population that prided itself, as the historian Andrew Heinze has found, on its ability to consume the same products as other Americans.[23] The problem for delicatessens was that supermarkets sold many of the same items that they carried. By 1957, 83 percent of supermarkets sold cooked meats and potato salad, 67 percent sold coleslaw, and 61 percent sold baked beans. And almost two-thirds of these supermarkets prepared these items in the store itself rather than depending on any outside vendors.[24]

As a result, from 1929 to 1954, the number of delicatessens (of all types, not just Jewish ones) dropped nationwide by more than a quarter from around 11,000 to only 8,000. By contrast, the number of supermarkets, or "combination markets," rose sharply from 115,000 to 188,000. By 1960, supermarkets sold 70 percent of the nation's groceries.[25] Waldbaum's, founded by the Polish Jewish immigrant Ira Waldbaum, catered to a customer base of middle-class Jews. The business journalist Leonard Lewis compared Waldbaum to Moses; Waldbaum led Jews on their exodus from Brooklyn to the Long Island suburbs. By doing so, Lewis noted, Waldbaum's became the "unofficial supplier to the children of this new promised land."[26]

The historian Mark Zanger has noted that ethnic foods tend to become "softer and whiter" in the process of assimilating to mainstream American foodways.[27] The flabby, bland, light-colored cold cuts sold in supermarket packages bore little resemblance to the chewy, spicy, dark-red slices of meat found in a traditional deli. While the average per capita consumption of meat in New York was more than three pounds a week in the 1950s, the trend was away from the type of meat traditionally served in a deli. According to Jerry Freirich, the owner of a kosher-meat-processing company, New Yorkers had become partial to lean meat that was not too spicy or salty, as compared to the South, where, he said, fattier, spicier, and saltier meats were still preferred.[28]

As the historian Marilyn Halter has noted, it was initially assumed by marketers that ethnic shoppers "would seek out local immigrant businesses involved in small-scale food production and retailing rather than consuming the products of corporate giants."[29] But for the most part, Americans of all stripes, including relatively new immigrants, eagerly embraced "ethnic" products sold by large food corporations. This made it difficult for mom-and-pop delis to compete. Sam Novick, a longtime salesman for a number of kosher meat companies, including Public National Kosher, City Kosher (founded by his father), and Hebrew National, put it bluntly: "The supermarket was part and parcel of the ruination of the neighborhood deli."[30]

On the other hand, some supermarkets saw delis as a threat and sought to block them from renting space in a shopping center in which the supermarket was an anchor tenant. This attitude reflected long-standing tensions between small retail stores and supermarkets; the attorney Manny Halper recalled that as a child in the Bronx, he once heard his rabbi give a sermon exhorting housewives not to buy meat from the supermarkets but to patronize their local butchers instead. Halper started writing leases in New York in 1960, enabling retail stores, including scores of Jewish delis, to move from city streets to suburban shopping centers. But he insisted that he never prepared a lease for a supermarket on Long Island without including a clause permitting a Jewish deli in the same shopping center. "The deli never posed any kind of threat," he said, "particularly a kosher deli, which sold different kinds of merchandise than the supermarket did."[31]

Whether the precipitous decline in Jewish deli owners' business could be attributed to the rise of the supermarket or not, it caused rage among them. In New York, their antagonism toward supermarkets allegedly grew so intense that they committed antitrust violations. If a kosher meat company agreed not to sell to local supermarkets such as Dilbert's, Kubrick's, Royal Farms, and Dan's Supreme, then the Jewish delis in that neighborhood would purportedly band together and buy all their meat exclusively from that company. Companies that sought to sell to the supermarkets anyway, the government claimed, were threatened with violence. Fred Molod, a deli owner's son who had become a lawyer for the Brooklyn branch of the Delicatessen Dealer's Association, defended the delis. Molod brought a large map of Brooklyn into the courtroom, pushing colored pins into the map to mark the locations of the delis. He then put the deli owners on the stand to testify that there had been no unlawful cooperation. The government backed down from most of its allegations.

Here She Is . . . Miss Hebrew National Salami

With the decline of the deli and the mainstreaming of Jews into society, the kosher meat companies also realized that they needed a new marketing strategy. By such publicity stunts as sending salami-scented ads through the mails and anointing a "Miss Hebrew National Salami" and a "Miss Hebrew National Frankfurter" (the latter on the occasion of the company's billionth hot dog sold), Hebrew National used sexual associations and offbeat humor to market its products beyond the Jewish community.

Sex in American advertising was, of course, nothing new; the historian Tom Reichert has found that it dates back to the 1850s, when drawings of nudes were first used to sell tobacco.[32] But, with the advent of *Playboy* in 1953 and the many men's magazines that followed in its wake, sexual images became more prominent and accepted in American culture. Sausages, because of their phallic shape, especially lent themselves to titillating advertising. While Jeanne Williams, a.k.a. "Miss Hebrew National Frankfurter of 1952," simply cradled a long hot dog above her ample cleavage and was surrounded by pendulous hot dogs in the background, Zion's "Queen of National Hot Dog Week of 1955," Geene Courtney, wore frankfurters, sausages, and kielbasa as a crown on her head, as a belt around her waist, as a scarf-like chain thrown over her left shoulder, and as bracelets around her wrists, as if in some kind of sexual bondage.[33] (As the activist Carol Adams has argued, meat has long been—and continues to be—advertised in our culture in ways that degrade women and that mirror pornography. According to Adams, "viewing other beings as consumable is a central aspect of our culture."[34])

Nevertheless, Hebrew National, in an ironic counterpoint to playing up the sexual undertones of its products, also emphasized the associations with purity, healthfulness, and cleanliness that many Americans associated with the word *kosher*. The company used the *Good Housekeeping* seal in its print advertising, along with a picture of a ribbon showing that the company had been commended by the consumer service bureau of *Parents* magazine. One ad campaign on New York City subways depicted a young boy balancing a Hebrew National salami on his head; the ad copy claimed that the food could be part of a healthy diet.[35]

Painted highway billboards, many located on commuter routes throughout the metropolitan area, focused on the company's new use of a distinctive blue-and-yellow string to connect its sausages and frankfurters to one another. Ads on subways and buses, in addition to in delicatessens and supermarkets themselves, hawked the kosher meats. Newspaper ads ran not just in New York but in cities such as Providence, Pittsburgh, Hartford, Cleveland, and Washington, DC.

The company also sponsored 80 percent of the radio and television coverage of the 1953 and 1954 elections on the major radio networks—ABC, CBS, NBC, and WOR; it used the slogan "Make Election Night Party Night" to encourage listeners to organize gatherings and serve the company's products. By promoting an association between Jewish food and voting, the company allied itself with ideals of patriotism and democracy. This fit with prevailing ideas about the role of consumption as a mark of good citizenship. According to the historian Lizabeth Cohen, "the new postwar era of mass consumption deemed that the good purchaser devoted to 'more, newer, better' was the good citizen," that one "simultaneously fulfilled personal desire and civic obligation by consuming."[36]

Hebrew National also produced as part of its marketing strategy a plethora of advertising items that reflected the ongoing acculturation process of the second and third generations of American Jews. These ranged from books of score sheets for gin rummy and canasta (popular card games that Jews played both at home and when they vacationed in the Catskills and in Miami Beach) to little, white, plastic trash bags with its logo and the slogan "Bag it and help keep our highways clean." These give-aways implicitly recognized that Jews wanted to maintain their connection to their heritage and participate in the life of society on an equal basis with other Americans.[37]

Hebrew National was also a major sponsor of the many popular radio and late-night television programs on CBS hosted by Arthur Godfrey. Both Godfrey and the comic Steve Allen gave out free Hebrew National salamis to their studio audiences; free provisions were also distributed at telethons, benefit performances at Madison Square Garden, and other large-scale charity events. Meanwhile, parents were targeted through a campaign in which consumers were asked to send in examples of situations that their children tended to avoid (such as the dentist's office, barber shop, music lessons, or bathtub) but for which a Hebrew National hot dog might serve as an effective bribe.[38]

In a radio spot on the most popular Jewish station in New York, WEVD (named for Eugene V. Debs, the socialist leader), a jaunty jingle by the Pincus Sisters announced that "for that old fashioned flavor that all the folks favor, try Hebrew National meats." Customers who sought authentic Jewish food for their parties, late-night dinners, and other social occasions were urged to "be rational" and "serve meats made by Hebrew National."[39] One advertising campaign solicited sandwich "recipes" from Jewish New Yorkers who were then featured in its advertising along with their creations. Another campaign focused on the supposed favorite sandwiches of celebrities such as the actress Molly Picon and the comedian Morey Amsterdam. Not to be outdone, Zion Kosher sponsored a "name that cantor" contest on radio station WEVD; identifying a cantor from his singing alone would win prizes in delicatessen products.

The clever mass marketing of Jewish foods also embraced the rye bread used to make delicatessen sandwiches. Henry S. Levy & Sons was a kosher bakery on Thames Street in Brooklyn that had long supplied kosher delicatessens; in an ad in the early 1930s in the *Mogen Dovid Delicatessen Magazine*, it trumpeted its fifty years in the business contributing to "firm, even, tender sandwiches that look better and taste better" and adver-

Ordinary New Yorkers with their sandwich creations depicted in a 1950s
Hebrew National promotional booklet (Collection of Ted Merwin)

tised twenty-four-hour deliveries to all parts of the city.[40] But
by the 1960s, with sales falling precipitously, the company experimented with packaged rye, pumpernickel, and raisin breads
in an effort to broaden its customer base, especially among
non-Jews—a strategy that apparently alienated many of the
bakery's Orthodox customers. Howard Zieff at the Doyle Dane
Bernbach advertising firm developed a series of ads featuring
non-Jewish models, including an American Indian chief, an
altar boy, a Japanese man, and an African American boy, eating
deli sandwiches on rye with the tag line, written by Judy Protas,
"You Don't Have to Be Jewish to Love Levy's Real Jewish Rye."[41]
The African American activist Malcolm X liked the one with
the African American boy so much that he had his own picture
taken standing next to it.

As Zieff later wrote, "We wanted normal-looking people,
not blond, perfectly proportioned models. I saw the [Ameri-

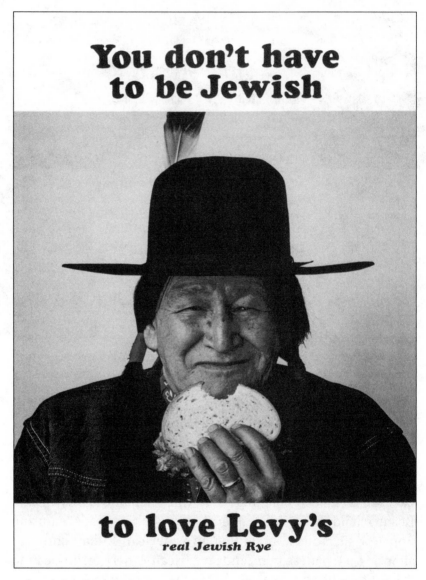

Levy's Rye Bread subway advertisement from the 1960s with American Indian eating a delicatessen sandwich (Courtesy of Bimbo Bakeries)

can] Indian on the street; he was an engineer for the New York Central. The Chinese guy worked in a restaurant near my Midtown Manhattan office. And the kid we found in Harlem. They all had great faces, interesting faces, expressive faces." What he sought, he said, were "faces that gathered you up."[42] In the same way, Jewish food was starting to "gather up" a non-Jewish clientele, thus expanding the popularity of Jewish culture in America in ways that would only accelerate in the coming decades.

Jews Redefining Themselves as a Religious Group

From the 1956 release of Cecil B. DeMille's *The Ten Commandments* to the rise of evangelical preachers such as Billy Graham, religion was resurgent in many Americans' lives during the postwar era. The economic prosperity that fueled the rise of the suburbs, the growing focus on family life in the generation of the baby boomers, and the ascendancy of a militant anticommunism—all of these seemed to require legitimation in religious terms. At the same time, fear about the instability of life in an age of hydrogen bombs also led many Americans, including Jews, to seek comfort from religion. Best-selling books by religious leaders from Rabbi Joshua Liebman (*Peace of Mind*) to Norman Vincent Peale (*The Power of Positive Thinking*) capitalized on the need for reassurance that many Americans felt. Liebman's book in particular, according to the historian Jonathan Sarna, "heralded Judaism's emergence as an intellectual, cultural, and theological force within postwar American society."[43] But as Judaism took on a kind of high-mindedness and serious of purpose, Jews began to define themselves less as an ethnic group and more as a religious one, as a "faith" that was the equal of Protestantism and Catholicism.

One sees this shift in the Academy Award–winning 1947 film *Gentleman's Agreement*, in which Gregory Peck plays a journalist who pretends to be Jewish in order to write a magazine article on anti-Semitism; he adopts none of the cultural or ethnic aspects of Judaism but simply announces that he is

Jewish by religion.[44] The rise of religion preempted Jewish ethnicity by substituting the social life of the synagogue for that of
the delicatessen. True, as the sociologist Will Herberg noted,
this newfound religiosity was often void of true meaning; it
was a "religiousness without religion, a religiousness with almost any kind of content or none, a way of sociability or 'belonging' rather than a way of reorienting life to God."[45] But it
sped the acculturation of Jews into American society by putting Judaism on an equal footing with other religious groups.
This was summed up in the title of Herberg's influential book
Protestant–Catholic–Jew, in which he argued that Jews had become part of Christian America by emphasizing the religious
rather than cultural aspects of their identity.

In order to find a specifically Jewish means of fitting into a
society that placed a premium on morality and public religious
behavior, Jews built palatial suburban synagogues as fortresses
against assimilation. (Some people jokingly referred to this as an
"edifice complex.") While relatively few members—including,
surveys showed, the congregational lay leaders—were interested
in attending services more than a few times a year, the synagogue could generally muster a good turnout with a Saturday-
night cultural program or Sunday-morning bagel brunch.

Even as Jews downplayed their ethnicity, then, Jewish food
remained a central component of postwar Jewish identity. In
Treasury of Jewish Humor, published in the early 1950s, the
folklorist Nathan Ausubel used the term "Culinary Judaism" to
refer to a food-based Jewish identity and detailed the lengths to
which Jews went to devour their favorite dishes, including delicatessen meats.[46] As the sociologist Seymour Leventman put it,
a "gastronomic syndrome" could be diagnosed among Jews, one
that "lingers on in the passion for bagels and lox, knishes, blintzes, rye bread, kosher or kosher-style delicatessen, and good
food in general."[47]

In order to survive the transformed gastronomic landscape in
which the relatively few Jewish delicatessens that opened in the
suburbs found themselves, they needed to appeal to non-Jews as

well as Jews. But they also did not want to alienate their base of Jewish customers by serving food that was so nonkosher that it would offend them. It was this balancing act, the historian Ruth Glazer (who later became Ruth Gay, when she married the historian Peter Gay) recalled, that her father engaged in when he opened an "unreconstructed" delicatessen at the end of a subway line in Queens. A kosher delicatessen sporting a sign with Hebrew letters, he was informed, would turn these non-Jews against him from the beginning. And most of the Jews no longer kept kosher or wanted to be seen eating in a kosher establishment.

So he opened a "kosher-style" delicatessen, in which traditional Jewish foods were served but the meat was not kosher. Jewish women felt free to come in to ask for advice on how to prepare Jewish food, while increasing numbers of non-Jews, who originally viewed the deli as a "curiosity," submitted to the entreaties of Jewish friends to come in and order pastrami, a word that they often mispronounced in amusing ways. Nevertheless, according to Glazer, the store became for Jews and non-Jews alike a "symbol of traditional Jewish living," despite its departures from fidelity to Jewish dietary law.[48] If the fare at Glazer's father's delicatessen created such harmony between the Jews and non-Jews of the town, the New Haven attorney Samuel Persky joked, perhaps anti-Semitism could be combated if, rather than "distributing educational pamphlets dedicated to the truth about the Jew, we can so manage it that every rock and rill in this land of liberty be permeated by the gracious aroma of hot corned beef and pastrami."[49]

The Rise of Ethnic Food

With the assassination of President John F. Kennedy, the rise of the civil rights movement, and the involvement of the country in Vietnam, the carefree ethos of the early 1960s began to dissipate. The burgeoning interest in multiculturalism, however, meant that ethnic food rose in popularity; the food historian Warren Belasco has insightfully compared the rise of ethnic food with the popularity of oak furniture—both spoke to consumers' desire for the sense of security that they identified with traditional ways of life.[50] Belasco attributes the interest in ethnic food to a host of factors, including the spread of foods from one ethnic group to another (for example, "in-migrating blacks [who] sampled out-migrating kosher foods"), the growth of tourism, and the presentation of ethnic foods in the mass media—especially in relation to ethnic movie and television stars.[51]

Indeed, people in the 1960s counterculture who resisted the "cultural imperialism" that was destroying local foodways around the globe and replacing them with standardized American foods founded a "countercuisine" based largely on ethnic foods. As Belasco puts it, while the first generation had made food from scratch, the second generation sought "old-style sauces to put on American meats and vegetables," and the third generation purchased "fully processed convenience foods with an Old World aura that could be supplied with a few spices and a picturesque aura."[52] Many ethnic foods were produced by large corporations, including the Pizza Hut chain and R. J. Reynolds' Chun King line of Oriental food; Chun King trumpeted a "new mood in food" as the impetus for the spread of Chinese food throughout the land.[53]

Delicatessen foods were no exception to the commodification of ethnic foods; in 1968, Hebrew National was sold to Riviana Foods, which was itself acquired by Colgate-Palmolive, a soap and toothpaste company.[54] (The Pines family bought it back in 1980; by 1986, the company was producing half a million frankfurters a day in its plant in Maspeth, Queens.)[55] Savvy young entrepreneurs who founded smaller ethnic-food companies could make a quick profit by selling out to bigger companies.[56] Jewish foods, like other ethnic foods, were commodified and torn from their original social context. The pastry-wrapped "deli sandwiches" sold under the Campbell's Pepperidge Farm and Nestlé's Stouffer's brands had as much relationship to a real New York delicatessen sandwich as frozen burritos did to authentic Mexican cuisine.

But it was Chinese food that most captivated American Jews. According to the blogger Peter Cherches, Chinese food was a "birthright" for Brooklyn Jews of his generation; he recalls being "weaned on chicken chow mein."[57] And if a rabbi needed to find ten Jews for a *minyan* (prayer quorum), what better place to look than in the local Chinese restaurant? In an updating of the phenomenon of "cross-over eating" found by Donna Gabaccia at the turn of the twentieth century, one ethnic group began to define itself through the consumption of another ethnic group's food.[58] The critic Neil Postman recalled that the shopping district in Flatbush, where he grew up during the Depression, boasted appetizing stores, two kosher delicatessens, three candy stores, and a "very popular" Chinese restaurant. On Friday nights, he and his older siblings had a ritual of bringing a dollar to the Chinese restaurant to buy three dinners for thirty cents each, which included egg drop soup, an egg roll, and chow mein.[59]

Many theories have been propounded to explain the intense Jewish fondness for Chinese food. Gaye Tuchman and Harry Gene Levine, the authors of a landmark study on the subject of New York Jews eating Chinese food, noted that Chinese food was appealing to Jews who, while not keeping strictly kosher (or keeping kosher at home but not away from home), avoided the overt consumption of pork and shellfish. Tuchman and Levine dubbed it "safe *treyf*"—food that was so thoroughly diced and chopped that it was not recognizable as nonkosher. Chinese food thus, according to Tuchman and Levine, became a "flexible open-ended symbol, a kind of blank screen on which [Jews] projected a series of themes relating to their identity as modern Jews and as New Yorkers"[60]—one that replaced the equally blank screen or palimpsest of the pastrami sandwich. Through the consumption of Chinese food, Tuchman and Levine suggest, Jews were able to perceive themselves as more sophisticated and urbane, despite the fact that the food was inexpensive and relatively simple. As the British social anthropologist Allison James notes, in writing of magazines and television programs about foreign cuisines, such cultural products paved the way to a "culinary, expatriate, cosmopolitanism."[61]

Others have speculated that Jews felt an affinity to the Chinese, since both were ethnic outsiders in Christian America. The Chinese are often called the "Jews of the East," and in America they became even more marginalized. Tuchman and Levine note that eating in Chinese restaurants "did not raise the issue of Jews' marginal position in a Christian society" because the Chinese were even more marginal than the Jews were.[62] Indeed, Jewish patrons could feel superior to the Chinese. They could even insult the waiter, turning the tables on the treatment they received in Jewish delicatessens.

As Philip Roth put it in his 1967 novel *Portnoy's Complaint*, "Yes, the only people in the world whom it seems to me the Jews are not afraid of are the Chinese. Because, one, the way they speak English makes my father sound like Lord Chesterfield; two, the insides of their heads are just so much fried rice anyway; and three, to them we are not Jews but *white*—and maybe even Anglo-Saxon." The idea that Jews could be actually taken for Protestants by the Chinese was especially appealing: "Imagine! No wonder the waiters can't intimidate us. To them, we're just some big-nosed variety of WASP!"[63] Both the Jews and the Chinese operated on a different calendar than Christians did; this was why the biggest night of the year for Jews to eat out in Chinese restaurants was Christmas Eve, a night when most other restaurants were closed. But in addition to serving as this once-a-year gathering place, the Chinese restaurant to some extent also displaced the deli as the weekly Sunday-evening gathering spot for Jewish families.

Of course, Jews still knew, as much as they tried to pretend otherwise, that they were eating forbidden foods. As the old Yiddish saying goes, *Az men est chazzer, zol rinnen iber der bord*—"If you're going to eat pork, you might as well eat it until it runs over your beard." In other words, if you are going to sin, you should enjoy it! Guilt, according to a Canadian rabbi, is a "terrific condiment."[64] On the other hand, as the food scholar

Miryam Rotkovitz has noted, the very fact that Chinese food was taboo made the experience of eating in a Chinese restaurant more exciting; it "contributed to the exoticism of the experience."[65]

The craze among Jews for Chinese food led to the first cookbook of kosher Chinese food, written by Ruth and Bob Grossman; it presented whimsical recipes that mingled Jewish and Chinese ingredients, such as Foh Nee Shrimp Puffs, which were fried balls of gefilte fish served with hot mustard and plum sauce.[66] Furthermore, the opening of kosher Chinese restaurants made it possible for observant Jews—many of whom had grown up in nonkosher households in which Chinese food was a staple and only later embraced Orthodox Judaism—to enjoy Chinese food as much as their less religious coreligionists did.

The marriage of delicatessen and Chinese food had been solemnized on the Lower East Side at Schmulka Bernstein's (later Bernstein on Essex), a kosher delicatessen that was opened in 1932 by Sol Bernstein, who adopted his father's name—his father was a butcher and meat manufacturer—as the name of the restaurant. Starting with a small seven-table establishment on Rivington Street between Essex and Ludlow, he moved to 110 Rivington Street, with a factory in the same building, the factory entrance being on Essex Street. The deli expanded in the 1950s by breaking through the wall and taking over the factory space, pushing the factory out to Utica Avenue in Brooklyn.

Bernstein's daughter, Eleanor, was brought up in an apartment over the store. "My mother never forgave my father for going into the deli business," she recalled. "When they got married, he was planning to be a doctor, but once he got to medical school, the cadavers upset him. But he joked that he was still an M.D.—a meat dealer!" The deli became known for its specially spiced Romanian pastrami, which other delis tried to copy. It also smoked a lot of geese for the winter holidays; smoked goose was popular among Germans for Christmas and had thus become a favored Chanukah dish for German Jews. In 1960, Eleanor's father realized that Jews liked Chinese food, and he called an agency that sent him a Chinese chef one day a week. "The Chinese chef came in like a doctor with a little case," she said. "He wanted to use his own knives, but the rabbi told him that everything had to be kosher; he gave the chef a lesson about all the special rules. My father took the chef to the restaurant supply stores on the Bowery and bought him whatever he needed." As demand grew, the restaurant hired more Chinese chefs, until the fateful day when, as Eleanor put it, "a war broke out in the kitchen between the Shanghai and the Cantonese, and my father had to fire everyone—-which wasn't easy, because they were in a union—and start over." Over time, the restaurant grew to the point that there were 52 people working in the kitchen and a total of 220 in the store.[67]

The delicatessen had two different menus—one for the traditional Jewish offerings and one for the Chinese ones. A sample Chinese menu from Bernstein's on Essex St. from the early 1960s ("Where West Meets East for a Chinese Feast and Kashruth Is Guaranteed") trumpets the fact that "for the first time," the "Orthodox Jew or Jewess can taste the food specialties of the Orient," advising patrons to begin with soup before proceeding to appetizers—egg rolls, spare ribs, or "sweet and pungent" veal—and then on to the main course and dessert. The menu also suggests that each party order a variety of dishes to share, a practice that became so popular that later generations would take it for granted.[68]

Bernstein hired Chinese waiters and gave them tasseled skullcaps to wear, so they looked like Chinese Jews. He sent his chefs to famous Chinese restaurants such as Pearl's to try their dishes and adapt them to a kosher menu. Although Bernstein would never eat in a nonkosher restaurant, he would occasionally accompany his staff on these spying missions; he would order one of the restaurant's signature dishes and poke through the food with his chopsticks until he figured out the ingredients so that he could create a kosher version. Even in the Chinese menu at Bernstein's, the dishes frequently melded Chinese food—or at least the Americanized versions of Chinese food—with eastern

Customers eating at Bernstein's on Essex, the first kosher delicatessen to offer Chinese food (Copyright Bettmann/CORBIS)

European Jewish food. Among the specialties of the house were salami fried rice, egg foo yung with chicken livers, and Stuffed Chicken Bernstein—a half chicken stuffed with bamboo shoots, water chestnuts, and pastrami. Israeli beers and wines were on the drinks menu, along with German beers and domestic kosher wines.

Jews and Italian Food

Italian cuisine was also extremely popular in Jewish communities. Jews and Italians, who often looked similar, both arrived on these shores in large numbers in the last two decades of the nineteenth century. The Jewish section of the Lower East Side was right next to Chinatown, but it was also adjacent to the immigrant Italian section, known as Little Italy, which had a large Sicilian and Neapolitan population. Italians and Jews went to school together, played on teams together, and occasionally ate in each other's apartments, as in the chapter in Henry Roth's classic Lower East Side Jewish immigrant novel *Call It Sleep*, in which the main character, David Schearl, is served crabs by his new Italian friend, Leo. David is afraid to eat the unfamiliar, clearly nonkosher delicacy, but Leo, sucking on a claw, boasts, "We c'n eat anyt'ing we wants," adding, "Anyt'ing that's good."[69] At the turn of the century, according to Philip Taylor, "a Jewish boy . . . could easily recognize an Italian district into which he had strayed, by the sight of certain sausages and cheeses in shops."[70]

Italians in Red Hook and Canarsie were not far from the Jewish neighborhoods in Brownsville, Bensonhurst, and Brighton Beach. Jews and Italians were known for getting into conflict over religion, with frequent street fights between the children of the two groups. But by the 1950s, Daniel Rogov recalls, the Italian kids would tag along when the Jewish kids went on quests to eat a hot dog in each of the six delicatessens in the Brooklyn Heights area; if they got into a fight, it was "more like playing stickball" than actually fighting, in the days before gang wars with tire chains.[71]

Both Jews and Italians loved to eat, and both groups were enraptured by, and obsessed with, the sheer quantity of food that was available in America—the meat, the fish, the coffee, the rich desserts. They also both enjoyed a highly theatrical approach to dining. Mamma Leone's, the Italian restaurant in the theater district, had extravagant decor, nude statues, singing waiters, and huge quantities of highly Americanized Italian food including spaghetti and meatballs, veal Sorrentina, clams casino, and shrimp scampi. Jewish and Italian families both prized dinnertime as the most important daily occasion.

The historian John Mariani could be writing equally about Jews in noting that in Italian households "the dinner table, not the living room, was the center of political and social discourse that raged on for hours and into the night, until one or another family member collapsed on the couch."[72] Rabbi Eric Cytryn recalled that while there was a kosher deli right around the corner from his house in Westbury, Long Island, his family usually gravitated to a local Italian restaurant instead, even though since they kept kosher, they could not eat any of the meat or shellfish on the menu.[73]

Beginning in the 1970s, Italian restaurants became increasingly fashionable in New York. Mimi Sheraton, the *New York Times* restaurant critic who happened to be Jewish, relentlessly championed restaurants such as Il Nido and Il Monello that served upscale Northern Italian cuisine, which was a far cry from the pasta and red-sauce-based Southern Italian cuisine that was familiar to most Americans. Even the typical neighborhood Italian restaurant with the red checkered tablecloth and bottle of olive oil on the table was getting rid of its pizza oven and expanding its veal and chicken offerings.[74] Sheraton interviewed the comedian Alan King at Il Nido; he talked about growing up in a kosher home but later developing a taste for many different kinds of food, from Italian to Japanese.[75]

By the 1980s, fashion industry executives, or "fashionistas," many of whom were Jewish, patronized Tuscan restaurants, where they shook hands on deals to import high-end Italian silk garments and leather shoes made by Prada, Ferragamo, Versace, and other companies. One Italian restaurant in particular, Da Silvano, was a hangout of the crowd from *Vogue* magazine, where the nation's fashion styles were set.[76] By comparison, Jewish delis never developed into "white tablecloth"–type restaurants where important business deals would be struck. But despite the attraction of other ethnic cuisines, many Jews often felt themselves irresistibly pulled back to a deli. The Jewish sculptor Louise Nevelson, for example, favored Italian food (particularly lobster, veal, or angel's hair pasta with pesto sauce), although she also often sought out Mexican, Indian, and Japanese restaurants. But when she felt sad, she headed straight for a deli, where she enjoyed "mounds of sour pickles, pickled green tomatoes, rye bread and even pastrami if it's good and spicy."[77]

Multiculturalism and the Deli

With the 1976 publication of Irving Howe's *World of Our Fathers*, the first comprehensive history of immigrant Jewish life in New York, Jewish tourism to the Lower East Side boomed with suburban Jews trying to recapture their roots. This nostalgia- and heritage-based tourism was part of a larger multicultural movement within society that also boosted the popularity of the television miniseries *Roots* (about African American history). *World of Our Fathers* was published at the same time as the bicentennial of the United States, as the whole country was celebrating its past.

That past, for many Jews, led back to the Lower East Side. As Ari Goldman of the *New York Times* noted in 1978, the immigrant ghetto "has always been famous for its Sundays. The wares from the shops on Orchard Street spill out onto the sidewalks, the delicatessens on Essex Street can't make the pastrami sandwiches fast enough, and the smell of pickle brine is heavy in the air."[78]

New York Jews' "tourism" to the Lower East Side dates back to the 1920s, when the children of Jewish immigrants who had grown up in the neighborhood first turned the ghetto into a place of pilgrimage, converting, in the words of Jenna Weissman Joselit, a "slum" into a "shrine."[79] In 1954, the nineteen-year-old Polish Jewish immigrant Abe Lebewohl had gotten his first job working as a soda jerk in a Coney Island delicatessen. Eager to learn the business, he volunteered to spend his lunch breaks working behind the counter. Before long, he became a counterman. He then saved up enough money to buy a ten-seat luncheonette on East Tenth Street, which, by dint of years of labor and more than one major expansion, eventually blossomed into the Second Avenue Deli, the landmark delicatessen on the Lower East Side, complete with a room that paid tribute to Molly Picon (the beloved Yiddish actress) and a "Walk of Fame" outside in which Yiddish actors had stars imprinted on the sidewalk.

But the Lower East Side faded as a part of Jewish life as new immigrants, especially Puerto Ricans and Asians, moved in and the city redeveloped the district with high-rise buildings. By the 1970s, it was the grandchildren of Jewish immigrants who began this process anew, rediscovering the Lower East Side as a source for nostalgia. Especially on Sunday afternoons, Hasia Diner has written, Jews made the stores and restaurants of the Lower East Side into pilgrimage sites, places to take their children and to recapture their childhoods.[80] The humorist Calvin Trillin confessed in 1973 that he often repaired on Sundays to Katz's, where the countermen "always maintain rigid queue discipline while hand-slicing a high quality pastrami on rye." He described the forbidding sandwich makers as appearing practically to "loom over the crowd—casually piling on corned beef, keeping a strict eye on the line in front of them, and passing the time by arguing with each other in Yiddish."[81]

For the Second Avenue Deli's twentieth-anniversary celebration in 1974, the restaurant rolled back its prices to what they had been when it first opened. Customers flocked in for the fifty-cent corned beef sandwiches, thirty-cent bowls of matzoh ball soup, and nickel cups of coffee. Lebewohl kept coming up with new ways to get publicity. In 1975, with the city on the verge of bankruptcy, Lebewohl gave all the proceeds from two days of salami sales to the municipal coffers. And he ignored the late-1970s gasoline shortages by hiring a horse and buggy—covered with signs promoting the delicatessen—to make deliveries.[82]

The less that Jews and non-Jews consumed pastrami sandwiches on a regular basis, the more that delicatessen food became special—it was transformed back into a "delicacy" in Jewish culture. Which pastrami sandwich was the "best" became a topic of heated debate; in 1974, *New York* magazine held a Pastrami Olympics in which the height of each sandwich was

Cover of Pastrami 'n Things menu, showing *New York* magazine poster
of the 1973 Pastrami Olympics (Collection of Ted Merwin;
rights courtesy of *New York* magazine)

carefully measured, along with the weight of the bread, weight of the meat, and cost of the meat per pound; the winning deli was Pastrami 'n Things in Manhattan. And the *New York Times* restaurant critic Mimi Sheraton bought 104 corned beef and pastrami sandwiches in 1979 to discover her own favorite, in both taste and construction (she dubbed Pastrami King in Queens, the Carnegie Deli, and Bernstein on Essex the best of the lot; Katz's was at the bottom of the list).[83] But these competitions underscored the fact that pastrami had come full circle; it had become, as originally both in eastern Europe and on the Lower East Side, a special-occasion food—to be savored as an occasional treat rather than as a regular part of one's diet.

Nevertheless, the delicatessen sandwich remained an all-purpose, universally recognizable symbol of the city, as shown in a 1970 magazine advertisement for Coca-Cola in which a smiling cab driver leans out the window of his yellow cab, holding an overstuffed corned beef sandwich along with his bottle of soda. The tagline, "It's the real thing. Coke," in the context of the ad implies that the corned beef sandwich is "the real thing" as well—that it is an authentic symbol of New York.[84]

Samurai Deli

In John Belushi's classic 1976 "Samurai Deli" skit on *Saturday Night Live*, Belushi plays a delicatessen counterman as a Samurai sword-wielding lunatic. A customer, played by the Jewish comedy writer Buck Henry, is concerned that the corned beef sandwich that he has ordered will give him heartburn and high cholesterol, but the owner, who speaks only Japanese, is a purist; he threatens to commit hara-kiri when the customer asks him to trim off the fat.[85] The customer withdraws his request, but when he asks the counterman to break a twenty-dollar bill, the counterman does so with his sword, demolishing the counter in the process.

The stereotypes of the deli are neatly inverted in this parody. The deli is no longer viewed as a haven; the deli owner, rather than being kindly and talkative, is homicidal and inarticulate. (He speaks no English, like the immigrant delicatessen owners who spoke only Yiddish a century before.) The deli is a place of violence and fear, and the food that it serves is so unhealthy as to be downright poisonous. It is difficult to see which is more dangerous, the food itself or the lunatic who serves it. Alan Zweibel, who wrote the skit, told me that his idea was to invert the idea of the friendly local delicatessen, turning the act of ordering food there into a terrifying experience.[86]

The episode, which was one of many Samurai spoofs that Belushi and Henry did, spoke to the mushrooming anxiety about health and fitness that characterized the 1970s; it also ran just as reports of mercury contamination in supermarket products caused widespread alarm about the nation's food supply. A skepticism about the efficacy of modern medicine, along with a developing focus on self-improvement and self-fulfillment, left many people feeling more responsible for maintaining their own bodies. As Peter N. Carroll has written, the spread of terrifying new viruses and bacterial infections in the 1970s led to what he calls a "thorough reevaluation of the relationship of the human body to the natural environment."[87]

A huge diet and fitness industry developed, centered around providing health clubs, exercise equipment, nutritional supplements, and low-calorie foods. By the 1980s, according to the sociologist Barry Glassner, the fit body held a "signal position in contemporary American culture—as locus for billions of dollars of commercial exchange and a site for moral action."[88] As Jews, including the Orthodox, jumped on the health and fitness bandwagon, they looked to develop healthier, more gourmet versions of traditional Jewish dishes.

In line with Americans' newfound "duty" to their own bodies, an estimated one hundred million of them were dieting. Companies began marketing low-fat, low-cholesterol, and low-sodium foods; by the middle of the decade, these "diet foods" were a $700 million business, compared to a $250 million business in the late 1950s. While "reducing salons" first became popular in the 1950s, they had been marketed primarily to women. The new emphasis on fitness extended to men as well. It was recommended that both men and women "exercise in qualitatively the same ways (with the same movements, using the same equipment or games) and in the same quantities, they should eat the same healthful foods, and subscribe to the same values, such as naturalness, self-control, and longevity."[89] Athletic equipment was a $2-billion-a-year industry, while Jim Fixx's *The Complete Book of Running* was a runaway best-seller.

In such a climate, delicatessen foods were considered the opposite of what both men and women needed to eat in order to preserve their health. Six of the ten leading causes of death— including heart disease, cancer, obesity, and stroke—were linked to diet.[90] For those who were on a salt-restricted diet, the Consumers Union recommended, foods to be avoided included smoked or prepared meats such as bacon, bologna, corned beef, ham, liverwurst, luncheon meats, pastrami, pepperoni, and smoked tongue.[91] For those who insisted on continuing to eat deli meats, experts recommended switching to pastrami, salami, and bologna made from turkey. Putting delicatessens in the same category as fast-food eateries, the food columnist Barbara Gibbons called on both kinds of restaurants to "shape up!" reporting that the "disenchanted are staying away in droves after a decade of bad-mouthing from nutritionists, consumerists and food critics."[92]

Robert Atkins, who first introduced his high-protein, high-cholesterol, low-carbohydrate diet in 1972, bucked the trend by proclaiming that fatty foods were good for you. Atkins was in many ways simply adapting Dr. Irwin Stillman's high-protein diet from the late 1960s, which Stillman touted both in a best-selling book and on late-night television. But Atkins lauded Jewish deli food in particular, explaining that his diet permitted not just lox and eggs but "cold cuts galore—brisket, tongue, corned beef, pastrami, turkey." He warned that dieters "avoid the coleslaw; it's made with sugar," but he invited them to "make free with those crisp, fragrant new dill pickles."[93]

Beef consumption, which had increased every year until 1975, suddenly took a nosedive, as men between the ages of nineteen and fifty cut their intake of beef, including deli meats, by a third. Francis Moore Lappe's best-selling book *Diet for a Small Planet*, published in 1971, argued that by feeding grain to animals, whose meat contains far fewer nutrients than the feed does, the United States wasted tremendous natural resources and perpetuated world hunger. Nor was this wholesale destruction limited to this country's borders; the cutting down of the rain forests in Brazil was blamed on the need to graze cattle to satisfy the fast-food market in America. And cows were also blamed for producing so much methane gas, mostly from belching and farting during rumination, that the greenhouse effect was dramatically intensified.[94]

Some people argued that at least the deli food sold in supermarkets was healthier than that traditionally purveyed by delis. For example, while delis sold frankfurters with natural casings (made from sheep intestines), the supermarkets offered the healthier, skinless variety. "You got a snap from a deli hot dog that you couldn't get from a skinless one," Skip Pines of Hebrew National admitted, even as he banked on the supermarkets for his company's future. Pines himself stayed healthy through portion control; he ate a single hot dog every day for lunch and then snacked in the late afternoon on a slice of salami, which he tested for the three essential qualities of "flavor, grind, and nuance."[95]

In addition to marketing their deli products on the basis of health, supermarkets also continued to advertise them on the basis of quality, convenience, and price. In the late 1970s, a newspaper ad by the Stop & Shop Supermarket in the local newspaper in Norwalk, Connecticut, urged consumers to "set aside a special 'get out of the kitchen night'" on a weekly basis. "Everything we make in our kitchens is just as good as the best New York Deli, but a lot less expensive." The ad suggested a Reuben sandwich with corned beef, coleslaw, and pumpernickel with Russian dressing or a jumbo club sandwich of roast turkey breast, baked ham, and Swiss cheese on rye—with the meat sliced "fresh to order" by its "deli people."[96]

As the twentieth century wore on, humor about the unhealthiness of Jewish deli food took on a sharper, more satiric edge. In Leonard Bernstein's short story "Death by Pastrami," a funeral salesman named Fleishman markets his services to deli patrons just after they polish off six-inch-high sandwiches; he bribes the waiters to tell him who ordered pastrami. But as more salesmen discover the scheme, the people eating in the delis begin to feel too self-conscious to eat in the restaurants, and his business takes a nosedive.[97]

Finally, concerns about the deleterious effects of Jewish food on the body animate a *Seinfeld* episode in which George's father, played by the comedian Jerry Stiller (who earned an Emmy Award for his performance in the episode), panics that he has poisoned the members of a singles group by serving them spoiled *kreplach*, which triggers traumatic memories of his serving contaminated meat to his platoon during the Korean War.[98] The stereotype of delicatessen food as unhealthy, which had dogged it as far back as the immigrant period, now dominated most Jews' perceptions of this type of food.

"Comin' through the Rye": Delis in Popular Music

By creating Jewish parodies of popular songs, Jews fantasized that the whole world had become Jewish. The masters of this form of comedy, both of whom referred almost obsessively to deli food in their work, were Mickey Katz and Allan Sherman.

Katz began his career as a clarinetist in Cleveland but soon found work with the Spike Jones orchestra, which was known for its send-ups of popular songs. Katz first invented a klezmer-inspired, Yiddish version of "Home on the Range," which he followed with "The Yiddish Mule Train," "Kiss of Meyer," and "Duvid Crocket," all of which sold tens of thousands of copies. Much of his success came from the quality of his orchestra, which included Mannie Klein (later replaced by Ziggy Elman) on trumpet, Si Zentner on trombone, and Sam Weiss on the drums.

Jewish food was a constant theme of Katz's Rabelaisian humor. Josh Kun has noted that Katz's parodies are invariably based on the "'substratum laughter' produced by food—*gribbenes*, matzoh, schmaltz, pickles, kishka, bagels, latkes—and its digestive impact on those who consume it."[99] What could Jewish humor be based on, at a time when many Jews were not well versed in their own tradition? Even if they no longer spoke Yiddish and had never learned much Hebrew, they could speak deli—the universal language of American Jewishness. Kun views Katz as resisting Jewish assimilation by insisting on the Jew as outsider, as on the cover of one of his albums, *Borscht Jester*, in which the musician is shown in cap and bells, holding a salami.

Katz seemed unable to resist incorporating references to Jewish food in almost every song, no matter how incongruous the reference. In his recordings and performances, including a short-lived 1951 Broadway show called *Borscht Capades*, Katz performed songs such as "Halvah Hilarities," "Matzoh Ball Jamboree," "Farfel Follies," and "Chopped Liver" (based on "Moon River"). In his version of the end of Al Jolson's "Toot, Toot, Tootsie," he substituted "I'll send you some pickles and rye" for Jolson's famous extended warble "Goodby-y-ye." Katz combined klezmer with swing, calypso, polka, mambo, opera, and rock music. Katz's music provided what must have felt like an easy fix, a quick detour into memory lane before getting back on the road to success in American society.

Katz's successor in the business of Jewish song parodies, the aforementioned Allan Sherman, was born Allan Copelon in Chicago in 1924, the son of the racing-car driver and automobile-garage owner Percy Copelon and his wife, a flapper named Rose Sherman. Sherman's parents divorced when he was six years old; he lived with his mother and eventually adopted her maiden name. Expelled from the University of Illinois for breaking into a sorority (for the purpose, he said, of using the phonograph player), Sherman ended up performing song parodies at a bar in Chicago, before finding work in New York writing jokes for various radio and stage comedians, including Jackie Gleason and Jack E. Leonard. In the early days of television, he was also a writer for variety shows such as *Cavalcade of Stars* and *Broadway Open House.*

Sherman's first album, *My Son, the Folksinger,* took the nation by storm; it became the fastest-selling album in recording history, eventually selling more than a million copies. When this short, obese man with heavy glasses with a raspy voice took American folk or Broadway songs and set them to lyrics about deli food, he showed that Jews still maintained an ethnic consciousness even while Jewish culture appeared to be increasingly subsumed under the overarching Judeo-Christian ethos. In his song "Shticks of One Kind and Half a Dozen of the Other," on his 1962 album *My Son, the Celebrity,* he sang, "Do not make a stingy sandwich / Pile the cold cuts high / Customers should see salami / Coming through the rye." The salami (read: Jewishness) erupted through the rye (read: American society), bringing Jewish culture to the fore.

By changing "Moon River" (from the film *Breakfast at Tiffany's*) to "Chopped Liver," "With a Little Bit of Luck" (from the Broadway musical *My Fair Lady*) to "With a Little Bit of Lox," and "Water Boy" (a southern African American song) to "Seltzer Boy," Sherman exploited not just the humorous associations of delicatessen foods but the sense that Jews were transforming American culture in their own image. According to Sherman's biographer, Mark Cohen, while Sherman's delicatessen-themed musical *The Golden Touch* never made it to Broadway, its "suspicion of success, encouragement to remain true to oneself, and proud assurance that chopped liver and other homely hallmarks of Jewish life were worth keeping . . . remained the themes of Sherman's life."[100]

While the author Ken Kalfus has suggested that Sherman made Jewish humor "mainstream," he also notes that Sherman emphasized Jewish particularity. In Kalfus's words, it "expressed

Jews' apartness from American culture, at a time when the culture itself was about to go counter." Kalfus writes perceptively about the emphasis placed at the time on the "lovability of the loser," cataloguing such bumblers and bunglers—both real and fictional—as the 1962 Mets (40 wins, 120 losses), Alfred E. Neuman, Charlie Brown, and Jerry Lewis.[101] In any event, Sherman turned Jewish food into comic gold in a way that transcended its Yiddish origins and made it accessible and humorous to both Jewish and non-Jewish Americans. As the critic Gerald Nachman has pointed out, Sherman "resisted being branded a 'Jewish' performer, as his repertoire played to everyone. . . . His lyrics spread a generous helping of chopped liver over a slice of American cheese. The playful lyrics were a kick, but they also made fun of Jewish (and, by extension, all) middle-class American life in the early 1960s."[102]

Love, Sex with the Shiksa, and the Jewish Delicatessen

Another "danger," that of intermarriage with non-Jews, loomed ominously over the delicatessen. Eating nonkosher delicatessen food had long symbolized having the "forbidden pleasure" of sexual relations with non-Jewish partners. In the 1940s, the novelist Isaac Rosenfeld had famously observed the riveted passersby who watched beef fry (a kosher imitation of bacon) falling off the slicing machine of a window of a Lower East Side delicatessen. Rosenfeld wrote that a crowd, "several rows deep," constantly gathered to watch this spectacle—"oblivious of the burden of parcels, of errands and of business; no comments are made, they stand in silence, not to interfere with another's contemplation, as they follow the course of the slices, from the blade to the box."[103]

Rosenfeld viewed the trance that the people fell into not in religious terms but in sexual ones; he suggested that the beef fry is an "optical pun" on the concept of *treyf* and that Jews unconsciously associated eating *treyf* with sex with non-Jews—unlawful carnal knowledge, indeed! Rosenfeld insisted that anti-Semitism sprang from a misconception among non-Jews that Jews were "lecherous" and enjoyed "greater freedom from restraint." As Eve Jochnowitz interprets him, Rosenfeld "traces all of sexual pathology to the laws of kashrut," suggesting that "all anti-Semitism is rooted in gentile myths, all provoked by Jewish food, about Jewish superior sexuality."[104]

By the late 1980s, the Jewish-Christian intermarriage rate had skyrocketed from almost nothing at the beginning of the century to about 50 percent, as Jews increasingly sought non-Jewish partners and non-Jews felt more comfortable marrying Jews.[105] The trope of the Jewish man and the *shiksa* (a derogatory Yiddish term for a non-Jewish woman) had become especially familiar in popular culture, especially in the films of Woody Allen. Jewish delis often served as backdrops for relations between Jewish men and their non-Jewish girlfriends, as in *Annie Hall*, when the main character, Alvy Singer, takes his tall, midwestern girlfriend to the Carnegie Deli as a prelude to their having sex for the first time; she mistakenly orders a pastrami sandwich on white bread with mayonnaise (echoing a scene in the Broadway musical *Skyscraper* in which Julie Harris commits a similar faux pas in the Gaiety Delicatessen),[106] and he grimaces, as if remembering Milton Berle's classic joke that "every time someone goes into a delicatessen and orders a pastrami on white bread with mayo, somewhere a Jew dies."

Food and sex are frequently linked in Allen's films; as Allen's character in *Love and Death* quips when his lover invites him to her bedroom, "I'll bring the sauce." Or as Allen noted in a parodic *New Yorker* essay, on food in the world of philosophy, "As we know, for centuries Rome regarded the Open Hot Turkey Sandwich as the height of licentiousness; many sandwiches were forced to stay closed and only opened after the Reformation." (Indeed, the seventeenth-century philosopher Baruch Spinoza "dined sparingly because he believed that God existed in everything and it's intimidating to wolf down a knish if you think you're ladling mustard onto the First Cause of All Things.")[107]

But why has Alvy taken Annie to a deli in the first place, if not to shore up his own vulnerable ego? The delicatessen is the one place that is comfortable and familiar for the demasculinized Jewish man and where he can thus feel superior to her and her anti-Semitic family. His refraining from coaching her on what to order, and his thus allowing her to make a fool of herself in front of him, elevates him in his own eyes. It allows him to make love to her from a position of strength rather than of weakness and inferiority.[108] The historian Henry Bial views this scene from the dual perspectives of the Jews and non-Jews in the film audience, noting that the non-Jews "learn what it means to act Jewish as the film progresses. . . . Alvy's rolling eyes and horrified expression are an in-joke to some of his viewers and a 'teachable moment' to the rest."[109]

This dynamic is neatly reversed in the Katz's Deli scene in Rob Reiner's 1989 film *When Harry Met Sally*—a takeoff of the Woody Allen genre and of *Annie Hall* in particular—in which the non-Jewish woman, Sally, played by Meg Ryan, shows the egotistical Jewish man, Harry, played by Billy Crystal, that he is less masculine than he thinks he is because he cannot tell whether she is having an orgasm (and, in a sense, that she doesn't need him at all in order to have it). While the fake orgasm is not related specifically to the food that she is eating (she is eating a turkey sandwich, from which she carefully removes one slice of meat after another before consuming it), it is uniquely appropriate in the deli context—one has the sense that the humor would evaporate if it were shot in a Chinese restaurant with tinkling music in the background. The scene makes hay from the associations that Jewish food has with sex, with vulgarity, with unbridled bodily urges, with the lack of civility and restraint.

After all, the deli—with its casual vibe, lack of tablecloths, and raucous atmosphere—was a place where Jews had celebrated freedom from table manners, from the need to speak softly, and from the oppressive kinds of control over their own physical bodies that they needed to assert in the wider soci-

Meg Ryan and Billy Crystal in the "orgasm" scene in Katz's Delicatessen from the 1989 Rob Reiner film *When Harry Met Sally* (Licensed by Warner Bros Entertainment, Inc. All rights reserved.)

ety in order to prevent being viewed as vulgar, uncivilized, and uncouth.[110] In the context of the Lower East Side, where Jews had historically lived in overcrowded tenements that afforded little privacy, "private" sexual behavior was often much more "public" than most would have preferred, and the deli was an extension of this private space into the public realm.

Yet, despite Sally's explosive, seemingly definitive usurpation of the space, a Jewish woman defiantly has the last word: the well-dressed, elderly customer at the next table (played by the director's mother, Estelle Reiner) declares in a perfect deadpan, "I'll have what she's having."[111] And Jewish women do indeed reclaim the space in the 2007 documentary *Making Trouble*, in which four female stand-up comics—Judy Gold, Jackie Hoffman, Cory Kahaney, and Jessica Kirson—eat lunch at Katz's while paying tribute to three generations of female Jewish entertainers in American history, such as Fanny Brice, Sophie Tucker, Joan Rivers, and Gilda Radner.[112] But non-Jewish women again take center stage in a flash-mob video from November 2013, in which twenty female customers at Katz's simultaneously reenact the scene from the Reiner film.[113]

Broadway Danny Rose, Allen's black-and-white 1984 film about a hard-luck theatrical agent, opens with a scene of a group of aging Jewish comics—Corbett Monica, Sandy Baron, Jackie Gayle, and Will Jordan—sitting at a table in the Carnegie Deli, swapping anecdotes about their life on the road. They then reminisce about Danny Rose, the agent, played by Allen. Rose has been reduced to representing such clients as a blind xylophone player, a one-armed juggler, a couple who "fold" balloon animals, and a skating penguin dressed as a rabbi.[114] The film highlights the waning of secular Jewish culture, using the deli as a symbol of that decline. According to the film scholar Jeffrey Rubin-Dorsky, "what Allen locates in the Jewish world of the Catskills" and, by extension, the Carnegie Deli, "and what Danny Rose recreates with his ragtag band of odd 'acts,' is the sense of unforced community that existed among a people gathered together to share a culture that would inevitably disappear in the process of Americanization." Rubin-Dorsky is struck by Allen's finding a "nurturing spiritual connection to the Jewish past" through the reiteration of the link between Jewish comedy and Jewish food.[115]

Jewish masculinity is even more explicitly connected to deli sandwiches in "The Larry David Sandwich," an episode of *Curb Your Enthusiasm* in which the main character, Larry David, who grew up in Brooklyn but now lives in Hollywood, decides for once to pray at a synagogue for Rosh Hashanah but finds out that the tickets are sold out and that he will have pay a scalper to gain admittance. His attendance at the service proves to be disastrous and results in his being ejected, along with his non-Jewish wife, Cheryl. Larry seems not to care; he realizes that he prefers to spend his time at his favorite Jewish deli, Leo's, where he has finally achieved the signal honor of having a sandwich named after him.

The problem for Larry is that "his" special sandwich is not a traditional meat sandwich but one of sable and whitefish. In

Ed O'Ross and Larry David in "The Larry David Sandwich" from
season 5 (airdate 9/25/2005) of *Curb Your Enthusiasm*
(Courtesy of HBO / John P. Johnson)

being a kind of inauthentic deli sandwich, it thus subtly under-
mines Larry's claim to true celebrity, as well as his masculinity,
as symbolized by the lack of red meat in his sandwich. The latter point is underlined by the fact that Larry is also afraid to
shake hands with the deli owner, Leo, because Leo's handshake
is crushing.

Larry's attempts to trade sandwiches with Ted Danson,
whose namesake is a roast beef, coleslaw, and Russian dressing combo, are fruitless. Larry argues, naively, that Danson
should not care what the ingredients of his own sandwich are
since Danson doesn't frequent the deli as much as Larry does or
bring his father to eat there; Danson, after all, is not Jewish. But
Danson refuses the trade—the fish sandwich sounds terrible
and is much too ethnically Jewish, and, in any case, Danson
knows a good deli sandwich as well as Larry does. Nevertheless,

even as deli food became more mainstream, as *Curb* showed, it also maintained a strong connection to secular Jewish identity, as one of the few remaining links that Jews like Larry had to their Jewish heritage.[116]

The episode presents the deli as a more viable Jewish space than the synagogue, where the worshipers are shown as bored and impatient. By contrast, the deli is a shown as a place of fun, fellowship, and humor where commercialism can be openly celebrated in its connection to popular culture. While the same characters, including the deli owner, are also shown at the synagogue, the conversations among them revolve around the deli sandwiches, not the lofty spiritual matters that one might expect them to be discussing on the Jewish New Year.

For these characters to have sandwiches named after them makes them feel that they have achieved true recognition; having other people eating "their" sandwich causes tremendous pride and pleasure. To get "up on the board" in a synagogue might mean having your name on a plaque on the wall; this honor is acquired simply by giving money. But to be "up on the board" at the deli is a sign of real fame.

The Yuppies Rule: The Rise of Gourmet Kosher Food

Beginning in the 1980s, Modern Orthodox Judaism, which promoted the idea that Jews could participate equally in American society and yet still maintain fidelity to religious law, gained strength. While Hasidic Jews had colonized neighborhoods in Brooklyn beginning in the interwar period and had seen their numbers climb dramatically in the years after the Holocaust, it was Modern Orthodox Jews who experienced the most dramatic rise in both visibility and influence.

One leading Orthodox rabbi, Walter S. Wurzburger, was quoted in a front-page article in the *New York Times* noting that the "vigor as well as the image" of Orthodox Judaism had been "completely revitalized." Indeed, he crowed, "Gone are the predictions of the inevitable demise of what was widely dismissed as an obsolete movement that could not cope with the challenges of an 'open' society."[117]

The resurgence of Orthodox Judaism spelled trouble for the typical kosher delicatessen. Many modern Orthodox Jews lacked nostalgia for the forms of Jewish culture that had been so important to their second-generation parents. Unless a delicatessen were *glatt* kosher, meaning that it adhered to the most rigid standards (including closing on the Sabbath and the Jewish holidays), they would generally avoid eating in it. Even to be seen walking into a non-*glatt* kosher delicatessen exposed one to the risk of ostracism from the community, under the assumption that observers might be misled into eating there themselves.

Delicatessen food was widely perceived as low class. Bryan Miller, restaurant critic for the *New York Times*, noting the expansion of kosher dining options in the city, observed that Jews appeared eager to shed what he called the "gastronomic barbells" of delicatessen food. The hearty food served in delicatessens represented, he averred, the weight of the immigrant Jewish heritage, which Jews self-consciously cast off in the act of adapting their heritage to meet the needs of upward social and economic mobility.[118]

The more "yuppified" that Orthodox Jews became, the more that they tended to disdain the deli. Some restaurants combined deli favorites with other types of food; for example, Jacob's Ladder in Cedarhurst, Long Island, served not just kosher matzoh ball soup, chopped liver, cold cuts, and potted brisket of beef but also hamburgers, barbequed chicken wings, spareribs, and chicken fricassee. But others avoided deli food entirely and sold more cosmopolitan, gourmet fare. On the Upper West Side, Orthodox Jews flocked to Benjamin of Tudela (named after a globe-trotting medieval Spanish rabbi) for its kosher steaks, chops, duck, chicken, and fish. The restaurant's brick walls, charcoal-gray rugs, and bouquets of wildflowers all bespoke an affluent clientele.

Nanou, a kosher French restaurant in downtown Manhattan serving the cuisine of Provençal, featured roast duck with orange sauce on its menu, along with grilled veal chops with mushroom sauce. In the Riverdale section of the Bronx, owner Michael Posit took his nonkosher French restaurant named Dexter's and turned it into a kosher restaurant that served chicken breast stuffed with veal mousse and medallions of beef with a sauce made from red wines, shallots, and thyme.

Other kosher restaurants soon rushed to occupy the upscale market niche, including Café Masada and La Kasbah (both serving North African cuisine) and Levana (serving a mix of Italian and French cuisine, with sauces and condiments "painted" on the plate). On Ocean Avenue in Brooklyn, in a neighborhood formerly crammed with Jewish delis, the latest dining establishment was Little Budapest, a fancy Hungarian Jewish restaurant. And many Jews—and non-Jews—when they weren't eating out, took advantage of dozens of kosher cooking classes at the Ninety-Second Street Y, organized by Batia Louzon Plotch, a Sephardic woman from Tunisia who sought to expand the idea of kosher food. "What they knew about Jewish food was Eastern European," she said of her students. "In my family, Jewish food is couscous [on] Friday night."[119] A master Japanese chef, Hidehiko Takada, taught the course on sushi, and the Chinese cookbook author Millie Chan taught the course on Northern Chinese cuisine. Other chefs instructed budding chefs to prepare kosher versions of Thai, Persian, Iraqi, Northern Italian, and Indian food.

Another new trend was the kosher gourmet club, in which a group of couples met once a month in one of their homes, with each couple bringing a different dish from the cuisine of the month, which could be anything from Cajun to Hawaiian to Fiji. These would often be quite extravagant affairs, with each couple vying to bring the fanciest dish and the hosts finding the appropriate music, dress, and decor to accompany the chosen cuisine. One of the group members might even be responsible for giving a *d'var Torah* (minisermon, or commentary on the Torah) in keeping with the dinner's theme.[120]

At the same time that nonkosher deli food was growing in popularity among Jews and non-Jews alike, kosher food was also becoming more sophisticated and increasing its appeal. Trends toward kosher food that was healthy, international, and gourmet accelerated through the 1990s and into the first decade of the twenty-first century. On the Upper West Side of New York, one could eat in a kosher sushi restaurant one night and a kosher Mexican restaurant the next. A spate of new kosher cookbooks emphasized Sephardic cuisine, which is based much more on fruits and vegetables than is meat-heavy Ashkenazic cookery. The Jewish delicatessen began to seem increasingly like a throwback to an earlier age, its fare hopelessly prosaic, unhealthy, and low class. As the humorist Sam Levenson pointed out in a *Saturday Review* article that was reprinted for years on the back of the Second Avenue Deli's menu, the deli was a remnant of a world that was sadly "all but destroyed by upward mobility."[121]

Thus, by the turn of the millennium, the Jewish delicatessen had become, in the words of the writer Richard Jay Scholem, "almost as obsolete as the buggy whip," given "the healthy eating movement, with its emphasis on low fat, cholesterol and calorie food, the diminution and diffusion of this area's Jewish population and the coming of age of a new generation without nostalgic memories of Jewish deli food."[122] The journalist Joseph Berger found that a small number of delis, such as the Second Avenue and the Carnegie, still functioned as what he called "Disneylands for tourists or nostalgia seekers who want to savor a way of life that is passing on."[123]

Readers of *Harper's* "Facts about New York City" tongue-in-cheek statistics column learned in 1998 that while there were no fewer than thirty-one branches of the Astoria Federal Savings Bank at which automatic-teller transactions could be conducted in Yiddish, the number of kosher delis in the city had declined by 88 percent since 1965. While the continued vitality of the immigrant Jewish language might seem to go hand-in-hand with a continued appetite for eastern European Jewish food, the magazine failed to point out, however, that the Yiddish-speaking ATM machines were concentrated in Hasidic neighborhoods in Brooklyn, where few delicatessens were located.[124]

In the Bronx, a hundred delicatessens had dwindled to no more than three. Closed were the delis near the county court-house, the delis near the movie theaters on the Grand Con-course (themselves also boarded up), and the delis underneath the pool halls. Even Schweller's, which had been a neighbor-hood fixture on Jerome Avenue, shut its doors after sixty-five years in business. As the journalist Jonathan Mark put it, "Kid, we're not talking about little groceries that call themselves delicatessens. We're talking about the ma and pa *fleishig* res-taurants with seven or eight tables, where you sit down like a human being and have some soup, flanken in the pot, a pas-trami on rye the size of your fist with a side of Dr. Brown's Cel-Ray; delis where grilled franks and knishes are crackling just inside the steamed windows, and neon Hebrew letters shine into the night." Before Greek diners, pizza parlors or hamburger joints, Mark noted, "a kosher frank was what passed for fast food in this city."[125]

As Jewish waiters and countermen who retired or passed away were replaced by non-Jewish employees, the very na-ture of the deli-going experience changed; few waiters did a vaudeville act in the course of serving a bowl of soup and a sandwich. In some delis, according to David Sax, waiters from such far-flung places as Egypt, China, and Mexico "took on the role with aplomb," learning "the shtick and the banter that's passed down almost like Talmudic knowledge."[126] But in most delis, the waiter was trained to be just like a server in any other restaurant—unfailingly helpful and polite, a far cry from the obnoxious but highly entertaining Jewish waiter of old.

As the Jewish population of New York declined substantially, falling from two million in 1950 to about half that number by the early 1990s, many formerly Jewish neighborhoods saw new immigrant groups become dominant. The last kosher delica-tessen in Flushing, Flushing Delight on Union Street, closed in

1995, ending a four-decade-long presence of a kosher deli at that location. Instead of Jewish stores and restaurants, Chinese, Korean, and Indian businesses proliferated, catering to the needs of those immigrants. The Jewish population was aging, with very few younger Jews moving in to replace those who died or moved away. "With the neighborhood changing the way it is, there just wasn't enough business," Flushing Delight's owner, Paul Reilly, told the *New York Times*. "More and more people, when they go to Florida, they aren't coming back."[127]

Even Hebrew National had moved out of New York by the late 1980s; its relocation to Indianapolis was widely viewed as the end of an era. The announcement of the move sparked a labor dispute in which two hundred employees walked out of the company's factory in Maspeth, Queens, and in which a small bomb was placed in the car of one of the company's managers. It led to a pitched legal battle between Hebrew National and Schulem Rubin, the senior rabbi for New York State's kosher compliance division, who was accused by the company of waiting two years after a governmental inspection to give the company a failing grade on its kashrut standards; the company insisted that the state was retaliating against it for moving to the Midwest. The move showed that deli meats were just like steel, fabric, and other consumer products that used to be made in New York; they would increasingly come to be manufactured in places where companies could find cheaper labor and lower taxes.[128]

Hebrew National never recovered its reputation in the Orthodox community. Before long, most Orthodox Jews eschewed eating the company's products. Even many Conservative Jews did not eat Hebrew National meats for years, until in 2004, the company finally obtained a new certification, Triangle K. But even though Triangle K is actually under the supervision of an Orthodox rabbi, it is not *glatt*—the strictest standard of kosher—and thus not suitable for Orthodox Jews themselves.

By the early years of the twenty-first century, then, the deli was widely seen as a throwback to an immigrant or second-generation way of life, in which different values had held sway. Jews could not flatter themselves on their success in American society by eating the food of their parents and grandparents. Their nostalgia for that way of life was still present, but it was indulged on particular family occasions rather than on a frequent, regular basis. At the same time, Jews had discovered the cuisines of other cultures and had turned their back on their own style of cooking, which was perceived, in the main, as unhealthy, low class, and unappetizing.

As we shall see in the next and final chapter, the deli in the twenty-first century plays a sharply diminished role in Jewish culture, even as nostalgia for the delis of the past has become in itself an important part of Jewish identity. At the same time, Jewish food is mutating in unexpected ways, and those delis that still exist are trying a plethora of strategies, including focusing on sustainability and attempting to attract a customer base of non-Jews, to keep themselves afloat.

The changes in Jewish aspirations are summed up by a late twentieth-century advertising campaign by Manischewitz; the company printed a fictional letter written by Mrs. Manischewitz to her grandmother, in which she recalls her upbringing in the Bronx and *kvells* (expresses her pride) over her son's graduation from Brown. "Who would have believed," she asks in amazement, "from a *shtetl* to the Ivy League?"[129]

Conclusion

THE CONTEMPORARY JEWISH DELI— WHISTLING PAST THE GRAVEYARD

A couple goes out to eat one evening at the neighborhood kosher deli. They are amazed when a suave Chinese waiter, speaking perfect Yiddish, comes up to their table to take their order. On their way out, they ask the owner how he ever managed to train a Chinese waiter to speak Yiddish. "Shh," he tells them, "he thinks I'm teaching him English!"

The setting for this revealing joke is the Lower East Side, where most Jews (and Chinese) settled when they first arrived in the United States. Only in that neighborhood, where so many Jews lived in such close proximity to one another, could a non-Jewish immigrant possibly confuse the language spoken by everyone around him with the language of the American people. To think that anyone could confuse Yiddish and English—this was hilarious to Jews, given how much outside the mainstream Jews knew themselves to be. If only Yiddish and English *were* the same, then Jews might not suffer so acutely their exclusion from American society. The waiter believes that he is on the way to becoming an American—wait until he finds out the truth! The only nation that he is assimilating into is the Jewish one.

And yet that is precisely it: the deli *does* represent America for the clueless Chinese waiter. It is, after all, the only "America" he knows outside his own community. In this sense, he is not so unlike the immigrant Jews themselves, for whom the deli was to become a place in which they began to erect the framework for an American identity. The waiter was to get his revenge when his own cuisine trumped that of the delicatessen. (And of course, Asians have been recently dubbed the "new Jews" for their success in American society; they are viewed as achieving this success in much the same way that Jews did, through a combination of intellect, sacrifice, hard work, and determination.)

It seems appropriate, then, that in Ben's, a deli that boasts an Art Deco–style interior ("Who said a nosh can't be posh?" reads the sign behind the deli counter that lists the hors d'oeuvres), the well-heeled, mostly Jewish patrons are literally surrounded by the words of this joke, as if *embraced* by a past in which the deli truly was the central institution in Jewish life. By reading—and perhaps even telling to each other—the joke in English, the patrons of Ben's remind themselves how far they have come, how much they have transcended their own ancestors' immigrant origins, how much *they* have succeeded in becoming American.

✦ ▨ ✦

When the Second Avenue Deli reopened in midtown Manhattan in late 2007 after having closed two years earlier in the East Village, it did so with much fanfare. Even though a thousand new restaurants open in New York every year, it would be difficult to think of another restaurant opening that generated quite so much excitement and anticipation. Almost every media outlet in the city descended on the deli to cover what was trumpeted, in messianic terms, as the "second coming" of the Second Avenue Deli, which is arguably the most famous kosher deli in America—and also one of the last.

The drama of the story was inescapable. Abe Lebewohl, the beloved deli owner, was murdered in broad daylight in 1996 (in a still-unsolved crime) while taking the deli's receipts to the bank, leaving the business in the hands of his brother, Jack, who ran the deli until its demise, which he blamed on the skyrocketing real estate prices in the rapidly gentrifying East Village.

Now Jeremy Lebewohl, Jack's twenty-five-year-old son, had emerged like a dark-horse candidate to take over the family business. Since when did the younger generation want to take over a deli? Hadn't so many children of the owners of small ethnic businesses, including countless kosher delis, turned their back on the family business in order to become doctors, lawyers, and investment bankers? Would Jeremy be like his uncle—if he knew you were sick, would he show up in person at your apartment or dorm room with a bowl of chicken soup in his hand? Or would the new Second Avenue Deli be just a restaurant like any other? The story of the Second Avenue Deli encapsulated so many aspects of life in New York. Like a once-glorious sports team that had suffered a string of losing seasons but now had a scrappy new manager who was determined to win a pennant, the Second Avenue had a fighting chance once again. It had, you might say, a shot at redemption.

In fact, the Second Avenue Deli had for a long time worn the defiant, slightly pugnacious air of a survivor. It had opened originally in 1954, a good four decades after most Jews had moved away from the Lower East Side neighborhood, the immigrant ghetto known for its overcrowded, disease-ridden tenements and horrific sweatshops.

But the kosher deli, with its flashy lightbulb-bordered sign with faux-Yiddish letters, had insisted on serving the foods beloved of these same immigrants and their children, in the hopes of bringing them back for a taste of the old neighborhood. Both Jews and non-Jews made pilgrimages to the deli to soak up the atmosphere of the Jewish past. And Lebewohl was a well-known figure, given to outlandish publicity stunts such as creating busts of famous people in chopped liver, giving out free sausages when a baseball player hit a home run, and maintaining public friendships with a range of characters from Mayor Ed Koch to the pornographer Al Goldstein and pretty much everyone in between. From the handprints on the Walk of Fame outside the door to the Molly Picon room inside, the place glittered with the aura of celebrity while still trading on its down-at-the-heels East Village chic. It saw itself as having nurtured the growth of the downtown arts scene and particularly the emergence of off-Broadway in the 1960s.

The Second Avenue Deli had become a quintessential part of New York, its appeal extending to many non-Jews, including tourists from all over the world. I dined one evening in the old Second Avenue Deli when a group of Jewish artists and scholars whom I knew from New York University was replaced at the same table by a family wearing traditional African garb, as if they had just come from a meeting at the nearby United Nations. I regretted not having brought a camera; I would have liked to take pictures of the successive groups of people who occupied the same table at the deli over the course of a single evening. The photos would have said a lot not just about the deli but about the polyglot nature of the city.

Over time, then, the deli had come to stand for a whole host of places and experiences that New Yorkers (and others) felt had become endangered: for the Jewish Lower East Side, for the counterculture of the East Village (the demise of the Second Avenue Deli was compared by some observers to the recent shuttering of the punk music club CBGB's), for immigrant Jewish culture (*Yiddishkeit*), for mom-and-pop businesses, for fatty Jewish food. Its closing seemed to mark the end of an era in more ways than one.

It is little wonder that when the deli closed on Tenth Street, a disappointed blogger sighed, "Sic transit gloria matzoh balls."[1] The comic Jackie Mason, a Second Avenue Deli regular, joked, "It's almost like wiping out Carnegie Hall. . . . A sandwich to a Jew is just as important as a country to a gentile."[2] Its closing truly seemed to mark the end of an era, just as its rebirth two years later seemed nothing short of miraculous. But can any new deli bring back the days of yore? Or does it inevitably have what the journalist Ron Rosenbaum, writing for *Slate*, calls a "theme-park vibe, a whistling-past-the-graveyard-schmaltzy nostalgia for schmaltz"[3]—a cardboard-cutout version of the past?

The essayist Adam Gopnik has traced what he calls the "drying up" of Jewish comedy in New York to the period between the release of *Annie Hall* and the release of *Broadway Danny Rose*, in which the "black-and-white world of the comics shpritzing at the Carnegie Deli is frankly presented as a Chagall world, a folk-tale setting, the whole thing vanished." Gopnik connects this transition to the fading of New York ethnic life in general, from the Asian countermen slicing fish at Zabar's—the iconic gourmet Jewish food shop—on the Upper West Side to the lack of overt Jewish references on *Seinfeld*, where the "Jewish situations are mimed by rote, while the real energy of the jokes lies in the observation of secular middle-class manners."[4]

For years, part of the experience of going to the Carnegie Deli in New York was watching a wacky promotional video, *What a Pickle: The World's Greatest Deli Musical*, that played on a loop at the restaurant to divert those who were waiting on line. The video starts with the late owner, Milton Parker, shlepping around an immense pickle. It then switches to a black-and-white silent-movie format with intertitles and background music, in which one of the deli waiters is shown walking home after work and slipping on a pickle on the sidewalk, where he is helped up by a beautiful woman. He romances her by taking her for a picnic in Central Park with sandwiches from the Carnegie Deli. The video then shows the customers and waiters singing and dancing at the Carnegie, with a big-band theme of everyone "swinging" at the "Deli King." The waiter disastrously juggles the food in a rapid-paced patter song, showing off the immense portions, including the "world's biggest sandwiches" and "world's biggest matzo ball."[5]

Parker drops some names of celebrities and their favorite sandwiches, and then the video again switches modes, with "Barry Whitefish" (Wayne Lammers, who also codirected the video and wrote the lyrics), a Barry White look-alike clad entirely in white, who sings a mellow song about pastrami, kasha, and other deli specialties to his leggy blond date as they enjoy a candlelight dinner in the deli and go for a horse-and-buggy ride. After showing a brief segment on how the pastrami and cheesecake is prepared at the deli's plant in New Jersey, the scene returns once more to the deli, where customers around the dining room yell out their hometowns, states, or countries (everywhere from New Jersey to India and Japan), and the video ends with a sing-along (complete with a bouncing ball) to the tune "Till We Meet Again," including the words "Till We Eat Again / I'll be thinking of food until we meet again." Interposed in the middle of the song is a sequence of obviously non-Jewish waitresses, trying to insult the customers in stereotypically obnoxious fashion.

One of the most striking aspects of the video, which was produced in 1999, is how non-Jewish the Carnegie Deli seems. Other than the owner and manager, and perhaps the waiter who plays the main role, there is nary a Jewish person in the place—the waiters and customers almost all appear to be non-Jews. The clearly nonkosher food nevertheless does represent a link to Jewish tradition, but it is used either for Jews to romance non-Jews or for non-Jews to romance each other. The quality of the food seems much less important than the quantity, and the humorous aspects of the dining experience—the ridiculously huge portions, the funny-sounding names of the foods, the nasty waitresses, the boisterous fellow customers, the attempts of both staff and customers to be comedians, and the obsessive mock-seriousness with which the food is treated—come to the fore.

Thus, not only is it possible to find yourself in a video if you eat in the deli, but eating in the deli *is* like being on television—or in the movies. You are surrounded by pictures of celebrities, you eat the same foods that celebrities eat, and the entire atmosphere is one that performance theorists would call "ludic"—the playfulness is not incidental to the experience but constitutive of it. Rather than merely being a pleasant diversion while you wait on line, watching the video helps to create the frame for the dining experience, by giving the viewer a set of expectations and understandings that will condition the experience of the meal, which is tied up with notions of celebrity (and fantasies of being a celebrity), vaguely Jewishly coded foods (the pastrami, matzoh balls, etc.), and an overall sense of excess (the "world's biggest sandwiches"). But unlike Sammy's Rumanian Restaurant on the Lower East Side, a place that actually does incorporate comedy and music into the dining experience—a meal there is like a meal at a Jewish wedding or bar/bat mitzvah—the nonkosher Carnegie Deli seems to cater more to non-Jews than to Jews.

By contrast, because the kosher deli serves a mostly Jewish clientele, it is clearly an endangered species in New York; there are only about fifteen kosher delis left in the five boroughs—a 99 percent drop since the deli's heyday in the 1930s. Noah's Ark, the only remaining kosher deli on the Lower East Side, closed in 2013, as did Adelman's, which was one of only three kosher delis left in southern Brooklyn—a former mecca for kosher delis. But, especially given Manhattan real estate prices, which make it almost impossible for nonchain restaurants to survive, even kosher-style delis are not immune; the Stage Deli closed at the end of 2012, a victim both of the overall decline in people's appetite for Jewish deli foods and of rising retail rents that surpassed $1 million a year.[6]

While it may not be surprising that there are relatively few urban delis left, many suburban delis are suffering the same fate. Five kosher delis—two of which dated back to the 1950s—have closed on Long Island in just the past eighteen months, as fewer non-Orthodox Jews keep kosher and as deli food continues to give way to other, more multicultural alternatives. Scott Horowitz, the owner of the only kosher wholesaler left on Long Island, urges delis to reinvent corned beef and pastrami in new taste combinations—kosher tapas, for example. "If they taste it, they will like it," he told the journalist Stewart Ain. "It's not the staple it once was, and if they don't get the young people, there's no future in the business."[7] Steve Weiss, who owns Regal

Kosher Deli in Plainview, told me flatly that "younger people have lost the taste for deli. They eat sushi instead."[8]

Kosher food companies are thus increasingly marketing their products to non-Jews; in 2011, the media reported that Manischewitz has spent millions of dollars on advertisements that do not mention the words "Jewish" or "kosher." The ads ran in mainstream newspapers such as the *Washington Post* and the *Newark Star-Ledger*. According to company spokesperson Elie Jacobs, "There's a tagline we use, 'Bringing families to the table since 1888,' and we want to be part of that family with you whether it's Rosh Hashanah, Hanukkah, or Easter."[9] Now that Manischewitz has been sold to a huge equity firm, Bain Capital, it is seeking more than ever to find non-Jewish customers, just as Hebrew National and Levy's Rye Bread did beginning in the 1960s. In the words of the company's chief rabbi, Yaakov Y. Horowitz, Manischewitz desires to "promote 'kosher' as a quality-control designation, rather than simply a religious one."[10] The humorist Paul Rudnick parodied this strategy in the *New Yorker*, inventing ludicrous imaginary Manischewitz campaigns in which creamy horseradish with dill is left for Santa on Christmas Eve and James Bond serves home-style potato latkes to the queen of England.[11]

Even kosher delis in Manhattan have considerably broadened their fare in order to cater to the ever-widening Jewish palate. Mr. Broadway Bar and Grill, an upscale kosher deli in Herald Square that was built on the site of a 1920s kosher dairy restaurant, offers sushi, Chinese food, and Israeli food—as well as a full selection of wines and beers—along with its overstuffed pastrami sandwiches. A few blocks east, on East Thirty-Fourth Street, one finds Eden Wok—a kosher Chinese eatery—that sells kosher hot dogs in egg-roll wrappers, a kosher dairy restaurant called Tiberias, a kosher Baskin Robbins / Dunkin Donuts franchise, and Mendy's (part of a chain of kosher delis, including one in Grand Central Terminal) that has a menu that extends to burgers and shawarma.

In pondering the decline of the deli, I am influenced by the Yiddish scholar Jeffrey Shandler, who calls Yiddish a "postvernacular" language at this stage of its evolution in America—a language that relatively few Jews (outside of ultra-Orthodox neighborhoods in Brooklyn and upstate New York) speak but for which many Jews retain a sentimental attachment. In inventing this term, Shandler follows in the footsteps of David Hollinger, who developed the idea of "postethnic" identity, in which cultural affiliation is no longer a matter of genealogical descent but is instead a matter of consent—or, one could say, choice.[12]

In tribute to both of these scholars, I would like to call the deli "postgastronomic," in the sense that most Jews, even of Ashkenazic heritage, do not eat in delis on a regular basis any more, and deli food no longer plays a central role in American Jewish culture. At the same time, the deli itself could also be called "postcommunal," in that the deli no longer serves as a central gathering place for the Jewish community—even as deli foods such as pastrami continue to be icons of New York for both Jews and non-Jews alike.

The French Jewish publisher and scholar Pierra Nora, who is a Holocaust survivor, argues in his monumental seven-volume edited text about the relationship between memory and history that the historical basis on which society (in his case, French society, although he extends it to Western culture in general) has rested for centuries has been almost entirely eroded and replaced by what he calls *lieux de memoire* (places, sites, or realms of memory) that purport to open up a conceptual gateway to the past. Nora writes, "Museums, archives, cemeteries, festivals, anniversaries, treaties, depositions, monuments, sanctuaries, fraternal orders—these are boundary stones of another age, illusions of eternity." Furthermore, according to Nora, "It is the nostalgic dimensions of these devotional institutions that make them seem beleaguered and cold. They mark the rituals of a society without ritual."[13]

Nora, who escaped the Gestapo by jumping out the window of a school building, often refers to Jews in his book; at one point, he puts even the Tablets of the Law in the category of memorial objects. While he does not allude specifically to Jewish delicatessens—or any type of food stores or restaurants, for that matter—Nora refers to "nonpracticing Jews, many of whom have felt a need in recent years to explore memories of the Jewish past." Memory, for Nora, serves an essential role in the constitution of Jewish identity. "To be Jewish," Nora writes, "is to remember being Jewish."[14]

Delis, in Nora's terms, might be viewed as furnishing a kind of last rites for Ashkenazic Jewish culture, a culture that no longer functions as an organic part of New York Jewish life other than in the occasional klezmer concert or Yiddish theater production (increasingly translated into English and restaged in a contemporary, multicultural idiom). The ritual of deli-going, which used to be a weekly or even daily one, is virtually defunct in an age in which pastrami is available in every franchise sandwich store and the few remaining Jewish delis cater almost entirely to tourists.

The deli is a *lieu de memoire* in many senses. It functions as a kind of museum, a place where the past—or some concept of the past—can be exhibited and consumed. The overarching irony is that while the deli seems to gesture to, or even recapitulate, Jewish history both in eastern Europe and on the Lower East Side, we have seen that the deli was not an especially prominent part of Jewish life in either place. There is something undifferentiated about this historical consciousness, in that it takes little stock of important differences between the generations.

In a description of the typical deli counter in Brooklyn, Elliot Willensky catalogues the "ritualized row of glass cases," including a shorter one with different types of meat ("all cut on the bias, the better to show their stuff") and a taller one with metal trays of coleslaw, potato salad, chopped liver, and so on. He rhapsodizes about the huge jars of condiments, including sauerkraut, sweet or hot red peppers, green tomatoes, and pickles. The pickles, he recalls, ranged from "really" sour, "wrinkled and olive drab in color," to half sour, "plump, pimpled, still dark green, and almost white inside." Finally, he recalls the drinks and mustard, concluding that even when you took food home, it never tasted so good as in the deli itself, with its beloved sights, sounds, and smells.[15]

But nostalgia is not simply a wistful and passive embrace. As the sociologist Fred Davis has written, nostalgia is an active process; it is "one of the means—or better, one of the more readily accessible psychological lenses—we employ in the neverending work of constructing, maintaining, and reconstructing our identities."[16] For Davis, nostalgia is an active process—an expenditure of psychological energy in the service of remaking ourselves in the image of our own past, however we understand and appreciate that past.

Delis indeed attempt through their decor and ambience to spur nostalgia. Ronnie Dragoon, the owner of the Ben's chain, is opening new delicatessens, and not just in the New York area; in addition to breaking ground on one in Scarsdale (in Westchester County), he plans to open others in Washington, DC, and Boston. His delis, including one in Boca Raton, Florida, boast an extravagantly faux–Art Deco style, incorporating curved wood, burnished metal, frosted glass, mosaic tiles, bold colors, and ceilings with Chagall-like designs that could be part of the stage for a production of *Fiddler on the Roof*—an effect that is heightened by the Jewish folk music playing in the background—what Dragoon calls "melding a new style with an old feeling."[17]

Nevertheless, given the dearth of delis, finding food that satisfies the desire for Jewish nostalgia can be difficult. As the food critic Mimi Sheraton has complained, Jewish foods that are true to the classics of her youth are almost impossible to find nowadays, whether in or out of the city.[18] Rabbi Arthur Hertzberg mourned the loss of the corned beef that he remembered from his own youth. "When we were all on the Lower

East Side, every mom-and-pop store cured its own," he complained in 1999. "That was one thing. Now you get two-week-old corned beef, supermarket corned beef and corned beef and cheese—utter desecrations of Jewish soul food."[19]

Yet, authenticity is inherently a subjective concept—what rings true or feels right to one person does not necessarily seem that way to another. As Darra Goldstein, the former editor of the journal *Gastronomica*, has suggested, "If a dish resonates for us, evoking memories of another time or place, if it connects us with something beyond the present moment, then it should be considered authentic enough, even if its ingredients and methods have changed. . . . Food can take new forms in different times and places yet still remain genuine in spirit. We should continue to pay attention to tradition, to understand what's come before. But to remain vital, recipes, like people, need to change."[20]

A handful of new "hipster" delis, caught up in this passion for the authentic, are creating food that is variably described as gourmet, artisanal, or sustainable. Some of these delis, which the *New York Times* has oxymoronically dubbed "neo-retro," are now focused on sustainability; they include Kenny and Zuke's in Portland, Oregon; Kaplansky's in Toronto; Neal's in Carrboro, North Carolina; Wise Sons in San Francisco, Wexler's in Los Angeles; and Mile End in Brooklyn and Manhattan. These delis, according to one journalist, find "up-and-coming chefs riffing on their grandparents' pastrami sandwiches and matzo balls—while cooking up an antidote to the Jewish deli's widespread demise."[21]

These "riffs" include pickled bluefish instead of herring at DGS in Washington, DC, and an option of smoked beets instead of corned beef in the Reuben at General Muir in Atlanta—both of which also serve the Canadian dish poutine (french fries covered with cheese, gravy, and chunks of pastrami). Julia Moskin of the *Times* calls this trend "proof of a sudden and strong movement among young cooks, mostly Jewish-Americans, to embrace and redeem the foods of their forebears."[22] Jewish foods such as bagels and smoked fish that were identified in the past with appetizing stores are now subsumed under the catch-all designation of "deli"; in a recent roundup of Jewish food stores in New York, the journalist Michael Kaminer describes even bagel stores as "delis."[23]

A nine-course Shabbat dinner at the City Grit Restaurant organized by Mile End at the 2012 Food Network New York City Wine and Food Festival featured signature dishes from all of these establishments; the menu included smoked trout mousse, schmaltzed chanterelles, bone marrow matzoh ball soup, duck confit and wild-mushroom-stuffed cabbage, and a "deconstructed" babka for dessert.[24] Deli owners from across the country were themselves in attendance, and the meal was followed the next day by two back-to-back panel discussions at ABC Carpet, an upscale home-furnishings store—the first, moderated by Joan Nathan, was on the future of Jewish food; the second, moderated by David Sax, was on the future of the deli. The discussion itself, like the meat had been, was free-ranging, and it pointed up the inherently subjective nature of Jewish food, which seems to mean very different things to different people, depending on their ethnic (Ashkenazic or Sephardic) upbringing and family of origin. But the speakers seemed to agree that as Jews become more assimilated, their interest in Jewish food tends to decline.

The *Time* food columnist Josh Ozersky called the future of Jewish food an "existential issue," explaining that "Jewish food comes out of two things—theology and poverty, neither of which impinges on most Jews nowadays, who are secular to the bone." Given that his own grandmother's signature dish was roast pork, Ozersky confessed, it may be no surprise that many Jewish foods never attained what he called "totemic status" but that Jewish cooking remained focused on just a few foods—brisket, matzoh balls, bagels—that prevented it from developing a full-fledged cuisine. "It's like a rejected lover going over the same two letters over and over again," he mused.[25] As Ozersky has noted elsewhere, the Jewish deli "had *terroir*; now that it's become this isolated pocket, all these places that remain that have this New York character are constantly in danger of becoming, essentially, self-referential parodies." He called Katz's the "old-time, antiquarian classic" that all New York delis have as their reference point.[26] Without the New York Jewish *terroir* (the French term for the effect of landscape, geology, and climate on the foods and wines of a region), he wonders if the deli can survive.

Nevertheless, the trend toward sustainability in the world of the Jewish deli suggests that these old dishes have had new, organic life breathed into them. Karen Adelman, co-owner of Saul's in Berkeley, has told the *Times* that the deli betrayed its ancient Jewish roots long ago by moving away from traditional Jewish attitudes toward the earth, in which economy, creativity, and freshness ruled the day—meat and other food was not wasted, all parts of the animal were used, and vegetables were served in season.[27] These principles, she says, are honored at Saul's, where the portions are small, the beef is local and grass-fed, the pickles are only served during June to November, and the celery soda is made in house to avoid buying it from industrial food manufacturers. Adelman insists that the deli's origins are "scrappy and sustainable" and that along the way, the deli "got supersized along with everything else." Delis walk a fine line between appealing to customers' emotions (and taste buds) and to their ethical and environmental values. As Adelman puts it, "Everyone feels like they own this cuisine. It's connected to nostalgia, to comfort, to religion."[28]

Sustainability, however, is a moving target. Take the concept of "local," which is notoriously difficult to define. Noah Bernamoff, the owner of Mile End, has conceded that the amount of meat that he serves cannot be sourced from farms in upstate New York or even from the tristate area. He goes through a hundred briskets a week—each cow has two briskets, so he needs the meat of fifty cows, even though most local farms raise but 250 head of cattle each season. So while Bernamoff can source eggs, milk, and trout from farms in the Catskills, he is obliged to import most of his beef from the Midwest, using the "natural" (free from antibiotics and growth hormones) line of Black Angus beef from Creekstone Farms, which has surpassed Niman Ranch in recent years to supply many of the country's most upscale restaurants.[29]

Bernamoff insists on importing bagels from his native Montreal—they have become somewhat of a delicacy in New York. So Mile End's products may be mostly made from scratch (some items are almost impossible to make in house; for example, very few delis make their own hot dogs) with even the spices freshly ground, but they do not necessarily have a low environmental impact. As he told me, "I have to make a multitude of decisions that have a real economic cost. The full scope of sustainability has to include the viability of the business itself."[30]

Mile End, which opened in 2010 with only nineteen seats, operates on the philosophy that, according to Bernamoff, "It's not looking for shortcuts, and that's what the average deli became—how can we shortcut everything to lower our prices, because people won't pay more money but want bigger portions?"[31] Peter Levitt of Saul's has echoed this sentiment, noting that "large, cheap meat sandwiches are a losing proposition for any restaurant."[32] By reversing the custom of serving big portions for their own sake, Bernamoff is able to do everything by hand rather than by machine. But he said that customers need to understand that meat (especially grass-fed beef) is more expensive than ever and that the overstuffed sandwich is a thing of the past.

"Customers still want that overstuffed sandwich for ten bucks," Bernamoff conceded. "But we can't provide that. In the meantime, the famous delis like Katz's and Second Avenue make much more money, because they don't need the kind of skilled labor that I need in order to make everything from scratch." While he reported that close to a third of his revenue comes from the sale of smoked meat, he pays a dollar more per pound for it than the cost of commodity beef. "It's up to the customers to save the deli," Bernamoff said, "so that it won't feed upon itself and implode. The people who are most to blame [for the decline of the deli] are those who are throwing up their hands and asking where the delis went."[33]

Bernamoff, who along with his wife, Rae, recently published a cookbook of the dishes served at his restaurant, aspires to have Jewish food be compared favorably to other ethnic cuisines, which have attained gourmet status in America. "Why can't deli food be taken seriously?" he asked. Bernamoff speculated that because after the Second World War Jewish food was mostly made at home, the delis "had it easy." By adopting the use of supermarket convenience foods, delis took shortcuts even in the preparation of their specialties, like Italian restaurants serving spaghetti from a box. This gave the customers a dependable, standardized experience of eating in a deli. But the experience of eating at Mile End is "highly variable," Bernamoff conceded, because "you can only have the best sandwich if you know that you can also have the worst." Deli meats, he said, have become utterly "generic" through mechanization, so that "you can never have a bad sandwich, but you can also never have a great sandwich." He sees himself as restoring the very concept of the delicacy to the deli, noting that a delicacy was "something special that people appreciated, but were forced to eat in moderation. You need to move forward by looking back." Bernamoff views his deli's signature offering not as smoked meat but as schmaltz, the rendered chicken fat that he uses for cooking and baking and even as salad oil. He calls schmaltz the "symbol par excellence of the age-old resourcefulness of Jewish cooks, who were doing nose-to-tail cuisine centuries before it became a hip urban trend. Nothing wasted, everything savored."[34]

Bernamoff chose to open his restaurants in neighborhoods that are, as he put it, "not oriented toward traditional deli customers" but instead toward a younger, more adventurous clientele. Most of his customers are not Jewish; many are experiencing the taste of deli for the first time. "We're making food that is not about nostalgia," he said, "but simply about the experience of eating." He said that he is grateful to the food writers in New York, who have compared his restaurant not to other delis but to other non-Jewish restaurants that serve gourmet food.[35] He has also recently started selling craft beers, including smoked beer from a German brewery.[36]

Bernamoff also knows that eating in a Jewish deli is about much more than the food itself. Mile End self-consciously attempts to re-create what Bernamoff terms the "deli culture" of Montreal, what he calls "the culture of going out on Sundays and having bagels and lox, or getting eggs and bacon." He describes his family's tradition of eating out for Sunday brunch as "very ritualistic," explaining, "the strength of that ritual was what I was really trying to bring to Mile End when we first opened." He thoughtfully adds that in order for a restaurant to succeed, it has to embody the personality of its owner; the restaurant "has to be an extension of yourself, it has to represent those aspects of yourself that you want to celebrate. It's so much more than just serving food to people."[37] As he told the *Times*, "When I see tourists going into Katz's, I feel a kind of rage. This is the food of my people, and places like that are turning it into a joke."[38]

It is ironic that for Jewish deli food to be what Bernamoff calls the "food of my people," it needs to be prepared in a way that corresponds as much to contemporary (basically secular) values as to ancestral (mostly religious) ones. As he put it, even younger Jews nowadays "expect deli food, like holiday food, to be glued in time." What they do not realize, he said, is that these foods can be updated and still retain the "rustic, comforting, familiar" flavor and appearance of foods that are based in an ethnic culture, whether it be Jewish, Italian, or Chinese. "I have no Italian roots whatsoever," he said, "but I can still enjoy rich, warming Italian food."[39] Bernamoff's latest venture, Black Seed Bagels, brings Montreal-style bagels to New York, where they have begun to attract a wide following.

As in Israel, where gourmet pork and shellfish dishes are increasingly marketed to middle- and high-end Jewish customers, Jewish restaurants in New York have begun to incorporate aggressively nonkosher food into deli fare. While it is obviously nothing new for a (nonkosher) Jewish deli to serve such food, the emphasis here is self-consciously and ironically on identity and assimilation. This irony extends well beyond the world of delis; at JoeDough (a sandwich-shop version of the upscale restaurant JoeDoe), Irish American owner Joe Dobias serves The Conflicted Jew—chicken liver, onion, and bacon on challah. The late cookbook author Gil Marks, while comparing the consumption of such a concoction by a Jew to "an American eating a horse," also recognized that eating such a sandwich can represent an ongoing connection to tradition, if only in the act of struggling to free oneself from it. "You always retain your roots, to a certain extent, no matter how hard you try to reject them," he observed.[40]

Similar issues pertain to Traif, a restaurant in Williamsburg (where many ultra-Orthodox Jews live) owned by a Jewish chef named Jason Marcus, which pushes the envelope quite boldly by advertising itself as "celebrating pork, shellfish, and globally-inspired soul food." A recent dinner menu at Traif included shiso-bacon-wrapped skate tempura, scallop carpaccio, charred baby octopus, and braised Berkshire pork cheek. And for dessert? Donuts sprinkled with bacon crumbs. Marcus once confided that his restaurant is quite popular with ex-Hasidic Jews; a renegade Hasid even showed up in a van in the middle of the night for a take-out order of the eatery's pork specialties.[41]

Nor does one need to eat at a deli per se in order to eat foods inspired by the Jewish deli. Kutsher's Tribeca (an outpost of the famed Catskills hotel, the last of the great Jewish resorts in upstate New York), which calls itself a "modern Jewish American bistro," serves such entrees as pot-roasted beef flanken, wild mushroom and fresh ricotta kreplach, and—a modern version of gefilte fish—diced wild halibut poached in fish stock. It also serves a deli charcuterie platter (on a wooden board) of pastrami, smoked veal tongue, salami, duck pastrami, and chopped liver—most of which are cured and smoked in house—along with homemade celery soda.

Adeena Sussman of the *Forward* newspaper has dubbed such culinary reinventions "haute haimish grub"[42]—examples of which are cropping up everywhere in New York, such as the celebrity chef Jean-Georges Vongerichten's kasha varnishkes (served with veal meatballs) at ABC Kitchen, the caviar knish at Torrisi Italian Specialties, and the Deli Ramen at Josh Kaplan's restaurant, Dassara, a dish that is composed of Japanese noodle soup with matzoh balls and strips of smoked meat. Such newfangled Jewish dishes are not entirely new; one thinks of the fusion between Jewish and Chinese food that is exemplified by the pastrami egg rolls and Chinese hot dogs at Eden Wok. But the gourmetization of Jewish food represents a different stage in its evolution; it suggests that Jewish food is wide open to reinterpretation and that one can play with the boundaries between Jewish and non-Jewish food while also playing with the distinctions between the upscale and the ethnic. Perhaps the best example is at Vinegar Hill House in Brooklyn: the stuffed cabbage is filled with curried goat, lima beans, and spinach.[43]

Delis throughout the country continue to trade on the association of "New York" with deli authenticity. This appears to be a particularly trendy concept in the Southwest, where former New Yorkers—or their descendants—have opened Kenny and Ziggy's New York Delicatessen Restaurant in Houston, New York Deli News in Denver, Chompie's New York Deli in Phoenix, and many others. (Nor is this phenomenon limited to the United States; there are "New York" delis in London, Cardiff, Tokyo, Jakarta, and scores of other cities around the globe.) The "New York" deli connotes a turn-back-the-clock, back-to-the-source quality. It suggests a style of restaurant notable for overstuffed sandwiches, eastern European Jewish dishes, the delirious scent of pickle brine, and an ambience that is loud, crowded, busy, and lively.

Indeed, by advertising a store or restaurant as one serving "New York" food—whether deli sandwiches, bagels, or pizza—the owner implicitly suggests that this is where that type of food originated, where it reached its highest quality, or where it became most famous. Many of these restaurants also put New York memorabilia up on their walls, such as playbills, caricatures of stage stars, and photographs of New York landmarks.

Nor do "New York" delis need be very far from New York. The Carnegie Deli has an outpost in the Sands Casino in Bethlehem, Pennsylvania, where busloads of Chinese immigrants from New York arrive daily to play the slots—and perhaps eat a pastrami sandwich. Harold's New York Deli in Edison, New Jersey, takes the supersize concept to its logical extreme, serving sandwiches, soups, and cakes that are so mammoth that one is more than enough for an entire table of diners. The experience of eating at Harold's reminded an Asian American food blogger, Mary Kong-Devito, of *Alice in Wonderland*; she joked that she "felt like a shrunken Alice at The Mad Hattowitz's Tea Party." She described the matzoh ball soup as "over sixty ounces of chicken soup, carrots, celery, chunk white chicken and a matzo ball bigger than Leonard Bernstein's head." The sandwiches, she reported, are "so enormous that you could share with a village."[44]

It is also striking that delis, *especially nonkosher ones*, are persistently, if rather tongue-in-cheek, described in religious terms. One of the African American slicers at Katz's is nicknamed the "Reverend of Pastrami," as if the deli counter is his church and the customers his congregants. Perhaps not coincidentally, the "reverend" presides over the same deli that *New York* magazine described as a "shrine, the soul of American Jewish cuisine" when it was rumored a few years ago that the building in which Katz is housed was being bought by real estate developers.[45] That the Jewish deli became an analogue to the synagogue, or even to the Temple in Jerusalem, has been suggested throughout this book. But it is striking that the deli sandwich is still imbued with so much quasi-religious symbolism, and it speaks to the intensity of the ambivalence that so many secular Jews still have about their religion, to the extent that this kind of humor still carries a charge.

Given that Jews are no longer a reliable customer base for Jewish delis, the delis that are going strong appeal largely to tourists. After reopening in midtown on Third Avenue and Thirty-Third Street, the Second Avenue Deli (still using its trademark sign of faux Hebrew or Yiddish letters) recently added a second branch on First Avenue and Seventy-Fifth Street. These locations, neither of which is actually on Second Avenue, have a very different vibe from the East Village; the Lower East Side, countercultural feel that the deli enjoyed for so many years is gone. To the extent that New York remains a city of distinct neighborhoods (this is a question in itself, given gentrification, the rise in real estate prices, and the proliferation of chain stores and franchises), a deli that is wrenched out of its original location and plopped down in a different part of the city is like a plant that has to grow new roots.

The very idea that the deli's name and the food that it offers are more important than its physical location represents a reversal of the whole concept of the traditional deli, where both the menu and the quality of the food were both fairly standard whatever deli you visited, and what mattered far more was where the deli was and the social network that it nurtured and that supported it in turn. The idea that you could put the Second Avenue Deli anywhere in the city and it would still be the Second Avenue Deli suggests that a deli is all about the food and the ambience and not about its embeddedness in community. The deli's customers thus pay for the privilege of becoming walking advertisements for the restaurant, while also showing off that they know where to get a good pastrami sandwich. Not that the neighborhood vibe doesn't exist at the Second Avenue Deli—people do seem to feel comfortable striking up conversations with total strangers who are sitting at neighboring tables. But, in a concession to contemporary restaurant etiquette, the waiters at the Second Avenue Deli, some of whom are old-time deli waiters, are instructed to be careful in dealing with customers and to refrain from insulting, or joking with, them.

The few kosher delis left in the outer boroughs do still serve, to some extent, as neighborhood hangouts. These include Jay and Lloyd's in Brooklyn, Ben's Best in Queens, and Liebman's in the Riverdale section of the Bronx. (There are no kosher delis left on Staten Island; Golden's, which was notable for having a real 1936 subway car plunked down in the middle of the restaurant, where it served as a small dining room, closed in early 2012.)[46] But in order to remain in business, even these off-the-beaten-track places have had to morph into "destination" restaurants; Ben's Best has been visited by George W. Bush, featured on Martha Stewart's television show, and appeared on the Food Network. This media attention gives Ben's Best the aura of celebrity that was so much a part of the appeal of the non-kosher delis in the theater district. But rather than helping the customer feel special, as Jews so badly needed to do in the early to mid-twentieth century, the deli makes the customer feel like a tourist to a shrine—to a place that has been sacralized by its media exposure.

Some of the nostalgia for the Jewish deli is for the time in which Jews from across the political and ideological spectrum regularly broke bread together. For a major split has regrettably occurred within the American Jewish community, with few Jewish contexts now present in which religious and secular Jews meet on a regular basis. In addition, most traditionally minded Jews are unwilling to eat in delis that are open on the Sabbath and Jewish holidays, and less observant Jews are unwilling to pay high prices (up to twenty dollars for a kosher soup-and-sandwich combination) for the privilege of eating kosher deli food. Except in smaller cities such as Memphis and St. Louis, where there are so few Jewish restaurants that the local kosher deli still attracts a wide range of customers, delis are less able to bridge differences between various types of Jews.

Ethnic Jewishness of the standard eastern European variety is on a steep decline. Few Jews speak Yiddish any more, except in ultra-Orthodox enclaves in Brooklyn and upstate New York, where it remains the everyday language. Jewish theaters throughout the country struggle to find an audience. Films and television shows that include Jewish characters may have Jewish references but rarely have Jewish themes. Non-Jews often seem more attracted to Judaism than Jews themselves are, as reflected in an episode of *Curb Your Enthusiasm* in which Larry David's character's non-Jewish wife makes a Passover seder, despite his contemptuous attitude toward the ritual. In many ways, Jews seem to be waving farewell to the religion and culture that once sustained them and that once undergirded so much of American culture in general.

One has only to glimpse the long lines of tourists waiting outside the Carnegie Deli in Times Square to appreciate that "destination" delis still play a role, if only to provide a taste of New York history to hungry tourists. The few remaining midtown delis, with their extravagant decor and overstuffed sandwiches, are still part of the uplifting of excess, the over-the-top quality of our popular culture. But the Jewishness of the Jewish deli has somewhat evaporated; indeed, a perusal of one hundred reviews revealed the mention of the word "Jewish" in only a small fraction of them. Much more likely to be mentioned was the fact that *When Harry Met Sally* was filmed there, suggesting that a knowledge of the deli scene in the film conditions customers' experience of eating there as much as anything else.

Many Ashkenazic Jews have embraced Middle Eastern and Mediterranean food in recent years, trading fatty deli foods for lighter dishes cooked in olive oil—dishes that tend to feature fruits and vegetables rather than meat. The longing for Jewish deli also reflects the fact that many "deli" foods—the term has become quite elastic—have now become so much a part of the overall American diet that soon few will remember that their consumption was once essentially limited to immigrant Jews and their children. Pastrami (or a cheap cut of beef that is spiced and smoked to resemble old-fashioned Jewish pastrami) is retailed at almost every Subway and Quiznos sandwich franchise, with posters showing how the meat is "piled high" on the bread, just as in a traditional Jewish deli. The mainstreaming of delicatessen food is almost complete. Not that certain deli dishes are likely to survive outside of New York and outside of a traditional delicatessen—foods like rolled beef, tongue, and stuffed derma (beef intestine filled with fat, flour, and water).

Even the Second Avenue Deli is now selling smoked fish, which was traditionally reserved for appetizing stores. The word "deli" has lost its exclusive connection to meat, even in New York, to the extent that among the most famous "delis" in New York are Zabar's (a take-out gourmet store and kitchenware emporium), Barney Greengrass (a bagel and smoked fish restaurant), and Russ and Daughters (an appetizing store).

Assimilation, neighborhood change, the diversification of the American Jewish population, the constantly widening range of food choices—all have had a deleterious effect on the deli. As a waiter at Ratner's reflected not long before the restaurant's closing, "This area was once home to the most densely populated Jewish community in the world, and home to the world's finest kosher cuisine. But these days, instead of high-rise chopped liver sandwiches on rye, we have high-rise buildings."[47]

As the delicatessen loses its primary place in American Jewish culture, Jewish food in general continues to assume an even greater place in the construction of American Jewish identity. There is much talk of "gastronomic" Jews or "bagel and lox Jews" (the term "pastrami Jew" has not yet been coined) who presumably connect to their Jewish identity chiefly through their stomachs. But, as discussed earlier, many Jewish foods—bagels are a prime example—have become so much part of the mainstream American diet that they have slipped their Jewish moorings. Outside of New York, even pastrami is bereft of its Jewish associations. At my local gas station in central Pennsylvania, I can buy a hot pastrami, brisket, or corned beef sandwich from the self-service kiosk, and it will be made to order before my gas has finished pumping.

Even in major cities, the delicatessen has become a museum piece, as exemplified in a 2006 exhibit in Philadelphia at the

National Museum of American Jewish History. "Forshpeis! A Taste of the Peter H. Schweitzer Collection of Jewish Americana" grouped memorabilia such as advertising signs, vintage kosher products, and cookbooks around iconic items such as a Formica-topped kitchen table and a deli counter. The counter was surrounded by menus, invoices, pickle crocks, a pillow in the shape of a Zion Kosher salami, and a counterman's paper hat reading "Ask for Mrs. Weinberg's Chopped Liver." And a Jewish food exhibit in Baltimore, "Chosen Food," which opened in 2011, featured items from my own collection, including a large neon sign from a shuttered New York deli called Pastrami Queen, a deli slicer and scale, and other memorabilia from delis throughout the country. Patrons could leave the exhibit and head around the corner to Attman's, one of the few old-time Jewish delis that still exist in that city.

David Sax rhapsodizes about the freshness of the food at the Second Avenue Deli, at a time when many delis serve frozen french fries and day-old bread; he is also impressed by its continuing to serve mostly forgotten Ashkenazic dishes such as *gribenes* (fried chicken skins) and *p'tcha* (calf's-foot jelly). But recapturing the past through food is tricky. As the food maven Arthur Schwartz pointed out to me, the experience of eating is about so much more than the actual food that one is consuming. This is why, he thinks, food "always tastes better on vacation." Paraphrasing a book on the cuisine of Naples, Schwartz averred that the best clam sauce that you ever ate is the one that you enjoyed in Italy, on a veranda overlooking the sea, with your lover whispering in your ear.[48]

In line with Schwartz's point about the context in which food is consumed, this book has examined some of the intangible aspects of the Jewish deli that made it such a crucial gathering space for the Jewish community—one that enabled it to sustain Jews not just physically but emotionally and socially as well. What are the Jewish "third places" of today? Aaron Bisman, the former head of JDub Records, which promoted Mattisyahu (the formerly Hasidic reggae singer), sees many younger Jews in their twenties and thirties as attracted to a "culture of choice" rather than a "religion of obligation." While the immigrant enclaves of the turn of the twentieth century were what he calls "bastions of Jewish life," he sees younger Jews as having "often lost the connection to their history, culture, and identity as Jews." He points out the paradox that while they often feel like outsiders in American culture, given the predominantly Christian influence in American society, they also often feel estranged from their Jewish identity, given that they are so assimilated into American society. Without either synagogue or deli, both of which promoted Jewish identity within an American milieu, how can Jews feel comfortable either as Americans or as Jews? Perhaps the third space concept no longer works in a technologized world, in which Bisman views the nascent forms of Jewish community as inherently "fluid," with "no borders," and "existing outside the walls of any particular space."[49]

Jews have become so integrated into mainstream culture that the deli is viewed as a throwback to an earlier era, in which unfamiliar Jewish foods symbolized the extent to which Jews were still aliens in American society. For example, in "So Jewtastic," a VH1 video about Hollywood stars, wrestlers, musicians, and other celebrities who openly celebrate their Jewish ethnicity, Jewish deli food is shown to be both unrecognizable and unpalatable by most Americans. The comedian Elon Gold asks a slew of patrons of various ethnicities at Canter's Deli in Los Angeles if they can recognize a particular Jewish food that he shows them—almost none of them know that it is gefilte fish. He then demonstrates a circumcision on a frankfurter. The segment implicitly mocks the idea that Jews still have a cuisine worth eating, an interesting perspective given that the video was sent to directors of Jewish Community Centers throughout the country to be used to inspire young Jews with pride in their heritage.

Some leaders of the American Jewish community insist that only by revitalizing the synagogue can Jewish communal life be restored. Gary Rosenblatt, publisher of the *New York Jewish Week*, views Jewish newspapers and magazines as a venue in which Jews from different backgrounds and varying levels of religious observance find both a voice and a place of discussion and debate. But Rosenblatt, who grew up in Annapolis, Maryland, finds a physical "third space" in the modern Orthodox synagogue in Manhattan where he prays every weekday morning before work in order to say *kaddish* for his recently deceased mother. The regulars at the morning *minyan*, he points out, seem to gather as much to *schmooze* as to pray.[50]

Others, such as Rabbi Daniel Smokler, a Hillel rabbi at New York University, point toward the primacy of Jewish text as a "Jewish commons" of its own. Smokler's argument is that while the "American commons is a practice rooted in shared space, the Jewish commons is a practice rooted in shared text." Smokler has been very successful in bringing together particular "affinity" groups of college students—Persian Jews at UCLA, gay Jewish men at NYU, and so on—to study sacred Jewish texts together. Smokler takes the idea of the third space and applies it to the activity of studying sacred text, of promoting what he calls a "good, serious conversation," one that "dignifies both the rich tradition of text and honors our own alienation from that tradition."[51] What an intriguing, paradoxical idea—that what Jews share above all is their "alienation" from their own heritage, their sense of being outsiders to their own religion. Isn't this to some extent what the deli, as a secular Jewish alternative to the synagogue, was always about?

Then again, the meaning of the deli has changed for each generation of American Jews. The delicatessen (or what we could think of a delicatessen, with a focus on pickled meats) was almost unknown in eastern European Jewish life and was also not well established on the Lower East Side at the turn of the twentieth century—despite the tremendous nostalgia with which the delicatessen came to be invested.

The delicatessen only came into its own as Jews came into *their* own—as the second generation discovered the pleasures of eating out and felt most comfortable doing so in each other's company. At its height in the interwar period, this Jewish gathering place was, paradoxically, a kind of way station, a staging ground or springboard for Jews to enter American life on equal terms with other Americans. The delicatessen nurtured their hopes and dreams, giving them a powerful sense of security and belonging. When the barriers to participation in American life fell in the wake of the Second World War, the meaning of the delicatessen changed yet again, becoming—especially for those Jews who remained in the New York area—just one choice of eatery among many.

As Jews moved to the suburbs, they also moved more into the mainstream of American society and ultimately turned their back on delicatessen food in favor of more gourmet, international, and healthier fare—even as the kosher meat companies sought to increase their market share by selling to non-Jews. By the turn of the twenty-first century, the delicatessen had long ceased to be a place where Jews gathered on a regular basis; indeed, there were few spaces that Jews, whether religious or secular, went to be with other Jews.

The story of the delicatessen exemplifies the overarching shifts that have taken place in American Jewish life, in which, even as the majority of Jews have become more secular (as the recent Pew Survey of American Judaism shows),[52] this secular identity has lost much of its actual content; the overwhelming majority of American Jews say that they are "proud" to be Jewish but do little in the way of connecting concretely to their tradition. Moreover, while the consumption of Jewish food is, for many Jews, one of the sole ways in which they relate to their heritage, this food is taking all kinds of forms nowadays, sometimes playing on "traditional" delicatessen fare but often incorporating ingredients and styles of cooking that bear little or no relation to that type of food. And so, as time goes on, the delicatessen fades further and further into the past as a viable space either for Jewish gathering or for Jewish gastronomy.

As long as both Jews and non-Jews want to eat "traditional" Jewish food, delis will always exist in our culture. If they die out, they will be resurrected and reinvented in some form in the future. But they will probably never occupy the centrality in American Jewish life that they once did, as they helped to bridge the world of the immigrants and their children with the promise and freedom of America.

Notes

Introduction

1. Mark Kurlansky, *Salt: A World History* (New York: Penguin, 1993).
2. Seth Wolitz, "The Renaissance in Kosher Cuisine," Policy Forum 18 (Jerusalem: Institute of the World Jewish Congress, 1999).
3. John Mariani, *America Eats Out: An Illustrated History of Restaurants, Taverns, Coffee Shops, Speakeasies, and Other Establishments That Have Fed Us for 350 Years* (New York: William Morrow, 1991), 75.
4. Quoted in Dinah Shore, *The Celebrity Cookbook* (New York: Price, Stern, Sloan, 1966), 38.
5. Quoted in Ted Merwin, "Homeland for the Jewish Soul," *New York Jewish Week* (7/26/2011).
6. Richard Condon, *And Then We Moved to Rossenarra* (New York: Dial, 1973), 114–120.
7. Daniel Stern, "Jewish New York," in Alan Rinzler, ed., *The New York Spy* (New York: David White, 1967), 31. See also Tom Wolfe, "Corned Beef and Therapy," in Rinzler, *New York Spy*, 9–19.
8. Hilton Als, "The Overcoat," *Transition* 73 (1997): 6–9. To make prospective donors laugh, black panhandlers (beggars) in New York in the 1990s asked passersby—many of whom were Jewish—to give them change for the "United Negro Pastrami Fund."
9. Joan Nathan, *Jewish Cooking in America* (New York: Knopf, 1998), 185; emphasis added.
10. Interview with the author, 1/15/2004.
11. Jonathan Rosen, *The Talmud and the Internet: A Journey between Worlds* (New York: Farrar, Straus and Giroux, 2000), 46.
12. Soupy Sales, *Soupy Sez: My Life and Zany Times* (New York: M. Evans, 2003), 176.

13. Gary Anderson, "The Expression of Joy as a Halakhic Problem in Rabbinic Sources," *Jewish Quarterly Review* 80.3–4 (1990): 234n35.

14. Bava Metzia 26B, with Rashi commentary about the association of mustard with royalty, derived from the story of Abraham's serving the angels a meal of three bull tongues with mustard (Gen. 18:1–15).

15. Edward Gibbon and Henry Hart Milman, *The Life of Edward Gibbon* (Paris: Baudry, 1840), 106.

16. See Bee Wilson, *Sandwich: A Global History* (London: Reaktion Books, 2010).

17. See Ted Merwin, "The Delicatessen as an Icon of Secular Jewishness," in Simon Bronner, ed., *Jewishness: Expression, Identity and Representation* (Oxford, UK: Littman Library of Jewish Civilization, 2008), 195–210.

18. Hasia Diner, *Hungering for America: Italian, Irish, and Jewish Foodways in the Age of Migration* (Cambridge: Harvard University Press, 2003), 201.

19. Diner, *Hungering for America*, 200.

20. Quoted in Ted Merwin, "Hold Your Tongue," *New York Jewish Week* (1/13/2006).

21. Gary Portnoy, who wrote the song with Judy Hart Angelis, grew up in a Jewish family that lived first in Brooklyn and later on Long Island. See Randolph Michaels, *Flashbacks to Happiness: Eighties Music Revisited* (Lincoln, NE: iUniverse, 2005), 145–149. I asked Portnoy if he thought about Jewish delis at all in writing the song, and he said that he did not but that his family did regularly drive into Manhattan to eat at Katz's Delicatessen. Email to the author, 5/09/2012.

22. Sharon Daloz Parks, *Big Questions, Worthy Dreams: Mentoring Young Adults in Their Search for Meaning, Purpose, and Faith* (San Francisco: Jossey-Bass, 2000), 10.

23. Sybil Taylor, *Ireland's Pubs* (New York: Penguin Books, 1983), 15.

24. Jennifer Nugent Duffy, *Who's Your Paddy? Racial Expectations and the Struggle for Irish American Identity* (New York: NYU Press, 2013), 113.

25. "Little Italy in New York," *New York Times* (5/31/1896), 32.

26. Arthur Schwartz, *Arthur Schwartz's New York City Food: An Opinionated History and More than 100 Legendary Recipes* (New York: Stewart, Tabori and Chang, 2008).

27. These sexual associations remain with us today. Unlike the penis, which tends to shrivel up in the bath, sausages and meats swell up when immersed in the salt water that "cures" or pickles them. (Both hard salami and pastrami are taken a couple of steps further, being showered with spices and then smoked.) The phrase "hide the salami," which refers to the disappearance of the penis in the vagina, is only one of many slang terms relating to the sausage, including a "salami party" or "salami factory," meaning a gathering where there are significantly more men than women in attendance. Common expressions for male masturbation are to "slap," "slam," or "stroke" the salami. And "Jewish corned beef," "Jewish national," and "kosher dill" are all slang phrases used to

refer to a circumcised penis. Is it any wonder that Meg Ryan's "orgasm" in *When Harry Met Sally* takes place in a Jewish deli?

28. Annie Polland and Daniel Soyer, *Emerging Metropolis: New York Jews in the Age of Immigration, 1840–1920* (New York: NYU Press, 2012), 133.

29. J. J. Goldberg, *Jewish Power: Inside the American Establishment* (New York: Basic Books, 1997), 29.

30. Chris McNickle, *To Be Mayor of New York: Ethnic Politics in the City* (New York: Columbia University Press, 1993), 185.

31. See Stephen J. Whitfield, "The Jewish Vote," *Virginia Quarterly Review* 62 (Winter 1986): 1–20.

32. Harpo Marx with Rowland Barber, *Harpo Speaks* (New York: Limelight, 2004), 166.

33. Interview with the author, 5/3/2009.

34. Laurie Ochoa, "Just What Is a Delicatessen Supposed to Look Like Anyway?," *Los Angeles Times* (3/11/1990), 99.

35. Quoted in Elaine Markoutsas, "Delis, the Originators of Fast Food: Pile on Ambience, Don't Hold the Mustard," *Chicago Tribune* (8/11/1977), A3.

36. Patric Kuh, "What's Not to Like?," *Los Angeles* (10/2007), 118–127.

37. Ira Wolfman, *Jewish New York: Notable Neighborhoods and Memorable Moments* (New York: Universe, 2003), 43.

38. Ted Merwin, "The New Heights of Nouvelle," *Jewish Week* (3/21/2008), A4–A5.

39. Quoted in Wendy Gordon, "Deli: Comfort Food for the WWII Generation," *Forward* (2/21/2012).

40. Arthur Schlesinger, "Food in the Making of America," in *Paths to the Present* (New York: Macmillan, 1949), 234–255.

41. See, for example, Warren Belasco, *Appetite for Change* (New York: Pantheon, 1990) and *Meals to Come: A History of the Future of Food* (Berkeley: University of California Press, 2006); Noah Bernamoff and Rae Bernamoff, *The Mile End Jewish Cookbook* (New York: Random House, 2012); Carole Counihan and Penny Van Esterik, eds., *Food and Culture: A Reader*, 2nd ed. (New York: Routledge, 2007); Counihan, *Food in the U.S.A.* (New York, Routledge, 2002); Darra Goldstein, ed., *The Gastronomica Reader* (Berkeley: University of California Press, 2010); Gil Marks, *Encyclopedia of Jewish Food* (New York: Wiley, 2010); Nick Zukin, *The Artisan Jewish Deli at Home* (Riverside, NJ: Andrews McMeel, 2013).

42. See Claude Lévi-Strauss, *The Raw and the Cooked* (Chicago: University of Chicago Press, 1983), 89.

43. Arjun Appadurai, "Gastro-Politics in Hindu South Asia," *American Ethnologist* 8.3 (1981): 494.

44. See Norbert Elias, *The Civilizing Process: Sociogenetic and Psychogenetic Investigations* (Oxford, UK: Blackwell, 2000).

45. Barry Kessler, "Bedlam with Corned Beef on the Side," *Generations*, Fall 1993, 2–7.

46. Michael Alexander, "The Meaning of American Jewish History." *Jewish Quarterly Review* 96.3 (2006): 426.

47. Sharon Lebewohl and Rena Bulkin, *2nd Avenue Deli Cookbook* (New York: Villard, 1999); Arthur Schwartz, *Arthur Schwartz's Jewish Home Cooking: Yiddish Recipes Revisited* (New York: Ten Speed, 2008); Maria Balinska, *The Bagel: The Surprising History of a Modest Bread* (New Haven: Yale University Press, 2009); Laura Silver, *Knish: In Search of the Jewish Soul Food* (Boston: Brandeis University Press, 2004); Jane Ziegelman, *97 Orchard: An Edible History of Five Immigrant Families in One New York Tenement* (New York: Harper, 2011); David Sax, *Save the Deli: In Search of Perfect Pastrami, Crusty Rye, and the Heart of Jewish Delicatessen* (New York: Mariner Books, 2010).

48. See Leah Koenig, "Goldbergers and Cheeseburgers: Particularism and the Culinary Jew," *Zeek*, Fall–Winter 2006, 13–22.

49. See Roland Barthes, *Elements of Semiology* (New York: Hill and Wang, 1968). See also Merwin, "The Delicatessen as an Icon of Secular Jewishness."

50. Telephone interview with the author, 1/17/07.

Chapter 1. *According to the Customer's Desire*

1. Personal collection of the author.

2. Interview with the author, 2/3/2010.

3. William Oldys and John Malham, *The Harleian Miscellany: or, A Collection of Scarce, Curious, and Entertaining Pamphlets and Tracts, as Well in Manuscript as in Print, Found in the Late Earl of Oxford's Library, Interspersed with Historical, Political and Critical Notes*, vol. 2 (London: Robert Dutton, 1809), 182.

4. Henry Finck, *Food and Flavor: A Gastronomic Guide to Health and Good Living* (London: John Lane, 1914), 99.

5. Interview with the author, 2/3/2010.

6. Jean-Paul Aron, *Art of Eating in France: Manners and Menus in the 19th Century* (Chester Springs, PA: Dufour, 1975), 24–25.

7. Abba Kanter, "Fun Der Kolbasa Biz Der Delicatessen Store" (From the Sausage to the Delicatessen Store), *Mogen Dovid Delicatessen Magazine* (11/1930), 19.

8. Harry Gene Levine, "Pastrami Land: The Jewish Deli in New York," *Contexts* (Summer 2007), 67, http://qcpages.qc.cuny.edu/~hlevine/Pastrami-Land.pdf. Rabbi Gil Marks speculates that the word *pastirma* was ultimately changed to *pastrami* in order to rhyme with *salami*. Gil Marks, *Encyclopedia of Jewish Food* (New York: Wiley, 2010), 450.

9. John Cooper, *Eat and Be Satisfied: A Social History of Jewish Food* (New York: Jason Aronson, 1993), 77.

10. David L. Gold, "When Chauvinism Interferes in Etymological Research: A Few Derivations on the Supposed Vulgar Latin Derivation of Rumanian *Pastrama*— *Pastrama*, a Noun of Immediate Turkish Origin (With Preliminary Remarks on Related Words in Albanian, Arabic, Armenian, English, French, Greek, Hebrew,

Judezmo, Polish, Russian, SerboCroatian, Spanish, Turkish, Ukrainian and Yiddish)," in *Studies in Etymology and Etiology*, ed. F. Rodríguez González and A. Lillo Buades (Alicante, Spain: University of Alicante, 2009), 271–375.

11. Cooper, *Eat and Be Satisfied*, 169.

12. Diner, *Hungering for America*, 164–165.

13. Sholem Aleichem, *Tevye the Dairyman and the Railroad Stories*, trans. Hillel Halkin (New York: Schocken, 1987), 14.

14. Molly Pulver Ungar, "From Zetz! to Zeitgeist: Translating 'Rumenye, Rumenye,'" in Pierre Anctil, Norman Ravvin, and Sherry Simon, eds., *New Readings of Yiddish Montreal / Traduire le Montreal Yiddish* (Ottawa, Canada: University of Ottawa Press, 2007), 118.

15. Mayer Kirshenblatt and Barbara Kirshenblatt-Gimblett, *They Called Me Mayer July* (Berkeley: University of California Press, 2007), 115.

16. Phyllis Glazer and Miriyam Glazer, *The Essential Book of Jewish Festival Cooking* (New York: HarperCollins, 2004), 243.

17. Yeskheskl Kotik, *Mayn Zikroynes* (My Memories) (Warsaw, 1913).

18. See Glenn Dynner, *Yankel's Tavern: Jews, Liquor, and Life in the Kingdom of Poland* (New York: Oxford University Press, 2013). See also Marni Davis, *Jews and Booze: Becoming American in the Age of Prohibition* (New York: NYU Press, 2012), 6.

19. Aharon Rosenbaum, "Memories of the Past," trans. Jerrold Landau, in M. Yari-Wold, ed., *Rzeszow Community Memorial Book* (Kehilat Raysha sefer zikaron) (Tel Aviv, 1967), available online at http://www.jewishgen.org/yizkor/rzeszow/rzeszow.html.

20. Phyllis Kramer, ed.,*1891 Galician Business Directory* (New York: JewishGen, 2000), http://www.jewishgen.org/databases/Poland/galicia1891.htm.

21. Gavriel Lindenberg, "Our Town as I Remember It," trans. Yehudis Fishman, in Sh. Meltzer, ed., *The Book of Horodenka* (trans. of *Sefer Horodenka*) (Tel Aviv, 1963), available online at http://www.jewishgen.org/yizkor/gorodenka/gor117.html.

22. David Shtokfish, *Jewish Mlawa: Its History, Development, Destruction* (trans. of *Mlawa Ha-Yehudit; Koroteha, HitpatKhuta, Kilyona Di Yidishe Mlawe; Geshikte, Oyfshtand, Unkum*) (Tel Aviv, 1984), available online at http://www.jewishgen.org/yizkor/mlawa/mla429.html/.

23. Ida Marcus-Kerbelnik and Bat-Sheva Levitan Kerbelnik, eds., *Kelme—An Uprooted Tree* (trans. of *Kelm—'Ets Karut*) (Tel Aviv, 1993), available online at http://www.jewishgen.org/yizkor/kelme/Kelme.html.

24. Referenced in Condon, *And Then We Moved*, 115.

25. Edwin Brooks, "The Romantic Origin of the Delicatessen Foods," *Chicago Jewish Food Merchant* (4/1936), 32.

26. "Love, Sausages, and Law," *New York Times* (3/27/1875), 3.

27. "Christmas Dainties: The German-American Must Have the Old Familiar Things That Come from the Fatherland," *New York Tribune* (12/16/1900), 3.

28. L. H. Robbins, "Rest for the Delicatessen Man?," *New York Times* (8/15/1937), 117.
29. "Klein Deutchland: Glimpses of Daily Life in the Recognized Little Germany of This Metropolis," *New York Herald* (11/11/1894), 2.
30. Edward Eggleston, "Wild Flowers of English Speech in America," *Century* 47.6 (1894): 853.
31. H. L. Mencken, *The American Language: An Inquiry into the Development of English in the United States* (New York: Knopf, 1921), 103n36. Among other English words that derived from German, Mencken listed *pumpernickel, lager-beer, wienerwurst, bock-beer,* and *schnitzel.* Mencken idealized German culture and was known, in other books, for making virulently anti-Semitic statements, such as that "the case against the Jews is long and damning; it would justify ten thousand times as many pogroms as now go in the world." H. L. Mencken, introduction to *The Anti-Christ*, by Friedrich Nietzsche (New York: Sharp, 1999), 14.
32. H. T. Webster, "They Don't Speak Our Language," *Forum and Century* 90.6 (1933), 62. For a list of contemporary deli terms, including *pistol* for pastrami, *CB* for corned beef, and *Coney* for hot dog, see Milton Parker and Allyn Freeman, *How to Feed Friends and Influence People: The Carnegie Deli* (Hoboken, NJ: Wiley, 2005), 59.
33. *Brooklyn Daily Eagle* (3/29/1885), 12.
34. Wong Chin Foo, "A Chinese Delicatessen Store," reprinted in *Bismarck (ND) Daily Tribune* (8/7/1891), 3.
35. "Queer Dishes in Shops," *New York Tribune*, illustrated supplement (12/12/1897),12.
36. Donna Gabaccia, *We Are What We Eat: Ethnic Foods and the Making of Americans* (Cambridge: Harvard University Press, 2000), 95.
37. Gabaccia, *We Are What We Eat*, 10–35.
38. George E. Walsh, "Queer Foreign Foods in America," *American Kitchen Magazine* 16 (11/1901): 65.
39. Walsh made an exception for German sausages, which he insisted "have no meaning whatever except to German-born people," since he averred that each type of sausage—such as *schinkenwurst, zugenwurst, blutwurst,* and *lieberwurst*—came from a particular German district and appealed mainly to those who hailed from that region. Walsh, "Queer Foreign Foods," 66.
40. Walsh, "Queer Foreign Foods," 67.
41. Forrest Chrissey, *The Story of Foods* (New York: Rand McNally, 1917), 463–472.
42. Moses Rischin, *The Promised City: New York's Jews, 1870–1914* (Cambridge: Harvard University Press, 1962), 56.
43. By 1917, according to a Jewish communal survey, it was estimated that one million Jews in the city were buying meat from kosher butchers and that the average consumption of meat was 156 pounds per capita. See *The Jewish Communal Register of New York City, 1917–1918* (New York: RareBooksClub, 2012), 319.

44. In 1886, baked beans also first became popular in London, after Henry John Heinz sold five cases of samples to Fortnum & Mason, the gourmet food store famous for its wide selection of canned goods.

45. Patricia Volk, "Deli," *American Heritage Magazine* 53.1 (2002), http://www.americanheritage.com/content/deli. See also Patricia Volk, *Stuffed: Adventures of a Restaurant Family* (New York: Vintage Books, 2002). Volk's descendants also went on to become inventors in their own right; his son developed the wrecking ball, while his equally entrepreneurial grandson, also named Sussman, concocted double-ended cigarette lighters and trash-can cleaners.

46. Marcus Ravage, *An American in the Making* (New York: Harper and Brothers, 1917), 88. D. H. Hermalin, writing at the turn of the twentieth century, estimated that throughout the city, Rumanian Jews—who numbered twenty-four thousand in New York—owned 150 restaurants, 200 wine cellars, and 30 coffeehouses. Hermalin described the fashion by which the Rumanians, "over a cup of black coffee and through the blue smoke curling up from their cigarettes . . . indulge in a game of cards or chess." D. H. Hermalin, "The Roumanian Jews in America," *American Jewish Yearbook* 3 (1901–1902): 101–102.

47. Esther Levy, *Jewish Cookery Book* (Philadelphia: W. S. Turner, 1871), 40. The first Jewish cookbook ever auctioned, it sold at Swann Auction Galleries in 2010 for $11,000. Gabriela Geselowitz, "Jewish Cooking, 19th Century Style," *New York Jewish Week* (3/24/2010). The first Yiddish cookbook in the United States was not published until the turn of the twentieth century; it was Hinde Amchanitzki's *Lehr-bukh vi azoy tsu kokhen un baken* (Cooking and Baking Textbook), first printed in New York in 1901. African and Middle Eastern Division, Library of Congress.

48. Levy, *Jewish Cookery Book*, 39.

49. See Paula Hyman, "Immigrant Women and Consumer Protest: The New York Kosher Meat Boycott of 1902," *American Jewish History* 70 (1980): 91–105.

50. See Jonathan Rees, *Refrigeration Nation: A History of Ice, Appliances, and Enterprise in America* (Baltimore: Johns Hopkins University Press, 2013).

51. Sammy Aaronson and Albert Hirshberg, *As High as My Heart* (New York: Coward-McCann, 1957), 18–19.

52. Rischin, *Promised City*, 80.

53. Andrew Heinze, *Adapting to Abundance* (New York: Columbia University Press, 1992), 16.

54. Anzia Yezierska, *Bread Givers* (New York: Persea Books, 1999), 165.

55. Alfred Kazin, *A Walker in the City* (New York: Harcourt Brace Jovanovich, 1951), 34.

56. The sociologist Shlomo Katz was reminded, he wrote, of the "distasteful and indelicate superabundance of Jewish restaurants, the staggering mounds of food in delicatessen stores in Jewish neighborhoods, the endearing diminutives applied to a *gut shtickele* ('fine piece of') something or another." Katz

suggested that the parents, by making their children fat, could make them "sufficiently buttressed against the hostile world." Shlomo Katz, "Heritage," in Elliot Cohen, ed., *Commentary on the American Scene* (New York: Knopf, 1953), 5–6.

57. David Nasaw, *Going Out: The Rise and Fall of Public Amusements* (New York: Basic Books, 1993), 13.

58. Sabine Haenni, *The Immigrant Scene: Ethnic Amusements in New York, 1880–1920* (Minneapolis: University of Minnesota Press, 2008), 5.

59. Maurice Hindus, *Green Worlds* (New York: Doubleday, Doran, 1938), 94–95.

60. Susan J. Matt, "A Hunger for Home: Homesickness and Food in a Global Consumer Society," *Journal of American Culture* 30.1 (2007): 13.

61. Quoted in Matt, "A Hunger for Home," 13.

62. Irving Howe, *World of Our Fathers* (New York: Harcourt Brace Jovanovich, 1976), 209.

63. Benjamin Reich, "A New Social Center: The Candy Store as a Social Influence," *Year Book of the University Settlement Society of New York*, 1899.

64. Bella Spewack, *Streets: A Memoir of the Lower East Side* (New York: Feminist Press of the City University of New York, 1995), 43.

65. Jillian Gould, "Candy Stores and Egg Creams," in Ilana Abramovitch and Seán Galvin, eds., *Jews of Brooklyn* (Waltham, MA: Brandeis University Press, 2001), 204.

66. Howe, *World of Our Fathers*, 237.

67. David Freedman, *Mendel Marantz* (New York: Langdon, 1925), 80.

68. Jewish refugees from Spain and Portugal had imported their way of deep frying fish—*pescado frito*—to England, prompting Thomas Jefferson to mention in a letter that he had eaten "fish fried in the Jewish fashion." See Claudia Roden, *The Book of Jewish Food: An Odyssey from Samarkand to New York* (New York: Knopf, 1996), 113. See also Alan Davidson, *The Penguin Companion to Food* (New York: Penguin, 2002), 359.

69. "Stalls for Fried Fish," *New York Times* (11/12/1899), 12.

70. John A. Jakle and Keith A. Sculle, *Fast Food: Roadside Restaurants in the Automobile Age* (Baltimore: Johns Hopkins University Press, 2002), 29.

71. Darra Goldstein, "Will Matzoh Go Mainstream? Jewish Food in America," in *The Jewish Role in American Life: An Annual Review*, vol. 4 (Los Angeles: Casden Institute, 2005).

72. See Harold P. Gastwirt, *Fraud, Corruption, and Holiness: The Controversy over the Supervision of Jewish Dietary Practice in NYC, 1881–1940* (Port Washington, NY: Kennikat, 1974).

73. See Maria Diemling, "As the Jews like to Eat Garlick: Garlic in Christian-Jewish Polemical Discourse in Early Modern Germany," in Leonard J. Greenspoon, Ronald A. Simkins, and Gerald Shapiro, eds., *Food and Judaism* (Omaha, NE: Creighton University Press, 2004), 218.

74. Sara Evans, *Born for Liberty* (New York: Free Press, 1997), 163.

75. Samuel Chotzinoff, *A Lost Paradise: Early Reminiscences* (New York: Arno, 1975), 184.

76. Isaac Reiss (Moishe Nadir), "Ruined by Success," translated from the Yiddish by Nathan Ausubel, in Ausubel, *Treasury of Jewish Humor* (New York: Doubleday, 1951), 36–39.

77. Classified section, *New York Herald* (2/19/1888), 19.

78. Annie Polland, *Landmark of the Spirit: The Eldridge Street Synagogue* (New Haven: Yale University Press, 2009), 96–97. Kosher meat is produced from biblically permitted animals (those that have cloven hoofs and that chew their cud), which are slaughtered with a single stroke of a sharp blade across the carotid artery, cut into pieces with a knife that has had no contact with dairy products, and then soaked and salted to remove any traces of blood.

79. Sholem Aleichem, *Motl Peyse dem Khazns Zun* (Motl Peyse, the Cantor's Son) (Jerusalem: Hebrew University Magnes Press, 1997). The translation is mine.

80. Ad for Barnet Brodie Genuine Kosher Meat Products, *Mogen Dovid Delicatessen Magazine* (8/1931), 18.

81. "Court Is Mystified by Delicatessen," *New York Times* (4/29/10), 3.

82. *Hyman Lipman v. Max Parker, et al.*, in M. E. McDonald, ed., *Lackawanna Jurist* 16 (1/29/1915–1/21/1916): 82–86.

83. Batya Miller, "Enforcement of the Sunday Closing Laws on the Lower East Side, 1882–1903," *American Jewish History* 91.2 (2003): 269–286.

84. *Soon v. Crowley*, 113 U.S. 703, 710.

85. Miller, "Enforcement of the Sunday Closing Laws," 278.

86. "Will Obey the Law," *New York Herald* (7/7/1895), 6. One wonders how many of the delicatessen owners were Jewish and likely closed their stores on Saturdays.

87. "Grew Eloquent on Delicatessen," *New York Herald* (7/30/95), 4.

88. "Overzealous on Excise," *New York Times* (8/27/1895), 8.

89. "'Delikatessen' on Sunday," *New York Times* (2/8/1899), 6.

90. "Sunday Delicatessen," *New York Times* (3/28/1899), 6.

91. May Ellis Nichols, "Exit the Maid," *Outlook* 125 (5/12/1920): 79.

92. "Raines Law Delicatessen," *New York Times* (2/7/1899), 5.

93. "Delicatessen Men's Festival," *New York Times* (7/31/1899), 7.

94. "Then and Now," *Life* (11/18/20), 921.

95. Chotzinoff, *Lost Paradise*, 182.

96. Kazin, *Walker in the City*, 34.

97. Ella Eaton Kellogg, *Science in the Kitchen* (Chicago: Modern Medicine, 1893), 29–31.

98. See Harvey Levenstein, *Fear of Food: A History of Why We Worry about What We Eat* (Chicago: University of Chicago Press, 2012), 32.

99. Sonia Kochman Davis, "A Dietician Looks at the Kosher Delicatessen Store and its Customers," *Jewish Criterion* (Pittsburgh, PA) (3/30/28), 59–62. For more on the perceived link between kosher food and poor health during the

1920s, see Kochman Davis, "The Kosher Diet—What It Is," *Jewish Criterion* (11/18/27), 41–42.

100. "To the White Coat and Apron Brigade," *Mogen Dovid Delicatessen Magazine* (6/1931), 7.

101. Barnett Brodie ad, *Mogen Dovid Delicatessen Magazine* (8/1931), 18.

102. Theodore Krainin, "'Kosher' and the Jewish Dietary Laws," *Jewish Forum* (1/23), 79.

103. Chelsea Delicatessen advertising card, collection of the author.

104. Diane Janowski, *Our Own Book—A Victorian Guide to Life—Homespun Cuisine, Health, Romance, Etiquette, Raising Children and Farm Animals* (Elmira, NY: New York History Review Press, 2008), 46; originally published by *Weekly Gazette and Press* (Elmira, NY), 1888. Delicatessen customer Bernard Cooper, who grew up in Los Angeles, recalled, "the glass bottles gave no clue as to the identity of Dr. Brown," but "I pictured him as a kindly white-coated man not unlike my dentist. In a pristine laboratory filled with bubbling test tubes and beakers, Dr. Brown concocted the amber elixir that washed away the saltiness of corned beef, cut the peppery after-burn of pastrami or kept me from choking on a throatful of brisket." Every swig of the beverage, he noted, was a "toast to the future, each bottle a triumph of science." Bernard Cooper, letter to the *New York Times* (3/10/1996).

105. Leah Koenig, "Cel-Ray Soda Grabs New Fans," *Forward* (7/18/2012).

106. LeRoy Kaser, "In the Delicatessen Shop, a Jewish Monologue," in *Dialect Monologues: Readings and Plays* (Dayton, OH: Paine, 1928), 146–147.

107. For more on Hebrew comics, see Ted Merwin, *In Their Own Image: New York Jews in Jazz Age Popular Culture* (New Brunswick: Rutgers University Press, 2006). The Yiddish accent sounds more German than Yiddish—very few non-Jewish comics strove to reproduce a bona fide Yiddish accent. Most of their audiences couldn't tell the difference anyway.

108. See Matthew Frye Jacobson, *Whiteness of a Different Color: European Immigrants and the Alchemy of Race* (Cambridge: Harvard University Press, 1999).

109. Quoted in Ronald T. Takaki, *Double Victory: A Multicultural History of America in World War II* (Boston: Back Bay, 2001), 188.

110. See Gastwirt, *Fraud, Corruption, and Holiness*.

111. Gastwirt, *Fraud, Corruption, and Holiness*, 122–123.

112. "Kosher Meat Man Held in High Bail," *New York Times* (4/20/1933), 25.

113. *People v. Jacob Branfman & Son*, 263 NYS 629, 147 Misc. 290 (City Court, 1933).

114. "The New Kosher Law," *Mogen Dovid Delicatessen Magazine* (6/1936), 1.

115. Gastwirt, *Fraud, Corruption, and Holiness*, 78–79.

116. "Ending a Scandal," *Yiddishes Tageblatt/Jewish Daily News* (4/5/1922), 8.

117. "75 Years Ago in the Forward," *Jewish Daily Forward* (3/9/2007).

Chapter 2. *From a Sandwich to a National Institution*

1. There are three published versions of this scene; the only one that contains the delicatessen references is the one that Groucho printed in his scrapbook, *The Groucho Phile*. But improvisation was an integral part of vaudeville, and since Groucho performed this scene for years, ad-libbing all the while, there is no way to know when the delicatessen references were introduced. Groucho Marx, *The Groucho Phile: An Illustrated Life* (New York: Galahad Books, 1979), 41.

2. See Samuel Zanvel Pipe, "Napoleon in Jewish Folklore," in *YIVO Annual of Jewish Social Science*, vol. 1 (New York: YIVO Institute for Jewish Research, 1946), 294; and Ronald Schechter, *Obstinate Hebrews: Representations of Jews in France, 1715–1815* (Berkeley: University of California Press, 2003), 226.

3. Deborah Dash Moore, *At Home in America: Second Generation New York Jews* (New York: Columbia University Press, 1981).

4. George Jean Nathan, "Clinical Notes: The Sandwich," *American Mercury* 8 (5–8/1926): 237–238.

5. Despite the popularity of competitive eating, its dangers are coming to public attention, especially after a man choked to death while competing in a hot-dog-eating contest in South Dakota on July 4, 2014. "Man Dies at South Dakota Hot Dog Eating Contest," *New York Times* (from the Associated Press) (7/8/2014).

6. Roger Abrahams, "The Language of Festivals: Celebrating the Economy," in Victor Turner, ed., *Celebration: Studies in Festivity and Ritual* (Washington, DC: Smithsonian Institution Press, 1982), 161–177.

7. Allan Sherman and Bud Burtson, *The Golden Touch*, unpublished ms., Du 27189 (registered on 4/2/51), Library of Congress, act 1, scene 1, p. 3. Thanks to Mark Cohen for sharing a copy of the manuscript with me. For a discussion of the musical, see Mark Cohen, *Overweight Sensation: The Life and Comedy of Allan Sherman* (Waltham, MA: Brandeis University Press, 2013), 58–66.

8. See Ted Merwin, "The American Dream, on Rye," *New York Jewish Week* (12/11/2012).

9. Jack Waldron, "Max's Delicatessen," undated ms., *T-Mss 2008–001, Smith and Dale Papers, Additions (1898–1987), Billy Rose Theater Collection, New York Public Library.

10. Marx, *Harpo Speaks*, 166.

11. Nathan, "Clinical Notes," 237–238.

12. Jim Heimann, *Make I Take Your Order? American Menu Design, 1920–1960* (San Francisco: Chronicle Books, 1998), 16.

13. Earl Wilson, "Famous Lindy's Waiters," *Beaver County (PA) Times* (9/19/1969).

14. Jerome Charyn, *Gangsters and Gold Diggers: Old New York, the Jazz Age, and the Birth of Broadway* (New York: Thunder's Mouth, 2003), 9.

15. Curled, tinted strips of paper—or cellophane—were emblematic of the delicatessen; the humorist George S. Kaufman, satirizing *Life* magazine's

"Calendar" for October 17, 1922, joked that it was that date when the "last New York delicatessen store [stopped] using colored paper sauerkraut for window decoration." Quoted in Simon Louvish, *Monkey Business: The Lives and Legends of the Marx Brothers* (New York: Macmillan, 2000), 166.

16. Montague Glass, "Kosher Restaurants," *Saturday Evening Post* (8/3/1929).
17. Arnold Manoff, "Reuben and His Restaurant—The Lore of a Sandwich," interview with Arnold Reuben, conducted on December 18, 1938, *American Life Histories: Manuscripts from the Federal Writers' Project, 1936–1940*, MSS55715: Box A722, Folklore Project, Life Histories, 1936–39, Manuscript Division, Library of Congress.
18. Nowadays, by contrast, fewer than two dozen shows open on Broadway each year.
19. For the Jewish involvement in Hollywood, see Neal Gabler, *An Empire of Their Own: How the Jews Invented Hollywood* (New York: Anchor Books, 1989). For the Jewish involvement in Broadway, see Merwin, *In Their Own Image*.
20. Rian James, *Dining in New York* (New York: John Day, 1930), 29.
21. Michael Alexander, *Jazz Age Jews* (Princeton: Princeton University Press, 2003), 63.
22. Manoff, "Reuben and His Restaurant."
23. Max Asnas, *Corned Beef Confucius* (Kimberly 11006, n.d.), LP.
24. Gutterman reported on plans, which did not come to fruition, to make a biopic about Asnas, with Edward G. Robinson considered for the lead. Gutterman quoted the sportswriter Murray Robinson to the effect that Asnas "moves serenely through a maze of comical woes which would unhorse a lesser spirit. Max has troubles with customers, partners, comedians, mustard pots, waiters, chefs, panhandlers, countermen, horse players and grammar. He beats them all down without drawing a deep breath." Leon Gutterman, "Our Film Folk," *Canadian Jewish Chronicle* (7/23/1954), 8.
25. Martin Kalmanoff (pseud. Marty Kenwood), Aaron Schroeder (pseud. Matt Kingsley), and Eddie White, "When Mighty Maxie Makes with the Delicatessen," undated ms., Martin Kalmanoff Papers, 1928–2002, Box 100, Folder 47, Billy Rose Theater Collection, New York Public Library.
26. Others claim that the iconic sandwich was invented by a cook in Reuben's Delicatessen, who named it after his boss. But the sandwich is also attributed to Reuben Kulakofsky, a wholesale grocer in Omaha, Nebraska, who played a weekly poker game with a group of men who fixed their own sandwiches to eat while they played. The Reuben eventually appeared on the menu of The Blackstone, a local hotel that was owned by Kulakofsky's poker buddy Charles Schimmel. The story about Annette Seelos is almost certainly fabricated, since Chaplin was making a film in Hollywood at the time, and in any event there is no record of an Annette (whom Reuben also referred to as "Anna") Selos appearing in any of Chaplin's films. Furthermore, just as there are a number of competing stories about how the Reuben came to be, there are many variations

on the Reuben. The 1920s menu lists a number of "Reuben" sandwiches, including Club a la Reuben Special, Reuben's Special, Reuben's Paradise, Reuben's Tongue Delite, and Reuben's Turkey Sandwich with Russian Dressing.

27. *Program for Ziegfeld Follies of 1931*, 17, Ziegfeld Follies File, Billy Rose Theater Collection, New York Public Library.

28. Quoted in Jane Stern and Michael Stern, *Roadfood Sandwiches: Recipes and Lore from Our Favorite Shops Coast to Coast* (New York: Houghton Mifflin Harcourt, 2007), 227.

29. Damon Runyon, *Guys and Dolls: The Stories of Damon Runyon* (New York: Penguin, 1992), 93. Oddly, Runyon seems to have associated delis with fish more than with meat; instead of writing that a character "ate" in a deli, he coined the expression "tore a herring." Woody Allen employs this expression in one of his novels. When Allen's narrator serves his nanny—who is writing a vituperative tell-all book about her employers—poisoned tea, she exclaims, "Gee, this is something new. We never tore a herring at eleven-thirty in the A.M." Woody Allen, *Mere Anarchy* (New York: Random House, 2008), 62.

30. Irving Berlin, "Puttin' on the Ritz," copyrighted 8/21/1929; introduced by Harry Richman and Joan Bennett in the film *Puttin' on the Ritz*, directed by Edward Sloman (United Artists Productions, 1930).

31. See Ralph Keyes, *I Love It When You Talk Retro: Hoochie Coochie, Double Whammy, Drop a Dime, and the Forgotten Origins of American Speech* (New York: Macmillan, 2009), 246.

32. See Merwin, *In Their Own Image*.

33. Leon de Costa, typescript of *Kosher Kitty Kelly*, Library of Congress, act 2, p. 11. For a longer discussion of the play, see Merwin, *In Their Own Image*, 105–109.

34. *Private Izzy Murphy*, directed by Lloyd Bacon (Warner Brothers, 1926).

35. See Ted Merwin, "The Performance of Jewish Ethnicity in Anne Nichols' *Abie's Irish Rose*," *Journal of American Ethnic History* 20.2 (2001): 3–37.

36. *The Delicatessen Kid*, directed by Walter Fabian (Universal, 1929).

37. See Ted Merwin, "Serving Up Food with Attitude," *New York Jewish Week* (4/3/2009).

38. The writer Sharon Rudnick has recalled that it was a "mixed blessing to get her because she was so incredibly slow. But she was so entertaining it made up for the service." Quoted in Sue Fishkoff, *Kosher Nation: Why More and More of America's Food Answers to a Higher Authority* (New York: Schocken, 2010), 91. When Kassner was encouraged to retire, she sued the deli for age discrimination; she won the suit, but only after she had already passed away at the age of eighty-three. Thomas Zambito, "Dead Waitress Wins Harass Suit," *New York Daily News* (4/30/2009).

39. Earl Wilson, "Famous Lindy's Waiters," *Beaver County (PA) Times* (9/19/1969).

40. Alan Richman, "Oldest Living," *GQ* (10/2000), http://www.gq.com/food-travel/alan-richman/200602/professonial-jewish-waiter. Spelling error in original.

41. Robert Sylvester, "The Broadway Gang Eats Here," *Saturday Evening Post* (7/15/1961), 51.

42. Dorothy Sue Cobble, *Dishing It Out: Waitresses and Their Unions in the Twentieth Century* (Urbana: University of Illinois Press, 1992), 34.

43. "No Hashers: Waitresses Must Have Tact and Charm," *Literary Digest* (5/1/1937), 26–27.

44. Levine, "Pastrami Land," 67.

45. "Pesach Burstein, Vol. 1," Pesach Burstein, Judaica Sound Archives, Florida Atlantic University, http://www.faujsa.fau.edu/burstein. Special thanks to Mike Burstyn (son of Pesach Burstein) and to Mark Altman for help in translating the song. Burstein's five albums of recordings for Columbia can be accessed through the Judaica Sound Archives on the website of the Florida Atlantic University. See also Eric Byron, "English Acquisition by Immigrants (1880–1940): The Confrontation as Reflected in Early Sound Recordings," *Columbia Journal of American Studies*, http://www.columbia.edu/cu/cjas/byron1.html (accessed 2/2/2009).

46. Ethel Somers, "Glorifying the Home Dinner," *Liberty* (1/29/1927), 67.

47. Untitled article, *Life* (11/1/1929), 16.

48. Daniel Fuchs, *Homage to Blenholt* (London: Constable, 1936), 242.

49. "With the Procession," *Everybody's Magazine* 10.1 (1904): 709.

50. L. H. Robins, "Rest for the Delicatessen Man?," *New York Times* (8/15/1937), 117.

51. Bertram Beinitz, "Our Town and Its Folk: A Delicatessen and Some Others," *New York Times* (3/29/1925), XX2.

52. "Says 'Delicatessen Wife' Is Grounds for a Divorce," *New York Times* (5/2/1925), 17.

53. "Poor Meals Break Homes," *New York Times* (9/16/1920), 8.

54. Florence Guy Seabury, "The Delicatessen Husband," in *The Delicatessen Husband: And Other Essays* (New York: Harcourt Brace, 1926), 31.

55. Seabury, "The Delicatessen Husband," 29.

56. Seabury, "The Delicatessen Husband," 42.

57. Silas Bent, *Machine Made Man* (New York: Farrar and Rinehart, 1930), 33.

58. Arthur Kober, "Nobody Can Beat Friedkin's Meats," in Harold U. Ribalow, ed., *A Treasury of American Jewish Stories* (New York: Thomas Yoseloff, 1958), 223.

59. Jo Sinclair, *Wasteland* (New York: Harper and Brothers, 1946), 105.

60. "News Plan," *Printer's Ink* 114 (3/24/1921), 79.

61. Montague Glass, "Welcome to New York: Fishbein and Blintz Discuss New York versus the Rest of the U.S.," *Life* 80 (8/31/1922), 20.

62. "Standard Meals? Enter the Delicatessen," *Baltimore Sun* (11/7/1926), E23.

63. "Standard Meals?," E23.

64. Robins, "Rest for the Delicatessen Man?"

65. Louise Gertner, "What New York Eats in the Hot Summer Days," *Yiddish Daily Forward* (7/27/1937), 4.

66. S. J. Wilson, *Hurray for Me* (New York: Crown, 1964), 98. In a review of the novel in the *Chicago Tribune*, the critic Digby Whitman wrote, "[It] glows with the unique warmth of what I can only call the tribal life of the underprivileged Jew." Digby B. Whitman, "Luminous Novel Re-creates Small Child's World," *Chicago Tribune* (2/23/1964), L1.

67. Thomas F. Dwyer to Benjamin Koenigsberg (6/16/1931), Benjamin Koenigsberg Collection, Box 11, Folder 1, Yeshiva University Archives. Reported numbers of kosher delicatessens fluctuated widely. Two years earlier, according to a report by the Jewish Telegraphic Agency, there were approximately two thousand nominally kosher delicatessens in New York City, along with ten thousand kosher butchers, although half of all these were found to be in noncompliance with strict kosher regulations. "Seek Greater Enforcement of Kashruth Laws in New York," *Jewish Criterion* (Pittsburgh, PA) (6/7/1929), 4.

68. Samuel Popkin, "The Delicatessen Industry," *Mogen Dovid Delicatessen Magazine* (5/1932), 12–13, Dorot Jewish Division, New York Public Library.

69. Popkin, "The Delicatessen Industry," 13.

70. David Ward and Oliver Zunz, *The Landscape of Modernity: New York City, 1900–1940* (Baltimore: Johns Hopkins University Press, 1997), 266.

71. See A. H. Raskin's review of Max Danish's *The World of David Dubinsky*, in which Raskin criticizes the book for failing to provide "an adequate sense of personal piquancy of a union leader as full of spice as the pastrami and pickled tomatoes he loves to munch at Lindy's or the Stage Delicatessen." A. H. Raskin, "The Man behind the Union," *New York Times* (11/10/1957), 306.

72. Daniel Rogov, "You Expected Maybe Pâté de Foie Gras?," in Daniel Rogov, David Gershon, and David Louison, *The Rogue's Guide to the Jewish Kitchen* (Jerusalem: Jerusalem Post Press, 1984), 23.

73. Laurie Ochoa, "Just What Is a Delicatessen Supposed to Look Like, Anyway?," *Los Angeles Times* (3/11/1990), 99.

74. Ruth Glazer, "West Bronx: Food, Shelter, Clothing," *Commentary* (6/1949), 582.

75. According to the report, 98 percent of cattle and also 98 percent of calves that were slaughtered in New York were killed according to the kosher laws; however, only about half of the meat consumed by the city's inhabitants was slaughtered locally. "Half of All Meat Used in New York Is Kosher," *Jewish Daily News* (5/29/1921), 16.

76. Jacob Cohn, *The Royal Table: An Outline of the Dietary Laws of Israel* (New York: Bloch, 1936).

77. "Dietary Laws of 'The Royal Table,'" *Literary Digest* 123 (1/2/1937), 28.

78. "Feeding the City," Works Progress Administration Study (8/15/1940), New York City Municipal Archives.

79. Interview with the author, 6/9/2005.

80. Jenna Weissman Joselit, *The Wonders of America: Reinventing Jewish Culture, 1880–1950* (New York: Picador, 2002), 177.

81. See Mordechai Kaplan, *Judaism as a Civilization: Toward a Reconstruction of American-Jewish Life* (New York: Jewish Publication Society of America, 1994). Rabbi Ezra Finkelstein, son of Louis Finkelstein, one of the most prominent rabbis of his day, recalls his father lunching during the mid-1920s at a kosher delicatessen with Cyrus Adler, then president of the Jewish Theological Seminary. Adler ordered a sandwich, while Finkelstein requested a cup of tea. An Orthodox Jewish passerby wearing a black hat and a long beard came into the restaurant and asked them, in Yiddish, if the restaurant hewed to strict standards of kashrut. Finkelstein, not wanting to get into a discussion of why he was having only a cup of tea (which could indeed indicate a lack of trust in the restaurant's standards with regard to food), shrugged his shoulders. The man took a look at Adler, who was clean shaven, and said to Finkelstein, in Yiddish, "So this other fellow is a non-Jew?" Ezra Finkelstein, e-mail to the author, 11/3/2010.
82. Moore, *At Home in America*, 75.
83. Moore, *At Home in America*, 76.
84. Willensky, *When Brooklyn Was the World*, 190.
85. Isidore P. Salupsky, "An Open Letter to the Storekeepers," *Mogen Dovid Delicatessen Magazine* (1/1932), 11.
86. Isidore P. Salupsky, "What a Delicatessen Man Should Remember," *Mogen Dovid Delicatessen Magazine* (6/1932), 11.
87. "Delicatessen—A Necessary Luxury," *Voice of the Delicatessen Industry* (1940), Center for Jewish History, YIVO Institute for Jewish Research.
88. Interview with the author, 1/7/2002.
89. Ruth Glazer, "From the American Scene: One Touch of Delicatessen," *Commentary* (3/1946), 62.
90. Interview with the author, 9/4/2007.
91. Interview with the author, 8/13/2003
92. Interview with the author, 2/12/2005.
93. Interview with the author, 2/10/2005.
94. Kazin, *Walker in the City*, 34.
95. Midrash Tanhuma, Genesis 1. The Torah refers to itself as *eish da'at*, "fiery law." Deuteronomy 33:2.
96. Naomi Seidman, "Alfred Kazin and the Great *Beyond*," JBooks.com, n.d., http://www.jbooks.com/interviews/index/IP_Seidman_Kazin.htm.
97. Kazin, *Walker in the City*, 40.
98. The irony of children watching shoot-'em-up films at the local movie theater was not lost on Goldfried, who knew that the headquarters of Murder Inc., the Italian-Jewish organized crime syndicate, was located in a nearby candy store called Midnight Rose's. But Goldfried was fearless. When Louis Capone (whom many mistakenly assumed to be related to Al Capone) and a group of his associates came in after Prohibition to persuade the deli owner to buy King's Beer, a brand that they controlled, he bravely told them to get lost.

99. Interview with the author, 4/2/2007.

100. Louis Menashe, "Sephardic in Williamsburg," in Ilana Abramovitch and Sean Galvin, eds., *The Jews of Brooklyn* (Lebanon, NH: University Press of New England, 2002), 117.

101. Quoted in Wendy Gordon, "Deli: Comfort Food for the WWII Generation," *Forward* (2/21/2012).

102. Interview with the author, 9/4/2007.

103. Kate Simon, *Bronx Primitive* (New York: Penguin, 1982), 117–118.

104. Leonard Bronstein, an Orthodox rabbi who certified many delis as kosher despite the fact that they were open on Saturday, told me that most kosher delicatessens "did their main business on Shabbos." He added that it was "always that way; the only date that they closed was Pesach [Passover]." Interview with the author, 6/30/2003.

105. Jeffrey Gurock, *Orthodox Jews in America* (Bloomington: Indiana University Press, 2009), 10.

106. Levine, "Pastrami Land," 67.

107. Susan Stamberg, "From Manhattan to Allentown to Washington, D.C.," in Alan King and Friends, *Matzo Balls for Breakfast and Other Memories of Growing Up Jewish* (New York: Free Press, 2004), 3.

108. Jay Cantor, *Great Neck* (New York: Vintage, 2003), 25; emphasis in original.

Chapter 3. Send a Salami

1. See Robin Platts, *Burt Bacharach and Hal David: What the World Needs Now* (New York: Collector's Press, 2002).

2. Hal David, radio interview with Terry Gross, 9/7/2012, http://m.npr.org/news/NPR+Music+Mobile/160748199.

3. "Topics of the Times," *New York Times* (5/25/1945), 18.

4. The average meal for a solider contained forty-three hundred calories, with a third of the total coming from fat. Amy Bentley, *Eating for Victory: Food Rationing and the Politics of Domesticity* (Urbana: University of Illinois Press, 1998), 94.

5. A. B. Genung, *Food Policies during World War II* (Ithaca, NY: Northeast Farm Foundation, 1951), 18.

6. Violet E. Dewey, "Hoard Rationing Memories," *Milwaukee Journal* (8/8/1973), 4.

7. Samuel Spiegler, *Your Life's Work* (New York: Riverdale, 1943), 146.

8. "Meat Rationing Will Have Effect on Restaurants," *Evening Independent* (3/24/1943), 12. In a bid to compel the OPA to modify the point system, delicatessen owners threatened to take advantage of a loophole in the regulations that permitted them to reduce the number of points needed for an item if the item was about to spoil. They plotted, in particular, to band together to slash the points for liverwurst. Jefferson G. Bell, "Point-Cutting War on Rationed Foods Is Begun in City," *New York Times* (4/4/1943), 1.

9. "Dinner Guests Set a Ration Puzzle," *New York Times* (3/24/1943), 18.

10. Ruth Corbett, *Daddy Danced the Charleston* (New York: A. S. Barnes, 1970), 119.

11. "Launch Bread and Gravy Month," *Super Market Merchandizing* (2/1945), 45.

12. Bentley, *Eating for Victory*, 92.

13. "Four Meat Concerns Guilty of OPA Charge," *New York Times* (12/2/1944), 17.

14. "Delicatessen Strike Off," *New York Times* (5/24/1945), 18.

15. "2 Meatless Days Ordered by Mayor; To Be Enforced, *New York Times* (1/22/1945), 1.

16. "All Delicatessens in City May Close," *New York Times* (9/22/1946), 43.

17. "Horse Meat Mart Here Soon Is Unlikely," *New York Times* (9/26/1946), 29.

18. Herbert Mitgang, "A Pledge of Remembrance," *New York Times* (12/17/1950), SM13.

19. Myrna Katz Frommer and Harvey Frommer, *It Happened in Brooklyn: An Oral History of Growing Up in the Borough in the 1940s, 1950s, and 1960s* (New York: Harcourt Brace, 1993), 11.

20. Telephone interview with the author, 10/18/2007.

21. Deborah Dash Moore, *To the Golden Cities: Pursuing the American Jewish Dream in Miami and L.A.* (Cambridge: Harvard University Press, 1996), 53.

22. Molly Picon, Scrapbook (1925–1932), Center for Jewish History, American Jewish Historical Society.

23. H. L. Kaplan advertisement in *Yiddishes Tageblatt / Jewish Daily News* (2/26/1917), 3.

24. Barry Kessler, "Bedlam with Corned Beef on the Side," *Generations*, Fall 1993, 2–7. See also Gilbert Sandler, *Jewish Baltimore: A Family Album* (Baltimore: Johns Hopkins University Press, 2000), 132–134.

25. Hillel Levine and Lawrence Harmon, *The Death of an American Jewish Community* (New York: Free Press, 1992), 24–25.

26. Mark Friedman, "Looking Back," *Historian* (newsletter of the Rogers Park / West Ridge Historical Society) 16.3 (2001): 2.

27. Bill Gleason, "Oscar Keeps Friendship with Yanks, Berra Strictly Kosher," *Chicago American* (4/23/1964).

28. Joseph Epstein, "Nostalgie de la Boeuf," *Commentary* (2/2010), 41.

29. Moore, *To the Golden Cities*, 59.

30. Orson Welles, "From Mars," *Commentary* (6/1946), 70.

31. Rich Cohen, *Tough Jews* (New York: Crown, 1999), 14.

32. Murray "Boy" Maltin, *1/4 Pound Lean* (Los Angeles: Boy's Own, 2001), 14.

33. Marcie Cohen Ferris, *Matzoh Ball Gumbo: Culinary Tales of the Jewish South* (Chapel Hill: University of North Carolina Press, 2005), 45.

34. Collection of the author.

35. Segal's boasted both a deli counter and a "dairy bar." Thus, while both meat and dairy were offered, none of the items on the menu combined the two. (Abe's Kosher Delicatessen in Scranton, Pennsylvania, continues this practice

to this day.) Among the offerings were an EDDIE beefILTON stew ("no HAM allowed") and a Kosher Bacon-Lettuce-Tomato Sandwich. The store was closed from sundown on Friday to sundown on Saturday, as well as on all Jewish holidays. Menu from Rosen's Delirama, author's personal collection. A picture of the store can be found in Scott Faragher and Katherine Harrington, *Memphis in Vintage Postcards* (Charleston, SC: Arcadia, 2000), 69.

36. Ferris, *Matzoh Ball Gumbo*, 45.
37. Harry Golden, *Only in America* (New York: Perma Books, 1958), 113.
38. Clive Webb, *Fight against Fear: Southern Jews and Black Civil Rights* (Athens: University of Georgia Press, 2001), 109–113.
39. Quoted in Moore, *To the Golden Cities*, 85.
40. Quoted in Joann Biondi, *Miami Beach Memories: A Nostalgic Chronicle of Days Gone By* (Guilford, CT: Globe Pequot, 2006), 27.
41. Gilbert Millstein, "Who's Who and Who's Ain't along Broadway," *New York Times* (12/31/1950), SM6.
42. Edward S. Shapiro, *We Are Many: Reflections on American Jewish History and Identity* (Syracuse: Syracuse University Press, 2005), 102.
43. Quoted in Biondi, *Miami Beach Memories*, 58.
44. Harry Gersh, "Kochalein: Poor Man's Shangri-La," *Commentary* (2/1949), 169.
45. Mimi Sheraton, *From My Mother's Kitchen* (New York: Harper and Row, 1979), 243.
46. Phil Brown, *Catskills Culture: A Mountain Rat's Memories of the Great Jewish Resort Area* (Philadelphia: Temple University Press, 2003), 43.
47. Brown, *Catskills Culture*, 17.
48. Brown, *Catskills Culture*, 89.
49. Interview with the author, 3/3/9/2007.
50. Jane Levi, "An Extraterrestrial Sandwich: The Perils of Food in Space," *Endeavor* 34.1 (2010), 7.
51. Levi, "An Extraterrestrial Sandwich," 6.
52. Quoted in Mary Roach, *Packing for Mars: The Curious Science of Life in the Void* (New York: Norton, 2010), 289.
53. *Independent Offices Appropriations for 1966: Hearings, Volume 9* (Washington, DC: U.S. Congress, 1965), 912. See also Barton C. Hacker and James M. Grimwood, *On the Shoulders of Titans: A History of Project Gemini* (Washington, DC: U.S. Government Printing Office, 2010).

Chapter 4. *Miss Hebrew National Salami*

1. "Restaurant!," *Mad* 16.16 (1964).
2. Joseph Weingarten, *An American Dictionary of Slang and Colloquial Speech* (New York: self-published, 1954).
3. See Jeffrey S. Gurock, *Jews in Gotham: New York Jews in a Changing City, 1920–2010* (New York: NYU Press, 2012), 102–103.
4. Howard Cosell, *Like It Is* (Chicago: Playboy, 1974), 281.

5. See Jim Sleeper, *The Closest of Strangers: Liberalism and the Politics of Race in New York* (New York: Norton, 1991).

6. Green Flag, *The Jewish Travel Guide: 1960* (London: Jewish Chronicle, 1960), 145.

7. "2 Boys, 16, Are Fatally Knifed by Lame Man in Store Robbery," *New York Times* (11/26/1964), 43.

8. Jonathan Rieder, *Canarsie: The Jews and Italians of Brooklyn against Liberalism* (Cambridge: Harvard University Press, 1987), 22.

9. "Department Stores and 'Chains' to Occupy Space in Final Unit of Glen Oaks Shops," *New York Times* (1/15/1950), R1. See also Lila Corwin Berman, "The Death and Life of Jewish Neighborhoods," *Sh'ma* (6/1/2014), http://shma. com/2014/06/the-death-and-life-of-jewish-neighborhoods/.

10. Edward S. Shapiro, *A Time for Healing: American Jewry since World War II* (Baltimore: Johns Hopkins University Press, 1995), 147.

11. Mickey Katz, *Mish Mosh* (Capitol Records, 1957), LP.

12. Greg Lawrence, *Dance with Demons: The Life of Jerome Robbins* (New York: Berkley Trade, 2002), 3.

13. Susan Thaler, "My Father, the Deli Man," *New York Times* (6/15/1985), 23.

14. Harry Gersh, "The Jewish Paintner," *Commentary* (1/1948), 64.

15. Jackie Mason, *I'm the Greatest Comedian in the World, Only Nobody Knows It Yet!* (Verve, 1962), LP.

16. Rachel Bowlby, *Carried Away: The Invention of Modern Shopping* (New York: Columbia University Press, 2001), 84.

17. Alan M. Kraut, "The Butcher, the Baker, the Pushcart Peddler: Jewish Foodways and Entrepreneurial Opportunity in the East European Immigrant Community, 1880–1940," *Journal of American Culture* 6.4 (1983): 80.

18. William M. Freeman, "The Old Standby Becomes a Luxury," *New York Times* (5/14/1961), F1.

19. Personal collection of the author.

20. Susan J. Thompson and J. Tadlock Cowan, "Durable Food Production and Consumption in the World- Economy," in Philip McMichael, ed., *Food and Agrarian Orders in the World-Economy* (Santa Barbara, CA: Greenwood, 1995), 36.

21. Jane Nickerson, "News of Food," *New York Times* (3/19/1947), 22.

22. Joselit, *Wonders of America*, 192.

23. See Heinze, *Adapting to Abundance*.

24. "Kosher Products Show Swift Rise," *New York Times* (1/2/1957), 86.

25. J. Tevere MacFadyen, "The Rise of the Supermarket," *American Heritage* (10–11/1985), 28.

26. Leonard Lewis, "Waldbaum, Suburb Star, Clinging to Ethnic Image," *Supermarket News* (1/14/1980), 1, 28.

27. Mark H. Zanger, "Ethnic Foods," in Andrew F. Smith, ed., *The Oxford Encyclopedia of Food and Drink in America* (New York: Oxford University Press, 2004), 436.

28. "Meat Processors Reaping Bonanza," *New York Times* (12/11/1955). This type of meat was associated with African American "soul food," rather than white Protestant fare. See Doris Witt, *Black Hunger: Soul Food and America* (Minneapolis: University of Minnesota Press, 2004).

29. Marilyn Halter, *Shopping for Identity: The Marketing of Ethnicity* (New York: Random House, 2000), 13.

30. Interview with the author, 1/14/2004.

31. Interview with the author, 12/15/2007.

32. See Tom Reichert, *The Erotic History of Advertising* (Amherst, NY: Prometheus Books, 2003).

33. See Keith Lovegrove, *Pageant: The Beauty Contest* (New York: teNeues, 2002).

34. Carol Adams, *The Pornography of Meat* (New York: Continuum, 2003), 12.

35. J. Leonard Shaub, executive vice president of the Rockmore Company (the ad agency employed by the company), said the ad's intention was to "emphasize the nutritional value of a product which a child always wants but shouldn't have too much of. But this is sometimes the only thing a parent can get him to eat, and if it's nutritional, he will be getting the food value he needs." "How Agency Helped Crash Non-Jewish Markets," *Advertising Agency Magazine* (7/6/1956), 27.

36. Lizabeth Cohen, *A Consumer's Republic: The Politics of Mass Consumption in Postwar America* (New York: Knopf, 2003), 119.

37. Collection of the author.

38. The campaign was called "What I Would Do for a Hebrew National Hot Dog." Found in "How Agency Helped Crash Non-Jewish Markets," 26.

39. *Music from the Yiddish Radio Project* (Shanachie, 2006), CD.

40. Levy's Rye Bread ad, *Mogen Dovid Delicatessen Magazine* (8/1931), 10.

41. Robert Glatzer, *The New Advertising: The Great Campaigns from Avis to Volkswagen* (New York: Citadel, 1970), 55.

42. Bernard Weinraub, "From Ordinary Faces, Extraordinary Ads," *New York Times* (2/21/2002). See also "Judy Protas, 91, Writer of Slogan for Levy's Real Jewish Rye," obituary in *New York Times* (1/12/2014), A22.

43. Jonathan Sarna, *American Judaism* (New Haven: Yale University Press, 2004), 272.

44. *Gentleman's Agreement*, directed by Elia Kazan (Twentieth Century Fox, 1948).

45. Will Herberg, *Protestant–Catholic–Jew: An Essay in American Religious Sociology* (Chicago: University of Chicago Press, 1955), 13.

46. Ausubel, *Treasury of Jewish Humor*, 355–356.

47. Quoted in Raphael Patai, *The Jewish Mind* (Detroit: Wayne State University Press, 1977), 452; Eli Lederhendler, *New York Jews and the Decline of Urban Ethnicity, 1950–1970* (Syracuse: Syracuse University Press, 2001), 110.

48. Gay, *Unfinished People*, 161.

49. Samuel Persky, "New England Testimony," *Commentary* (7/1946), 48.

50. Warren Belasco, "Ethnic Fast Foods: The Corporate Melting Pot," *Food and Foodways* 2 (1987): 1–29.

51. Belasco, "Ethnic Fast Foods," 10–11.

52. Quoted in Katherine J. Parkin, *Food Is Love: Food Advertising and Gender Roles in Modern America* (Philadelphia: University of Pennsylvania Press, 2006), 113.

53. Belasco, "Ethnic Fast Foods."

54. Herbert Koshetz, "Colgate Slates Riviana Merger," *New York Times* (2/13/1976), 59.

55. Lawrence van Gelder, "Deli Food on a Grand Scale: 500,000 Frankfurters a Day," *New York Times* (4/6/1986), B39.

56. Belasco, "Ethnic Fast Foods," 28.

57. Peter Cherches, "Chinese Food, the Early Years," *Word of Mouth* (blog) (1/2/2007), http://www.petercherches.blogspot.com/2007/01/chinese-food-early-years.html.

58. Nevertheless, the film director Mel Brooks remembered about when he was growing up in Brooklyn, "As long as [my mother] was cooking, we never went to a Chinese restaurant. I mean the pot roast, the knaydlach, the stuffed gedempte, all those things with a 'chuch' and 'chach' at the end—they melted in your mouth." Quoted in Hanna Miller, "Identity Takeout: How American Jews Made Chinese Food Their Ethnic Cuisine," *Journal of Popular Culture* 39.3 (2006): 432.

59. Myrna Katz Frommer and Harvey Frommer, *Growing Up Jewish in America: An Oral History* (New York: Bison Books, 1999), 88. The radio host Jesse Brown grew up in Toronto, but his experience is the same as many Jewish New Yorkers: "Why, in the Jewish neighborhood where I grew up, are there eight Chinese restaurants but no Chinese people? Why is Chun King's won ton soup as much a part of my culinary tradition as my grandma's matzoh ball soup? Why are my parents more likely to run into the Silversteins from next door at Lee Gardens in Chinatown than at the fruit market around the corner?" Jesse Brown, "Jews and Chinese Food" (audio), Jesse Brown's website, http://www.jessebrown.ca/radio.html (accessed 10/5/2007).

60. Gaye Tuchman and Harry G. Levine, "New York Jews and Chinese Food: The Social Construction of an Ethnic Pattern," in Barbara G. Shortridge and James R. Shortridge, eds., *The Taste of American Place: A Reader on Regional and Ethnic Foods* (Lanham, MD: Rowman and Littlefield, 1997), 166.

61. Allison James, "Cooking the Books: Global or Local Identities in Contemporary British Food Cultures?," in David Howes, ed., *Cross-Cultural Consumption: Global Markets, Local Realities* (New York: Routledge, 1996), 87.

62. Tuchman and Levine, "New York Jews and Chinese Food," 170. See also Andrew Coe, *Chop Suey: A Cultural History of Chinese Food in the United States* (New York: Oxford University Press, 2009); Jennifer 8. Lee, *The Fortune Cookie Chronicles: Adventures in the World of Chinese Food* (New York: Twelve, 1999); Joshua Eli Plaut, *A Kosher Christmas: 'Tis the Season to be Jewish* (New Brunswick: Rutgers University Press, 2012); and Haiming Liu,

"Kung Pao Kosher: Jewish Americans and Chinese Food in New York," *Journal of Chinese Overseas* 6 (2010): 80–101.

63. Philip Roth, *Portnoy's Complaint* (New York: Vintage, 1967), 90.
64. Jesse Brown, *Search Engine* radio show, April 24, 2007, http://www.neatorama.com/2007/04/24/jews-chinese-food/.
65. Miryam Rotkovitz, "Kashering the Melting Pot," in Lucy M. Long, ed., *Culinary Tourism* (Lexington: University of Kentucky Press, 2010), 175.
66. Ruth Grossman and Bob Grossman, *The Chinese-Kosher Cookbook* (New York: Pocket Books, 1999).
67. Interview with the author, 11/27/2009.
68. Bernstein's on Essex menu, personal collection of the author.
69. Henry Roth, *Call It Sleep* (New York: Farrar, Straus and Giroux, 1992), 320.
70. Quoted in Richard Juliani and Mark Hutter, "Research Problems in the Study of Italian and Jewish Interaction in Community Settings," in Jean A. Scarpaci, ed., *The Interaction of Italians and Jews in America* (Staten Island, NY: American Italian Historical Association, 1975), 47.
71. Interview with author, 7/7/2010.
72. John Mariani, "Everybody Likes Italian Food," *American Heritage* 40.8 (1989), http://54.201.12.217/content/"everybody-likes-italian-food". See also Mariani, *How Italian Food Conquered the World* (New York: Palgrave Macmillan, 2011).
73. Interview with author, 12/15/2007.
74. Mimi Sheraton, "A Twin Success in Italian Cuisine," *New York Times* (7/8/1983).
75. Mimi Sheraton, "From Alan King, Tales of a Happy Eater at Large," *New York Times* (10/28/1981).
76. See Mariani, *How Italian Food Conquered the World.*
77. Quoted in Mimi Sheraton, " The Food Tastes of Tastemakers," *New York Times* (11/3/1982), C1.
78. Ari L. Goldman, "Rivington St. Wine Tour," *New York Times* (1/13/1978), C15.
79. Jenna Weissman Joselit, "How a Slum Became a Shrine," *Jewish Social Studies* 2 (1996): 54–63.
80. Hasia Diner, *Lower East Side Memories* (Princeton: Princeton University Press, 2002), 99.
81. Calvin Trillin, "A Sunday-Morning Tale," *New Yorker* (2/24/1973), 114–115.
82. Patricia Wells, "Delivering the Goods, Any Way," *New York Times* (6/27/1979), C3.
83. Mimi Sheraton, *Eating My Words: An Appetite for Life* (New York: Harper Perennial, 2006), 26.
84. Ad for Coca-Cola, *Look* magazine (6/30/1970), 16.
85. "Samurai Deli," originally aired 1/17/1976, on *Saturday Night Live: The Best of John Belushi* (Lions Gate, 2005), DVD.
86. Interview with the author, 4/14/2010.

87. Peter N. Carroll, *It Seemed Like Nothing Happened: America in the 1970s* (New Brunswick: Rutgers University Press, 1990), 307.

88. Barry Glassner, "Fitness and the Postmodern Self," *Journal of Health and Social Behavior* 30 (6/1989): 183.

89. Glassner, "Fitness and the Postmodern Self," 186.

90. Carroll, *It Seemed Like Nothing Happened*, 310.

91. "Eating Right for Less: Salt and Fats Linked to Health," *Milwaukee Journal* (11/24/1975), 23.

92. Barbara Gibbons, "Slim Gourmet," *Reading Eagle* (4/13/1977), 41.

93. Robert C. Atkins, *Dr. Atkins' Diet Revolution* (New York: Bantam, 1981), 269–270.

94. See Frances Moore Lappe, *Diet for a Small Planet* (New York: Ballantine Books, 1971).

95. Isadore Barmash, "The Big Kosher Salami War," *New York Times* (6/6/1987), 37.

96. Stop & Shop advertisement, *The Hour* (Norwalk, CT) (5/25/1977), 15.

97. Leonard S. Bernstein, "Death by Pastrami," *Literary Review*, Spring 2001, reprinted in Leonard S. Bernstein, *The Man Who Wanted to Buy a Heart* (New York: UNO, 2012).

98. "The Fatigues," *Seinfeld*, season 8, episode 6, originally aired 10/31/1996 (Sony Pictures, 2012), DVD.

99. Josh Kun, "The Yiddish Are Coming; Mickey Katz, Antic-Semitism, and the Sound of Jewish Difference," *American Jewish History* 87.4 (1999): 368.

100. M. Cohen, *Overweight Sensation*, 88.

101. Ken Kalfus, "Shine On, Harvey Bloom," *Commonweal* (4/22/1994), 15.

102. Gerald Nachman, *Seriously Funny: The Rebel Comedians of the 1950s and 1960s* (New York: Pantheon, 2003), 19.

103. Isaac Rosenfeld, "Adam and Eve on Delancey Street," in *Preserving the Hunger: An Isaac Rosenfeld Reader*, ed. Mark Shechner (Detroit: Wayne State University Press, 1988), 146–147.

104. Eve Jochnowitz, "'Send a Salami to Your Boy in the Army': Sites of Jewish Memory and Identity at Lower East Side Restaurants," in Hasia R. Diner, Beth Wenger, and Jeffrey Shandler, eds., *Remembering the Lower East Side* (Bloomington: Indiana University Press, 2000), 212–225.

105. See Dana Evan Kaplan, *Contemporary American Judaism: Transformation and Renewal* (New York: Columbia University Press, 2009), 161–205.

106. *Skyscraper*, book by Peter Stone, lyrics by Sammy Cahn, and music by Jimmy Van Heusen, 1965 original cast recording (DRG, 2002), CD.

107. Woody Allen, "Thus Ate Zarathustra," *New Yorker* (7/3/2006).

108. Shepard Sobel, "From the Director," in *A Playgoer's Supplement to Hamlet*, Pearl Theatre Company, 2007–2008 season brochure, 8.

109. Henry Bial, *Acting Jewish: Negotiating Ethnicity on the American Stage and Screen* (Ann Arbor: University of Michigan Press, 2005), 98.

110. See Norbert Elias, *The Civilizing Process: Sociogenetic and Psychogenetic Investigations*, rev. ed. (Oxford, UK: Wiley-Blackwell, 2000).

111. *When Harry Met Sally*, directed by Rob Reiner (MGM, 1989), DVD.

112. *Making Trouble*, directed by Rachel Talbott (Jewish Women's Archive, 2007), DVD.

113. See "'When Harry Met Sally': Flash Mob Recreates Iconic Deli Scene," *Hollywood Reporter* (11/14/2013). For the video, see Improv Everywhere, "Harry Met Sally Orgasm Scene Prank—Movies in Real Live (Ep 7)," YouTube (11/12/2013), http://www.youtube.com/watch?v=shC016PnxPs.

114. *Broadway Danny Rose*, directed by Woody Allen (Orion Pictures, 1984), DVD.

115. Jeffrey Rubin-Dorsky, "The Catskills Reinvented (and Redeemed): Woody Allen's *Broadway Danny Rose*," *Kenyon Review* 25.3 (2003): 264–281. This deli connection is made throughout Allen's oeuvre; in *Bananas*, for example, Allen's character orders a thousand sandwiches with coleslaw from a band of revolutionaries in the jungle. *Bananas*, directed by Woody Allen (MGM, 2000), DVD.

116. "The Larry David Sandwich," *Curb Your Enthusiasm*, season 5, episode 1, originally aired 9/25/2005 (HBO Studios, 2006), DVD.

117. Kenneth A. Briggs, "Orthodox Judaism Is Buoyed by a Resurgence in New York," *New York Times* (3/29/1983), A1.

118. Bryan Miller, "Kosher Dining Out: The Options Grow," *New York Times* (10/8/1986), C1.

119. Jacqueline Rivkin, "The Ys of a Kosher Cooking School," *Kosher Gourmet* (3/1989), 6–7.

120. Jacqueline Rivkin, "Kosher Gourmet Clubs Provide Adventurous Eating," *Kosher Gourmet* (6–8/1987), 6.

121. Sam Levenson, "Oh Cuisine!," *Saturday Review* (3/1/1980).

122. Richard Jay Scholem, "A Stalwart of Old-Fashioned Deli Fare," *New York Times* (1/18/1998).

123. Joseph Berger, "As Delis Dwindle, Traditions Lose Bite," *New York Times* (5/15/1998), B1.

124. "Facts about New York City," *Harpers* (4/1998).

125. Jonathan Mark, "When the Bronx Had Delis," *New York Jewish Week* (3/15/1996).

126. Quoted in Ted Merwin, "Serving Up Food with Attitude." *Text/Context*, supplement to *New York Jewish Week* (4/3/2009), http://www.thejewishweek.com/special_sections/text_context/serving_food_attitude.

127. David M. Herszenhorn, "Knishes or Kimchi: Last Kosher Deli Closes on Union Street," *New York Times* (8/6/1995), C6.

128. Samuel Freedman, "Indiana Pastrami? Hebrew National Plans Move," *New York Times* (8/8/1986), B3.

129. Elliot Weiss, "Packaging Jewishness: Novelty and Tradition in Kosher Food Packaging," *Design Issues* 20.1 (2004): 48.

Conclusion

1. Quoted in Ted Merwin, "Hold Your Tongue," *New York Jewish Week* (1/13/2006).

2. Andy Newman, "Hold the Mustard, Maybe Forever," *New York Times* (1/6/2006), 1.

3. Ron Rosenbaum, "Where Is the Schmaltz of Yesteryear? Christmas Eve in a Jewish Deli," *Slate* (12/27/2007), http://www.slate.com/id/2180953.

4. Adam Gopnik, *Through the Children's Gate: A Home in New York* (New York: Random House, 2007), 64–65.

5. *What a Pickle: The World's Greatest Deli Musical*, directed by Henry Chalfant and Wayne Lammers (Tribabka Films, 1999), VHS.

6. See David Sax, "Shiva for the Stage Deli," *The Jew & the Carrot* (blog), *Forward* (11/30/2012), http://blogs.forward.com/the-jew-and-the-carrot/167020/shiva-for-the-stage-deli/. See also Ted Merwin, "The American Dream, on Rye," *New York Jewish Week* (12/11/2012).

7. Stewart Ain, "Kosher Delis Close across Long Island," *New York Jewish Week* (4/2/2014).

8. Interview with the author, 5/23/2014.

9. Andrew Adam Newman, "After 123 Years, Manischewitz Creates Kosher Food for Gentiles," *New York Times* (12/26/2011), B3.

10. William Alden, "Equity Fund Buys Maker of Matzos," *New York Times* (4/7/2014), B4.

11. Paul Rudnick, "Yummy" (Shouts and Murmurs), *New Yorker* (6/2/2014), 35. The idea of serving deli food to Christians on Christmas Eve also animates Mike Reiss's comical children's book about a deli owner who fills in for Santa Claus. See Mike Reiss, *How Murray Saved Christmas*, illustrated by David Catrow (New York: Puffin, 2004).

12. See Jeffrey Shandler, *Adventures in Yiddishland: Postvernacular Language and Culture* (Berkeley: University of California Press, 2005); and David Hollinger, *Postethnic America: Beyond Multiculturalism* (New York: Basic Books, 2006).

13. Pierre Nora, "Between Memory and History," in Lawrence D. Kritzman, ed., *Realms of Memory: Rethinking the French Past* (New York: Columbia University Press, 1996), 12.

14. Nora, "Between Memory and History," 11.

15. Willensky, *When Brooklyn Was the World*, 190.

16. Fred Davis, *Yearning for Yesterday: A Sociology of Nostalgia* (New York: Free Press, 1979), 31.

17. Interview with the author, 3/12/2008.

18. Mimi Sheraton, "Lost, Then Found—New York Classics," *New York Times* (7/31/2012), D1.

19. Quoted in R. W. Apple, "Bagging the Endangered Sandwich," *New York Times* (9/15/1999), F13.

20. Darra Goldstein, "From the Editor: Food from the Heart," *Gastronomica* 4.1 (2004), http://www.gastronomica.org/food-from-the-heart/.

21. Daina Beth Solomon, "Wexler's Brings the Deli Revolution to L.A.," *Forward* (5/7/2014).

22. Julia Moskin, "Everything New Is Old Again," *New York Times* (5/27/2014).

23. Michael Kaminer, "The New York Jewish Deli Meets the 21st Century, and the Results Are Geshmak," *Washington Post* (7/17/2014).

24. Devra Ferst, "Shabbat Dinner Faces the Future with Panache," *Forward* (10/17/2012).

25. Panel discussion at ABC Carpet, New York City Wine and Food Festival, 10/13/2012.

26. Josh Ozersky and David Sax, "Debating the Deli," *Jewish Daily Forward* video on Vimeo, http://vimeo.com/58913579 (accessed 3/21/2014).

27. Julia Moskin, "Can the Jewish Deli Be Reformed?," *New York Times* (4/14/2010), D1. See also Bonnie Hulkower, "Michael Pollan, Saul's Deli Secret Pastrami Hawker?," *Treehugger* (3/2/2010), http://www.treehugger.com/green-food/michael-pollan-sauls-deli-secret-pastrami-hawker.html.

28. Moskin, "Can the Jewish Deli Be Reformed?"

29. Glenn Collins, "Beef from Creekstone Farms Impresses New York Chefs," *New York Times* (3/24/2010), D1.

30. Interview with author, 10/13/2012.

31. Interview with the author, 10/19/2013.

32. Moskin, "Can the Jewish Deli Be Reformed?"

33. Interview with author, 10/19/2013.

34. Noah Bernamoff and Rae Bernamoff, *The Mile End Cookbook: Redefining Jewish Comfort Food from Hash to Hamantaschen* (New York: Clarkson Potter, 2012), 14.

35. Interview with author, 10/13/2012.

36. Margaret Eby, "Mile End, Russ and Daughters Both Plan Bars," *Forward* (9/22/2013).

37. Interview with Michelle Kiefer, 5/20/2011, Nona Brooklyn, http://nonabrooklyn.com/deli-defiant-mile-end%E2%80%99s-noah-bernamoff-does-it-his-way/#.UZNxJzfCuZA (accessed 8/15/2012).

38. Moskin, "Can the Jewish Deli Be Reformed?"

39. Interview with the author, 10/19/2012.

40. Lisa Keys, "High on the Hog," *Tablet* (2/5/2010), http://tabletmag.com/jewish-life-and-religion/25147/high-on-the-hog.

41. Josh Ozersky, "How Traif Came to Williamsburg," *Huffington Post* (12/15/2010), http://www.huffingtonpost.com/josh-ozersky/how-traif-came-to-william_b_796891.html.

42. Adeena Sussman, "Haimish to Haute in New York," *Forward* (3/28/2012).

43. See Sarah Zorn, "Our Favorite Jewish-ish Dishes," *Brooklyn Magazine* (11/12/2013).

44. Mary Kong-Devito, "Bigger Is Better at Harold's Deli," *Girl Meets Food* (blog) (12/7/2009), http://dc.eater.com/tags/girl-meets-food.

45. "Mother of Mercy! Is This the End of Katz's?," *New York* (5/17/2007), http://newyork.grubstreet.com/2007/05/mother_of_mercy_is_this_the_en.html.

46. "Food and Drink," in Kenneth M. Gold and Lori R. Weintrob, eds., *Discovering Staten Island: A 350th Anniversary Commemorative History* (New York: History Press, 2011), 88.

47. Bonnie Goodman, "The Higher East Side of New York," *PresenTense* (blog) (2/22/2008), http://presentense.org/node/389.

48. Interview with the author, 6/19/2007.

49. Interview with the author, 2/14/2008.

50. Interview with the author, 1/3/2014.

51. Daniel Smokler, "Toward a Third Space—New Dimensions of Jewish Education for Emerging Adults," paper presented at Hillel Conference at NYU (6/2010).

52. Pew Research, Religion & Public Life Project, *A Portrait of Jewish Americans* (10/1/2013), http://www.pewforum.org/2013/10/01/jewish-american-beliefs-attitudes-culture-survey/.

Selected Bibliography

Aaronson, Sammy, and Albert Hirshberg. *As High as My Heart*. New York: Coward-McCann, 1957.

Abrahams, Roger. "The Language of Festivals: Celebrating the Economy." In Victor Turner, ed., *Celebrations: Studies in Festivity and Ritual*, 161–177. Washington, DC: Smithsonian Institution Press, 1982.

Abramovitch, Ilana, and Seán Galvin, eds. *Jews of Brooklyn*. Waltham, MA: Brandeis University Press, 2001.

Adams, Carol. *The Pornography of Meat*. New York: Continuum, 2003.

Aleichem, Sholem. *Motl Peyse dem Khazns Zun* (Motl Peyse, the Cantor's Son). Jerusalem: Hebrew University Magnes Press, 1997.

———. *Tevye the Dairyman and the Railroad Stories*. Translated by Hillel Halkin. New York: Schocken, 1987.

Alexander, Michael. *Jazz Age Jews*. Princeton: Princeton University Press, 2003.

———. "The Meaning of American Jewish History." *Jewish Quarterly Review* 96.3 (2006): 423–432.

Allen, Woody. *Mere Anarchy*. New York: Random House, 2008.

Als, Hilton. "The Overcoat." *Transition* 73 (1997): 6–9.

Amchanitzki, Hinde. *Lehr-bukh vi azoy tsu kokhen un baken* (Cooking and Baking Textbook). New York, 1901.

Anderson, Gary. "The Expression of Joy as a Halakhic Problem in Rabbinic Sources." *Jewish Quarterly Review* 80.3–4 (1990): 221–252.

Appadurai, Arjun. "Gastro-Politics in Hindu South Asia." *American Ethnologist* 8.3 (1981): 494–511.

Aron, Jean-Paul. *Art of Eating in France: Manners and Menus in the 19th Century*. Chester Springs, PA: Dufour, 1975.

Atkins, Robert C. *Dr. Atkins' Diet Revolution*. New York: Bantam, 1981.

Ausubel, Nathan. *Treasury of Jewish Humor.* New York: Doubleday, 1951.

Balinska, Maria. *The Bagel: The Surprising History of a Modest Bread.* New Haven: Yale University Press, 2009.

Barthes, Roland. *Elements of Semiology.* New York: Hill and Wang, 1968.

Belasco, Warren. *Appetite for Change.* New York: Pantheon, 1990.

———. "Ethnic Fast Foods: The Corporate Melting Pot." *Food and Foodways* 2 (1987): 1–29.

———. *Meals to Come: A History of the Future of Food.* Berkeley: University of California Press, 2006.

Bent, Silas. *Machine Made Man.* New York: Farrar and Rinehart, 1930.

Bentley, Amy. *Eating for Victory: Food Rationing and the Politics of Domesticity.* Urbana: University of Illinois Press, 1998.

Bernamoff, Noah, and Rae Bernamoff. *The Mile End Cookbook: Redefining Jewish Comfort Food from Hash to Hamantaschen.* New York: Random House, 2012.

Bernstein, Leonard S. *The Man Who Wanted to Buy a Heart.* New York: UNO, 2012.

Bial, Henry. *Acting Jewish: Negotiating Ethnicity on the American Stage and Screen.* Ann Arbor: University of Michigan Press, 2005.

Biondi, Joann. *Miami Beach Memories: A Nostalgic Chronicle of Days Gone By.* Guilford, CT: Globe Pequot, 2006.

Bowlby, Rachel. *Carried Away: The Invention of Modern Shopping.* New York: Columbia University Press, 2001.

Brown, Phil. *Catskills Culture: A Mountain Rat's Memories of the Great Jewish Resort Area.* Philadelphia: Temple University Press, 2003.

Byron, Eric. "English Acquisition by Immigrants (1880–1940): The Confrontation as Reflected in Early Sound Recordings." *Columbia Journal of American Studies.* http://www.columbia.edu/cu/cjas/archives.html (accessed 2/2/2009).

Cantor, Jay. *Great Neck.* New York: Vintage, 2003.

Carroll, Peter N. *It Seemed Like Nothing Happened: America in the 1970s.* New Brunswick: Rutgers University Press, 1990.

Charyn, Jerome. *Gangsters and Gold Diggers: Old New York, the Jazz Age, and the Birth of Broadway.* New York: Thunder's Mouth, 2003.

Chotzinoff, Samuel. *A Lost Paradise: Early Reminiscences.* New York: Arno, 1975.

Chrissey, Forrest. *The Story of Foods.* New York: Rand McNally, 1917.

Cobble, Dorothy Sue. *Dishing It Out: Waitresses and Their Unions in the Twentieth Century.* Urbana: University of Illinois Press, 1992.

Coe, Andrew. *Chop Suey: A Cultural History of Chinese Food in the United States.* New York: Oxford University Press, 2009.

Cohen, Elliot, ed. *Commentary on the American Scene.* New York: Knopf, 1953.

Cohen, Lizabeth. *A Consumer's Republic: The Politics of Mass Consumption in Postwar America.* New York: Knopf, 2003.

Cohen, Mark. *Overweight Sensation: The Life and Comedy of Allan Sherman.* Waltham, MA: Brandeis University Press, 2013.

Cohen, Rich. *Tough Jews*. New York: Crown, 1999.

Cohn, Jacob. *The Royal Table: An Outline of the Dietary Laws of Israel*. New York: Bloch, 1936.

Condon, Richard. *And Then We Moved to Rossenarra*. New York: Dial, 1973.

Cooper, John. *Eat and Be Satisfied: A Social History of Jewish Food*. New York: Jason Aronson, 1993.

Corbett, Ruth. *Daddy Danced the Charleston*. New York: A. S. Barnes, 1970.

Cosell, Howard. *Like It Is*. Chicago: Playboy, 1974.

Counihan, Carole. *Food in the U.S.A.* New York: Routledge, 2002.

Counihan, Carole, and Penny Van Esterik, eds. *Food and Culture: A Reader*. 2nd ed. New York: Routledge, 2007.

Davis, Fred. *Yearning for Yesterday: A Sociology of Nostalgia*. New York: Free Press, 1979.

Davis, Marni. *Jews and Booze: Becoming American in the Age of Prohibition*. New York: NYU Press, 2012.

Diemling, Maria. "As the Jews Like to Eat Garlick: Garlic in Christian-Jewish Polemical Discourse in Early Modern Germany." In Leonard J. Greenspoon, Ronald A. Simkins, and Gerald Shapiro, eds., *Food and Judaism*. Omaha, NE: Creighton University Press, 2004.

Diner, Hasia R. *Hungering for America: Italian, Irish, and Jewish Foodways in the Age of Migration*. Cambridge: Harvard University Press, 2003.

———. *Lower East Side Memories*. Princeton: Princeton University Press, 2002.

Diner, Hasia R., Beth Wenger, and Jeffrey Shandler, eds. *Remembering the Lower East Side*. Bloomington: Indiana University Press, 2000.

Duffy, Jennifer Nugent. *Who's Your Paddy? Racial Expectations and the Struggle for Irish American Identity*. New York: NYU Press, 2013.

Dynner, Glenn. *Yankel's Tavern: Jews, Liquor, and Life in the Kingdom of Poland*. New York: Oxford University Press, 2013.

Elias, Norbert. *The Civilizing Process: Sociogenetic and Psychogenetic Investigations*. Oxford, UK: Blackwell, 2000.

Evans, Sara. *Born for Liberty*. New York: Free Press, 1997.

Faragher, Scott, and Katherine Harrington. *Memphis in Vintage Postcards*. Charleston, SC: Arcadia, 2000.

Ferris, Marcie Cohen. *Matzoh Ball Gumbo: Culinary Tales of the Jewish South*. Chapel Hill: University of North Carolina Press, 2005.

Finck, Henry. *Food and Flavor: A Gastronomic Guide to Health and Good Living*. London: John Lane, 1914.

Fishkoff, Sue. *Kosher Nation: Why More and More of America's Food Answers to a Higher Authority*. New York: Schocken, 2010.

Freedman, David. *Mendel Marantz*. New York: Langdon, 1925.

Frommer, Myrna Katz, and Harvey Frommer. *Growing Up Jewish in America: An Oral History*. New York: Bison Books, 1999.

———. *It Happened in Brooklyn: An Oral History of Growing Up in the Borough in the 1940s, 1950s, and 1960s*. New York: Harcourt Brace, 1993.

Fuchs, Daniel. *Homage to Blenholt*. London: Constable, 1936.

Gabaccia, Donna. *We Are What We Eat: Ethnic Foods and the Making of Americans*. Cambridge: Harvard University Press, 2000.

Gabler, Neal. *An Empire of Their Own: How the Jews Invented Hollywood*. New York: Anchor Books, 1989.

Gastwirt, Harold P. *Fraud, Corruption, and Holiness: The Controversy over the Supervision of Jewish Dietary Practice in NYC, 1881–1940*. Port Washington, NY: Kennikat, 1974.

Gay, Ruth. *Unfinished People: Eastern European Jews Encounter America*. New York: Norton, 2001.

Genung, A. B. *Food Policies during World War II*. Ithaca, NY: Northeast Farm Foundation, 1951.

Gibbon, Edward, and Henry Hart Milman. *The Life of Edward Gibbon*. Paris: Baudry, 1840.

Glassner, Barry. "Fitness and the Postmodern Self." *Journal of Health and Social Behavior* 30 (6/1989): 180–191.

Glatzer, Robert. *The New Advertising: The Great Campaigns from Avis to Volkswagen*. New York: Citadel, 1970.

Glazer, Phyllis, and Miriyam Glazer. *The Essential Book of Jewish Festival Cooking*. New York: HarperCollins, 2004.

Glazer, Ruth. "The Jewish Delicatessen: The Evolution of an Institution." *Commentary* (3/1946): 58–63.

———. "West Bronx: Food, Shelter, Clothing." *Commentary* (6/1949): 578–585.

Gold, David L. *Studies in Etymology and Etiology*. Edited by F. Rodríguez González and A. Lillo Buades. Alicante, Spain: University of Alicante, 2009.

Gold, Kenneth M., and Lori R. Weintrob, eds. *Discovering Staten Island: A 350th Anniversary Commemorative History*. New York: History Press, 2011.

Goldberg, J. J. *Jewish Power: Inside the American Establishment*. New York: Basic Books, 1997.

Golden, Harry. *Only in America*. New York: Perma Books, 1958.

Goldstein, Darra, ed. *The Gastronomica Reader*. Berkeley: University of California Press, 2010.

———. "Will Matzoh Go Mainstream? Jewish Food in America." In *The Jewish Role in American Life: An Annual Review*, vol. 4. Los Angeles: USC Casden Institute, 2005.

Gopnik, Adam. *Through the Children's Gate: A Home in New York*. New York: Random House, 2007.

Gould, Jillian. "Candy Stores and Egg Creams." In Ilana Abramovitch and Séan Galvin, eds., *Jews of Brooklyn*, 202–205. Waltham, MA: Brandeis University Press, 2001.

Grossman, Ruth, and Bob Grossman. *The Chinese-Kosher Cookbook*. New York: Pocket Books, 1999.

Gurock, Jeffrey S. *Jews in Gotham: New York Jews in a Changing City, 1920–2010*. New York: NYU Press, 2012.

———. *Orthodox Jews in America*. Bloomington: Indiana University Press, 2009.

Hacker, Barton C., and James M. Grimwood. *On the Shoulders of Titans: A History of Project Gemini*. Washington, DC: U.S. Government Printing Office, 2010.

Haenni, Sabine. *The Immigrant Scene: Ethnic Amusements in New York, 1880–1920*. Minneapolis: University of Minnesota Press, 2008.

Halter, Marilyn. *Shopping for Identity: The Marketing of Ethnicity*. New York: Random House, 2000.

Heimann, Jim. *Make I Take Your Order? American Menu Design, 1920–1960*. San Francisco: Chronicle Books, 1998.

Heinze, Andrew. *Adapting to Abundance*. New York: Columbia University Press, 1992.

Herberg, Will. *Protestant–Catholic–Jew: An Essay in American Religious Sociology*. Chicago: University of Chicago Press, 1955.

Hermalin, D. H. "The Roumanian Jews in America." *American Jewish Yearbook* 3 (1901–1902): 101–102.

Hindus, Maurice. *Green Worlds*. New York: Doubleday, Doran, 1938.

Hollinger, David. *Postethnic America: Beyond Multiculturalism*. New York: Basic Books, 2006.

Howe, Irving. *World of Our Fathers*. New York: Harcourt, Brace, Jovanovich, 1976.

Hyman, Paula. "Immigrant Women and Consumer Protest: The New York Kosher Meat Boycott of 1902." *American Jewish History* 70 (1980): 91–105.

Jacobson, Matthew Frye. *Whiteness of a Different Color: European Immigrants and the Alchemy of Race*. Cambridge: Harvard University Press, 1999.

Jakle, John A., and Keith A. Sculle. *Fast Food: Roadside Restaurants in the Automobile Age*. Baltimore: Johns Hopkins University Press, 2002.

James, Allison. "Cooking the Books: Global or Local Identities in Contemporary British Food Cultures?" In David Howes, ed., *Cross-Cultural Consumption: Global Markets, Local Realities*, 77–92. New York: Routledge, 1996.

James, Rian. *Dining in New York*. New York: John Day, 1930.

Janowski, Diane. *Our Own Book—A Victorian Guide to Life—Homespun Cuisine, Health, Romance, Etiquette, Raising Children and Farm Animals*. Elmira, NY: New York History Review Press, 2008. Originally published by *Weekly Gazette and Press* (Elmira, NY), 1888.

Jochnowitz, Eve. "'Send a Salami to Your Boy in the Army': Sites of Jewish Memory and Identity at Lower East Side Restaurants." In Hasia R. Diner, Beth Wenger, and Jeffrey Shandler, eds., *Remembering the Lower East Side*, 212–225. Bloomington: Indiana University Press, 2000.

Joselit, Jenna Weissman. "How a Slum Became a Shrine." *Jewish Social Studies* 2 (1996): 54–63.

———. *The Wonders of America: Reinventing Jewish Culture, 1880–1950*. New York: Picador, 2002.

Juliani, Richard, and Mark Hutter. "Research Problems in the Study of Italian and Jewish Interaction in Community Settings." In Jean A. Scarpaci, ed., *The*

Interaction of Italians and Jews in America. Staten Island, NY: American Italian Historical Association, 1975.

Kaplan, Dana Evan. *Contemporary American Judaism: Transformation and Renewal*. New York: Columbia University Press, 2009.

Kaplan, Mordechai. *Judaism as a Civilization: Toward a Reconstruction of American-Jewish Life*. New York: Jewish Publication Society of America, 1994.

Kaser, Arthur LeRoy. "In the Delicatessen Shop, a Jewish Monologue" In *Dialect Monologues: Readings and Plays*, 146–147. Dayton, OH: Paine, 1928.

Kazin, Alfred. *A Walker in the City*. New York: Harcourt Brace Jovanovich, 1951.

Kellogg, Ella Eaton. *Science in the Kitchen*. Chicago: Modern Medicine, 1893.

Kessler, Barry. "Bedlam with Corned Beef on the Side." *Generations*, Fall 1993, 2–7.

Keyes, Ralph. *I Love It When You Talk Retro: Hoochie Coochie, Double Whammy, Drop a Dime, and the Forgotten Origins of American Speech*. New York: Macmillan, 2009.

Kirshenblatt, Mayer, and Barbara Kirshenblatt-Gimblett. *They Called Me Mayer July*. Berkeley: University of California Press, 2007.

Kober, Arthur. "Nobody Can Beat Friedkin's Meats." In Harold U. Ribalow, ed., *A Treasury of American Jewish Stories*, 217–224. New York: Thomas Yoseloff, 1958.

Koenig, Leah. "Goldbergers and Cheeseburgers: Particularism and the Culinary Jew." *Zeek*, Fall–Winter 2006, 13–22.

Kotik, Yeskheskl. *Mayn Zikroynes* (My Memories). Warsaw, 1913.

Kraemer, David. *Jewish Eating and Identity through the Ages*. New York: Routledge, 2008.

Kraut, Alan M. "The Butcher, the Baker, the Pushcart Peddler: Jewish Foodways and Entrepreneurial Opportunity in the East European Immigrant Community, 1880–1940." *Journal of American Culture* 6.4 (1983): 71–83.

Kun, Josh. "The Yiddish Are Coming; Mickey Katz, Antic-Semitism, and the Sound of Jewish Difference." *American Jewish History* 87.4 (1999): 343–374.

Kurlansky, Mark. *Salt: A World History*. New York: Penguin, 1993.

Lappe, Frances Moore. *Diet for a Small Planet*. New York: Ballantine Books, 1971.

Lawrence, Greg. *Dance with Demons: The Life of Jerome Robbins*. New York: Berkley Trade, 2002.

Lebewohl, Sharon, and Rena Bulkin. *The 2nd Avenue Deli Cookbook*. New York: Villard, 1999.

Lederhendler, Eli. *New York Jews and the Decline of Urban Ethnicity, 1950–1970*. Syracuse: Syracuse University Press, 2001.

Lee, Jennifer 8. *The Fortune Cookie Chronicles: Adventures in the World of Chinese Food*. New York: Twelve, 1999.

Levenstein, Harvey. *Fear of Food: A History of Why We Worry about What We Eat*. Chicago: University of Chicago Press, 2012.

Levi, Jane. "An Extraterrestrial Sandwich: The Perils of Food in Space." *Endeavor* 34.1 (2010): 6–11.

Levine, Harry Gene. "Pastrami Land: The Jewish Deli in New York City." *Contexts* (Summer 2007): 67–69.

Levine, Hillel, and Lawrence Harmon. *The Death of an American Jewish Community*. New York: Free Press, 1992.

Lévi-Strauss, Claude. *The Raw and the Cooked*. Chicago: University of Chicago Press, 1983.

Levy, Esther. *Jewish Cookery Book*. Philadelphia: W. S. Turner, 1871.

Liebman, Joshua Loth. *Peace of Mind*. New York: Simon and Schuster, 1946.

Lindenberg, Gavriel. "Our Town as I Remember It." Translated by Yehudis Fishman. In Sh. Meltzer, ed., *The Book of Horodenka* (translation of *Sefer Horodenka*). Tel Aviv, 1963.

Liu, Haiming. "Kung Pao Kosher: Jewish Americans and Chinese Food in New York." *Journal of Chinese Overseas* 6 (2010): 80–101.

Louvish, Simon. *Monkey Business: The Lives and Legends of the Marx Brothers*. New York: Macmillan, 2000.

Lovegrove, Keith. *Pageant: The Beauty Contest*. New York: teNeues, 2002.

Maltin, Murray "Boy." *1/4 Pound Lean*. Los Angeles: Boy's Own, 2001.

Marcus-Kerbelnik, Ida, and Bat-Sheva Levitan Kerbelnik, eds. *Kelme—An Uprooted Tree*. Translation of *Kelm—'Ets Karut*. Tel Aviv, 1993.

Mariani, John. *America Eats Out: An Illustrated History of Restaurants, Taverns, Coffee Shops, Speakeasies, and Other Establishments That Have Fed Us for 350 Years*. New York: William Morrow, 1991.

———. "Everybody Likes Italian Food." *American Heritage* 40.8 (1989). http://54.201.12.217/content/"everybody-likes-italian-food."

———. *How Italian Food Conquered the World*. New York: Palgrave Macmillan, 2011.

Marks, Gil. *Encyclopedia of Jewish Food*. New York: Wiley, 2010.

Marx, Groucho. *The Groucho Phile: An Illustrated Life*. New York: Galahad Books, 1979.

Marx, Harpo, with Rowland Barber. *Harpo Speaks*. New York: Limelight, 2004.

Matt, Susan J. "A Hunger for Home: Homesickness and Food in a Global Consumer Society." *Journal of American Culture* 30.1 (2007): 6–17.

McDonald, M. E., ed. *Lackawanna Jurist* 16 (1/29/1915–1/21/1916): 82–86.

McMichael, Philip, ed. *Food and Agrarian Orders in the World-Economy*. Santa Barbara, CA: Greenwood, 1995.

McNickle, Chris. *To Be Mayor of New York: Ethnic Politics in the City*. New York: Columbia University Press, 1993.

Meltzer, Sh., ed. *The Book of Horodenka*. Translation of *Sefer Horodenka*. Tel Aviv, 1963.

Menashe, Louis. "Sephardic in Williamsburg." In Ilana Abramovitch and Séan Galvin, eds., *The Jews of Brooklyn*, 115–119. Lebanon, NH: University Press of New England, 2002.

Mencken, H. L. *The American Language: An Inquiry into the Development of English in the United States.* New York: Knopf, 1919.

———. Introduction to *The Anti-Christ,* by Friedrich Nietzsche. New York: Sharp, 1999.

Merwin, Ted. "The Delicatessen as an Icon of Secular Jewishness." In Simon Bronner, ed., *Jewishness: Expression, Identity and Representation,* 195–210. Oxford, UK: Littman Library of Jewish Civilization, 2008.

———. *In Their Own Image: New York Jews in Jazz Age Popular Culture.* New Brunswick: Rutgers University Press, 2006.

———. "The Performance of Jewish Ethnicity in Anne Nichols' *Abie's Irish Rose.*" *Journal of American Ethnic History* 20.2 (2001): 3–37.

Michaels, Randolph. *Flashbacks to Happiness: Eighties Music Revisited.* Lincoln, NE: iUniverse, 2005.

Miller, Batya. "Enforcement of the Sunday Closing Laws on the Lower East Side, 1882–1903." *American Jewish History* 91.2 (2003): 269–286.

Miller, Hanna. "Identity Takeout: How American Jews Made Chinese Food Their Ethnic Cuisine." *Journal of Popular Culture* 39.3 (2006): 430–465.

Moore, Deborah Dash. *At Home in America: Second Generation New York Jews.* New York: Columbia University Press, 1981.

———. *G.I. Jews.* Cambridge: Harvard University Press, 2006.

———. *To the Golden Cities: Pursuing the American Jewish Dream in Miami and L.A.* Cambridge: Harvard University Press, 1996.

Nachman, Gerald. *Seriously Funny: The Rebel Comedians of the 1950s and 1960s.* New York: Pantheon, 2003.

Nasaw, David. *Going Out: The Rise and Fall of Public Amusements.* New York: Basic Books, 1993.

Nathan, Joan. *Jewish Cooking in America.* New York: Knopf, 1998.

Nora, Pierre. "Between Memory and History." In Lawrence D. Kritzman, ed., *Realms of Memory: Rethinking the French Past.* New York: Columbia University Press, 1996.

Oldys, William, and John Malham. *The Harleian Miscellany: or, A Collection of Scarce, Curious, and Entertaining Pamphlets and Tracts, as Well in Manuscript as in Print, Found in the Late Earl of Oxford's Library, Interspersed with Historical, Political and Critical Notes.* Vol. 2. London: Robert Dutton, 1809.

Parker, Milton, and Allyn Freeman. *How to Feed Friends and Influence People: The Carnegie Deli.* Hoboken, NJ: Wiley, 2005.

Parkin, Katherine J. *Food Is Love: Food Advertising and Gender Roles in Modern America.* Philadelphia: University of Pennsylvania Press, 2006.

Parks, Sharon Daloz. *Big Questions, Worthy Dreams: Mentoring Young Adults in Their Search for Meaning, Purpose, and Faith.* San Francisco: Jossey-Bass, 2000.

Patai, Raphael. *The Jewish Mind.* Detroit: Wayne State University Press, 1977.

Peale, Norman Vincent. *The Power of Positive Thinking.* New York: Prentice Hall, 1953.

Pipe, Samuel Zanvel. "Napoleon in Jewish Folklore." In *YIVO Annual of Jewish Social Science*, vol. 1, 294–304. New York: YIVO Institute for Jewish Research, 1946.

Platts, Robin. *Burt Bacharach and Hal David: What the World Needs Now*. New York: Collector's Press, 2002.

Plaut, Joshua Eli. *A Kosher Christmas: 'Tis the Season to be Jewish*. New Brunswick: Rutgers University Press, 2012.

Polland, Annie. *Landmark of the Spirit: The Eldridge Street Synagogue*. New Haven: Yale University Press, 2009.

Polland, Annie, and Daniel Soyer. *Emerging Metropolis: New York Jews in the Age of Immigration, 1840–1920*. New York: NYU Press, 2012.

Ravage, Marcus. *An American in the Making*. New York: Harper and Brothers, 1917.

Rees, Jonathan. *Refrigeration Nation: A History of Ice, Appliances, and Enterprise in America*. Baltimore: Johns Hopkins University Press, 2013.

Reich, Benjamin. "A New Social Center: The Candy Store as a Social Influence." *Year Book of the University Settlement Society of New York*, 1899.

Reichert, Tom. *The Erotic History of Advertising*. Amherst, NY: Prometheus Books, 2003.

Reiss, Isaac (Moishe Nadir). "Ruined by Success." Translated from the Yiddish by Nathan Ausubel. In Nathan Ausubel, ed., *Treasury of Jewish Humor*, 36–39. New York: Doubleday, 1951.

Ribalow, Harold U., ed. *A Treasury of American Jewish Stories*. New York: Thomas Yoseloff, 1958.

Richman, Alan. "Oldest Living." *GQ* (10/2000). http://www.gq.com/food-travel/alan-richman/200602/professonial-jewish-waiter.

Rieder, Jonathan. *Canarsie: The Jews and Italians of Brooklyn against Liberalism*. Cambridge: Harvard University Press, 1987.

Rischin, Moses. *The Promised City: New York's Jews, 1870–1914*. Cambridge: Harvard University Press, 1962.

Roach, Mary. *Packing for Mars: The Curious Science of Life in the Void*. New York: Norton, 2010.

Roden, Claudia. *The Book of Jewish Food: An Odyssey from Samarkand to New York*. New York: Knopf, 1996.

Rogov, Daniel. "You Expected Maybe Pâté de Foie Gras?" In Daniel Rogov, David Gershon, and David Louison, *The Rogue's Guide to the Jewish Kitchen*. Jerusalem: Jerusalem Post Press, 1984.

Rosen, Jonathan. *The Talmud and the Internet: A Journey between Worlds*. New York: Farrar, Straus and Giroux, 2000.

Rosenbaum, Aharon. "Memories of the Past." Translated by Jerrold Landau. In M. Yari- Wold, ed., *Rzeszow Community Memorial Book* (Kehilat Raysha sefer zikaron). Tel Aviv, 1967.

Rosenfeld, Isaac. *Preserving the Hunger: An Isaac Rosenfeld Reader*. Edited by Mark Shechner. Detroit: Wayne State University Press, 1988.

Roth, Henry. *Call It Sleep*. New York: Farrar, Straus and Giroux, 1992.

Roth, Philip. *Portnoy's Complaint*. New York: Vintage, 1967.

Rotkovitz, Miryam. "Kashering the Melting Pot." In Lucy M. Long, ed., *Culinary Tourism*. Lexington: University of Kentucky Press, 2010.

Rubin-Dorsky, Jeffrey. "The Catskills Reinvented (and Redeemed): Woody Allen's *Broadway Danny Rose*." *Kenyon Review* 25.3 (2003): 264–281.

Runyon, Damon. *Guys and Dolls: The Stories of Damon Runyon*. New York: Penguin, 1992.

Sales, Soupy. *Soupy Sez: My Life and Zany Times*. New York: M. Evans, 2003.

Sandler, Gilbert. *Jewish Baltimore: A Family Album*. Baltimore: Johns Hopkins University Press, 2000.

Sarna, Jonathan. *American Judaism*. New Haven: Yale University Press, 2004.

Sax, David. *Save the Deli: In Search of Perfect Pastrami, Crusty Rye, and the Heart of Jewish Delicatessen*. New York: Mariner Books, 2010.

Schechter, Ronald. *Obstinate Hebrews: Representations of Jews in France, 1715–1815*. Berkeley: University of California Press, 2003.

Schlesinger, Arthur. *Paths to the Present*. New York: Macmillan, 1949.

Schwartz, Arthur. *Arthur Schwartz's Jewish Home Cooking: Yiddish Recipes Revisited*. New York: Ten Speed, 2008.

———. *Arthur Schwartz's New York City Food: An Opinionated History*. New York: Stewart, Tabori and Chang, 2008.

Seabury, Florence Guy. "The Delicatessen Husband." In *The Delicatessen Husband: And Other Stories*, 28–42. New York: Harcourt Brace, 1926.

Shandler, Jeffrey. *Adventures in Yiddishland: Postvernacular Language and Culture*. Berkeley: University of California Press, 2005.

Shapiro, Edward S. *A Time for Healing: American Jewry since World War II*. Baltimore: Johns Hopkins University Press, 1995.

———. *We Are Many: Reflections on American Jewish History and Identity*. Syracuse: Syracuse University Press, 2005.

Sheraton, Mimi. *Eating My Words: An Appetite for Life*. New York: Harper Perennial, 2006.

———. *From My Mother's Kitchen*. New York: Harper and Row, 1979.

Shore, Dinah. *The Celebrity Cookbook*. New York: Price, Stern, Sloan, 1966.

Shtokfish, David. *Jewish Mlawa: Its History, Development, Destruction*. Translation of *Mlawa Ha-Yehudit; Koroteha, HitpatKhuta, Kilyona Di Yidishe Mlawe; Geshikte, Oyfshtand, Unkum*. Tel Aviv, 1984.

Silver, Laura. *Knish: In Search of the Jewish Soul Food*. Boston: Brandeis University Press, 2004.

Simon, Kate. *Bronx Primitive*. New York: Penguin, 1982.

Sinclair, Jo. *Wasteland*. New York: Harper and Brothers, 1946.

Sleeper, Jim. *The Closest of Strangers: Liberalism and the Politics of Race in New York*. New York: Norton, 1991.

Spewack, Bella. *Streets: A Memoir of the Lower East Side*. New York: Feminist Press of the City University of New York, 1995.

Spiegler, Samuel. *Your Life's Work*. New York: Riverdale, 1943.

Stamberg, Susan. "From Manhattan to Allentown to Washington, D.C." In Alan King and Friends, *Matzo Balls for Breakfast and Other Memories of Growing Jewish*. New York: Free Press, 2004.

Stern, Daniel. "Jewish New York." In Alan Rinzler, ed., *The New York Spy*, 31–39. New York: David White, 1967.

Stern, Michael, and Jane Stern. *Roadfood Sandwiches: Recipes and Lore from Our Favorite Shops Coast to Coast*. New York: Harcourt Houghton Mifflin, 2007.

Takaki, Ronald T. *Double Victory: A Multicultural History of America in World War II*. Boston: Back Bay, 2001.

Taylor, Sybil. *Ireland's Pubs*. New York: Penguin Books, 1983.

Thompson, Susan J., and J. Tadlock Cowan. "Durable Food Production and Consumption in the World- Economy." In Philip McMichael, ed., *Food and Agrarian Orders in the World-Economy*, 35–54. Santa Barbara, CA: Greenwood, 1995.

Tuchman, Gaye, and Harry Gene Levine. "New York Jews and Chinese Food: The Social Construction of an Ethnic Pattern." In Barbara G. Shortridge and James R. Shortridge, eds., *The Taste of American Place: A Reader on Regional and Ethnic Foods*, 163–184. Lanham, MD: Rowman and Littlefield, 1997. Available online at http://qcpages.qc.cuny.edu/~hlevine/SAFE-TREYF.pdf.

Ultan, Lloyd, and Barbara Unger. *Bronx Accent: A Literary and Pictorial History of Borough*. New Brunswick: Rutgers University Press, 2006.

Ungar, Molly Pulver. "From Zetz! to Zeitgeist: Translating 'Rumenye, Rumenye.'" In Pierre Anctil, Norman Ravvin and Sherry Simon, eds., *New Readings of Yiddish Montreal/Traduire le Montreal Yiddish*. Ottawa, Canada: University of Ottawa Press, 2007.

Volk, Patricia. *Stuffed: Adventures of a Restaurant Family*. New York: Vintage Books, 2002.

Ward, David, and Oliver Zunz. *The Landscape of Modernity: New York City, 1900–1940*. Baltimore: Johns Hopkins University Press, 1997.

Webb, Clive. *Fight against Fear: Southern Jews and Black Civil Rights*. Athens: University of Georgia Press, 2001.

Webster, H. T. "They Don't Speak Our Language." *Forum and Century* 90.6 (1933): 57–62.

Weingarten, Joseph. *An American Dictionary of Slang and Colloquial Speech*. New York: self-published, 1954.

Whitfield, Stephen J. "The Jewish Vote." *Virginia Quarterly Review* 62 (Winter 1986): 1–20.

Whiting, John. "Authentic? Or Just Expensive?" In Richard Hosking, ed., *Authenticity in the Kitchen: Proceedings of the Oxford Symposium on Food and Drink*. Oxford, UK: Oxford Symposium, 2006.

Willensky, Elliot. *When Brooklyn Was the World, 1920–1956*. New York: Harmony, 1986.

Wilson, Bee. *Sandwich: A Global History*. London: Reaktion Books, 2010.

Wilson, S. J. *Hurray for Me*. New York: Crown, 1964.

Witt, Doris. *Black Hunger: Soul Food and America*. Minneapolis: University of Minnesota Press, 2004.

Wolfe, Tom. "Corned Beef and Therapy." In Alan Rinzler, ed., *The New York Spy*, 9–19. New York: David White, 1967.

Wolfman, Ira. *Jewish New York: Notable Neighborhoods and Memorable Moments*. New York: Universe, 2003.

Wolitz, Seth. "The Renaissance in Kosher Cuisine." Policy Forum 18. Jerusalem: Institute of the World Jewish Congress, 1999.

Yezierska, Anzia. *Bread Givers*. New York: Persea Books, 1999.

Zanger, Mark H. "Ethnic Foods." In Andrew F. Smith, ed., *The Oxford Encyclopedia of Food and Drink in America*. New York: Oxford University Press, 2004.

Ziegelman, Jane. *97 Orchard: An Edible History of Five Immigrant Families in One New York Tenement*. New York: Harper, 2011.

Zukin, Nick, *The Artisan Jewish Deli at Home*. Riverside, NJ: Andrews McMeel, 2013.

Index

About the Author

Ted Merwin is Associate Professor of Religion and Judaic Studies and Founding Director of the Milton B. Asbell Center for Jewish Life at Dickinson College. He writes about Jewish culture for the *New York Jewish Week* and other major newspapers and magazines.